MADEIRA

ALEX LIDDELL

Madeira

The Mid-Atlantic Wine

HURST & COMPANY, LONDON

First published in 1998
by Faber and Faber Limited
All rights reserved
© Alex Liddell, 1998
Second revised edition, 2014
© Alex Liddell, 2014
Printed in India

Distributed in the United States, Canada and Latin America by
Oxford University Press, 198 Madison Avenue, New York, NY 10016,
United States of America.

ISBNs 9781849043342 *paperback*
      9781849044530 *hardback*

This book is printed using paper from registered sustainable
and managed sources.

www.hurstpublishers.com

In memory of my very good friend Dieter Bohrmann, who shared my love of madeira.

CONTENTS

CONTENTS

CONTENTS

CONTENTS

PART IV: PRESENT AND FUTURE

LIST OF MAPS

ABOUT THE AUTHOR

Alex Liddell was born in Glasgow in 1934. He pursued an academic career as a university lecturer in philosophy and politics until 1987, after which he became a wine investment advisor in Europe until 1991, when he became a director of a wine-importing firm in London. In addition to numerous articles on wine and wine travel, he is the author of *Port Wine Quintas of the Douro* and *The Wines of Hungary*. He has a longstanding interest in madeira and fortified wine.

ACKNOWLEDGEMENTS

FIRST EDITION

I have many people to thank for the help they gave me in the preparation of this book.

First and foremost, I wish to express my thanks to Belmagri SA for making a generous financial grant towards the costs of publishing this book. I also wish to acknowledge and tender thanks for help received from the following: Artur de Barros e Sousa, Lda; H. M. Borges, Sucrs., Lda; Henriques & Henriques Vinhos, SA; Madeira Wine Co., SA; Pereira D'Oliveira (Vinhos), Lda; Silva Vinhos, Lda; Vinhos Barbeito (Madeira), Lda; Vinhos Justino Henriques, Filhos, Lda; the Instituto do Vinho da Madeira, which kindly provided hospitality; the Serviços de Produção Agrícola of the Direcção Regional da Agricultura; the Direcção Regional de Estatística; and the Direcção Regional de Turismo.

Many individuals very kindly gave me unstintingly their time, their knowledge, and often their hospitality. Amongst these I should particularly like to thank the following: Francisco Albuquerque, Ferdinando de Bianchi, Richard Blandy, João Brazão, João Brito, João César, John Cossart, Sigfredo da Costa Campos, Ivo Couto, John Crook, Isabel Dantas, Luisa Dias, David Fairlie, Manuel Eugénio Fernandes, Mário Fernandes, Manuela de Freitas, Ricardo de Freitas, Patrick Grubb, Duncan McEuen, João Pedro Marques, Anthony Miles, Artur and Edmundo de Olim, Aníbal and Luís D'Oliveira, Constantino Palma, Américo Pereira, João Abel Santos, Catherine Scott, Henrique Seabra, Susan Seldon, Duarte da Silva, Jacques Faro da Silva, James Symington and Alberto Vieira.

I wish to thank the following for having allowed me to quote from books of which they own the copyright, or from manuscripts in their possession: Richard Blandy, Blandy's Madeiras, Lda, John Cossart, Christie's of London, Ricardo de Freitas, William Leacock, the Madeira Wine Company, and Susan Seldon.

I should especially like to thank Ernest Halberstadt, who read through drafts of Chapters 10 and 11, and who saved me (a non-chemist) from some blunders. Julian Jeffs, the editor of the series of which this book forms a part, and John Cossart read through the entire first draft of this book. They gave me much helpful advice and saved me from some stupid errors. I am greatly in their debt, but I need hardly add that the opinions expressed in this book are my own, and that Julian Jeffs and John Cossart do not necessarily agree with any of them: indeed, they sharply dissent from some of them.

SECOND EDITION

In preparing this new edition I have had invaluable help from the following people to whom I wish to offer my grateful thanks. For any errors that appear in the text I, not they, have responsibility.

Francisco Albuquerque, Sebastian Ballard, Christopher Blandy, Ivo Couto, José Eduardo Eiras Dias, Michael Dwyer, Luís Faria, Mário Fernandes, Helena Borges Fontes, Ricardo da Freitas, Isabel Borges Gonçalves, Humberto Jardim, Artur de Olim, Luís D'Oliveira, Paula Cabaço Silva, Bárbara Spínola, Jacques Faro da Silva, Juan Teixeira, and José Vouillamoz.

I also wish to thank the staffs of IVBAM, of the shippers in Madeira, and of my publisher, C. Hurst and Co., for their kind assistance in various ways.

Finally, although I have made efforts to contact the copyright holders of material quoted in the original book in order to request the continuance of the permissions granted then for the re-publication of their properties here, it has not in all cases been possible to trace them. I apologize to them, or their successors, for that, and hope that they will forgive the presumption I have made that they would indeed have granted continuance of the original permission.

PREFACE TO THE FIRST EDITION

'I know of no wine of its class that can beat Madeira when at its best ... In fact, I think Madeira and Burgundy carry combined intensity and complexity of vinous delights further than any other wines.'[1] Such is the glowing eulogy penned by George Saintsbury in his *Notes on a Cellar-Book*. Yet it has to be admitted that, in the century which has elapsed since these words were written, the reputation of madeira has not just diminished amongst amateurs of wine: it has all but totally disappeared.

The first madeira I ever tasted was a Cama de Lobos 1789, which I purchased only because its date, shared with the French Revolution, fired my romantic imagination and excited my curiosity. How, I wondered, could a wine from the eighteenth century possibly have survived into the twentieth? This was in 1958, when I was up at Oxford, and I had found it on a list of old vintage madeiras offered for sale by Avery's, the long-established Bristol wine merchant. I have the original invoice in front of me as I write. It cost £3.75 a bottle, which was an immense sum for me in those days, but curiosity prevailed over financial caution. In fact, for good measure I bought two bottles, just in case I enjoyed it.

I shall never forget the ravishment of that first taste. Its powerful and explosive attack, rich complexity of flavour, rapier-like dry finish, and long, intense aftertaste were quite beyond anything I had hitherto experienced. I was hooked for life—and rapidly invested in three more bottles, one of which still remains in my cellar.

I even had the impertinence to write to Avery's to ask how they could be sure that the date of the wine was really 1789. How much less alluring, I insinuated, if it had happened to be 1788. The terse, slightly rebuking reply merely stated that 'it was in cask from 1789 until early in the present century when it was transferred into demijohns from which it was bottled, as we say, a year or so ago'.[2] How, the letter seemed to say, could you doubt the word of a firm such as ours? We have a reputation to maintain.

So began the fascination which madeira has had for me over the last forty years. I am in no doubt that Saintsbury is correct. At its best—which is an important qualification—madeira makes a statement about the vine which is almost unparalleled. Every serious wine lover owes it to himself to discover its delights. If I can communicate some of my own enthusiasm for madeira and thereby bring into the fold those of my readers who do not yet know that they have been missing one of the world's great wine experiences, I shall be well satisfied. Despite my enthusiasm, however, my book is far from being uncritical; some of my friends on the island may even think it goes too far in the opposite direction. Sadly, although the fortunes of madeira, like port, have always been subject to fluctuating fashions of taste, the decline of madeira in the twentieth century has been partly a self-inflicted injury.

I first went to Madeira a quarter of a century ago, in 1973. The island, and to some extent the wine, were both very different in these days. That was before the 1974 Portuguese revolution, still referred to today by many older people as 'the times of misery'. Poverty was rife and, in the north of the island, people without shoes were a not uncommon sight. Much of the cheaper madeira was of deplorable quality, and almost entirely made from the hybrid vines which are now banned.

The visitor to Madeira as the century nears its end finds a very different situation. The entry of Portugal into the EU has, within the past ten years, provided considerable aid for development of the infrastructure, and this is now rapidly transforming the island. Tourism, the mainstay of Madeira's economy, has increased by 75 per cent during this period.[3] With hotel and time-share building proceeding apace, it looks set to increase further with the extension of the airport to accommodate jumbo jets. There has been enormous development to the west of the capital, Funchal. New fast roads have made communication quicker and easier, and a general air of prosperity is starting to prevail.

Within the same period there have also been encouraging changes in the wine scene. As recently as 1992, in a book about Portuguese wine, an English writer painted a bleak picture for the future of the island's wine industry and warned, with considerable justification, that 'it looks as though madeira could be facing terminal decline'.[4] Not all the reasons for gloom have yet been dispelled, but this present book, even if sometimes critical, is far from being an obituary notice. Indeed, the portents for the future are now distinctly brighter.

There are few books exclusively about madeira, and in English there have been none in print for several years now. Noël Cossart's *Madeira* remains fascinating and unbeatable for its wealth of personal reminiscence and the authoritativeness which comes from having spent a lifetime in the trade. I gladly acknowledge my own inevitable and considerable indebtedness to such a rich source of information. But Cossart retired from the wine trade a quarter of a century ago, and some of what he wrote about the production of madeira was already out of date when his book first appeared in 1984. Since then the pace of change has accelerated as much for madeira as for other things, and an up-to-date book is now more than ever necessary.

The first part of this book is concerned with the history of the wine and its trade. The sources for such a history are extensive, and happily they are now beginning to attract the attention of scholars. I have had to rely mainly on secondary sources, and my use of primary materials in a book of this scope has, of necessity, had to be very limited. However, Dr Alberto Vieira has completed a proper, detailed history of madeira, and this will shortly be published, with a large photographic record of the trade, on CD-ROM in both Portuguese and English. I fully acknowledge my debt to his source book of documentary material on the history of the wine, and his courtesy in answering my many questions. Professor David Hancock, of the Department of History at Harvard, is shortly to publish a book on the central importance of madeira in the development of the British North American colonies, and this will plug another gap in our knowledge. My own contribution, within the confines of a general book on madeira, is necessarily comparatively brief, but I believe that it sheds some new light on certain aspects of the wine's history.

I have made extensive use of guidebooks and reports published by visitors to Madeira up to the end of the nineteenth century. These visitors were not for the most part specialists in wine matters. They were often reliant on what others told them, and doubtless made mistakes about some of the information they were given. Moreover, this was the age of plagiarism and much has simply been diligently copied from earlier publications—even word for word! Such sources, therefore, have to be used with caution. Nevertheless, I have used as much direct quotation as possible in Part I of the book, in the belief that the words of those who lived through historical events can often bring them to life for the reader as no later commentator can.

Inevitably, a book of this sort has to contain a number of statistics which can easily prove wearisome to the reader. Those which relate to the geology and climate of the island I have put in an appendix. Lists of export totals are likewise tedious, but general trends are interesting. I have therefore adopted and extended a graphical form of representation used by Lemps in his book *Le Vin de Madère*—and hereby make grateful acknowledgement of the fact—to display exports from Madeira for the last two centuries, and this also appears as an appendix.

A note on spelling conventions and terminology

'Madeira' with an upper-case M refers to the island, and with a lower-case m refers to the wine.

Câmara de Lobos and Cama de Lobos are alternative names for the same place. I have preferred the former, except when referring to wine originating from Câmara de Lobos, which by tradition seems always to be called Cama de Lobos.

I have relied on the context to make it clear when I am referring to a grape variety and when I am referring to the wine which is made from it. However, there are alternative correct spellings in Portuguese of some of the grape varieties. Thus we have *Malvasia* and *Malvazia*. Nowadays, the former is most often used to refer to the grape, whilst for many years the latter has been used as the spelling for the wine. Nobody seems to know why this is so, but I have adopted the same convention. Other alternative spellings are *jacquet* and *jacquez*, and *sercial* and *cerceal*. I have chosen the former in both cases.

I use Portuguese spelling in preference to anglicized versions for two of the wines, although there is nothing wrong with these in context. Thus I refer to Boal rather than to Bual, and to Malvazia rather than to Malmsey, except in quotations or when shippers have used the anglicized form on their labels.

Sercial, Verdelho, Boal and Malvasia used to be called the *castas nobres*, or noble varieties. This phrase, although convenient, is now old-fashioned. I have, therefore, adopted the following terminology:

Classical varieties: meaning Sercial, Verdelho, Boal and Malvazia.

Traditional varieties: meaning these four varieties and, additionally, Terrantez and Bastardo.

In Portuguese all syllables and vowels are pronounced. The stress invariably falls on vowels with accents, failing which on the penultimate vowel.

PREFACE TO THE SECOND EDITION

Madeira first appeared in 1988 as one of the Faber Books on Wine and later formed part of Mitchell Beazley's Classic Wine Library series. Much has happened in the intervening fifteen years with regard to both the development of the island and its wine. Improvements to the infrastructure of the island largely funded by EU grants have transformed Funchal harbour, the airport and the road system. Tourism, now indisputably the major player in Madeira's economy, has expanded so much that the increase in hotel accommodation has had a big impact on the look and character of Funchal's Lido area and some other parts of the island. The regulatory body of wine production and export—formerly the *Instituto do Vinho da Madeira* (IVM)—has been merged with what used to be the *Instituto do Bordado, Tapeçarias e Artesanato da Madeira* (IBTAM) to form the *Instituto do Vinho, do Bordado e do Artesanato da Madeira* (IVBAM). There have been changes in the vineyards as the impact of 'reconversion' has reduced the dominance of the so-called 'direct producers' in the north of the island, and the development of *colheita* madeiras and the extension of the range of aged madeiras have diversified the choice of styles available to the public. One producer (Silva Vinhos Lda) included in the first edition no longer exists, but two others have emerged. All of this has rendered some of the detail in the first edition of *Madeira* either redundant, inadequate or inaccurate, so an up-date of the text—mainly in Parts II, III and IV—has become urgent, and this new edition addresses this need.

Although I have left the text of Part I largely untouched, it may be useful to mention a few of the more important publications that have appeared since *Madeira* first came out. In the historical field two books deserve attention. David Hancock's long-awaited *Oceans of Wine*—already anticipated in the first edition—explores in enormous and fascinating detail the impact of the madeira wine trade on American society between 1640 and 1815. For those who can read Portuguese, Alberto Vieira's *A Vinha e o Vinho na História da Madeira—Sécolos XV a XX* is a characteristically complete and painstaking historical survey that contains statistical information not obtainable from other published sources (although it was anticipated that this work would appear as a CD-ROM and online, neither, unfortunately, has come to pass). For the general reader, *Madeira Wine*, Vieira's collaboration with Constantino Palmer and António Homen-Cardoso, provides a beautifully illustrated, mainly historical text with only a brief consideration of current wine production. Marcus Binney's *The Blandys of Madeira 1811–2011* is largely about individual members of the family, but throws considerable incidental light on its involvement in the wine trade—just one of the Blandys' many commercial enterprises.

Emanuel Berk has produced a new edition of Noël Cossart's irreplaceable *Madeira—The Island Vineyard*, with the original text unchanged, but with useful new appendices including a survey of madeira prices at auction. In my own text I have changed the page references to Cossart's book to correspond with Berk's edition.

Finally, mention must be made of Trevor Elliott's *The Wines of Madeira*. This useful book, the only one to deal with madeira wine production in detail that has appeared since my own, is crammed with information and aptly illustrated mainly with the author's own photographs.

Madeira was never intended to be in any sense a buyer's guide. More than ever before, what is available to buy changes quickly. I have therefore forsworn, apart from the odd exceptional case, comments on current madeiras. Chapter 13 has been retained, without additions, to illustrate some of the contentions made in the preceding chapter. Nor is this a book about table wine. However, in this case, it would clearly be odd if there were no mention of it, so I have said what I have to say in Appendix 5.

Until the early twentieth century it was common practice to measure madeira volumetrically in pipes, both for production and for export, after which metric measurement became the norm. Although this makes for an awkward transition for the reader (see page 88), I have simply followed trade practice for a number of reasons. As indicated in the Glossary entry for *pipa* (pipe), there have been a variety of types of pipe in use over the centuries, leaving an (admittedly small) element of doubt about the preciseness of the term as a unit of volumetric measurement. Moreover, in the historical part of this book I rely heavily on quotations from contemporary sources which measure both production and export volumes in pipes. Translation into putative metric terms would, therefore, have been cumbersome and a little speculative. Conversely, to have attempted to achieve some consistency by converting metric measurements in twentieth century statistics back into pipes would have been retrograde and merely quaint. However, the reader who wishes to make a general comparison between modern and earlier export volumes should find Appendix 3, explained in the next paragraph, of some assistance.

Since the book was first published, Dr Vieira has compiled the most complete lists available of annual production and annual exports of madeira over several centuries. The graph of exports shown in Appendix 3 is now based on Dr Vieira's figures. The intention of this graph, which calibrates volumes in terms both of pipes and hectoliters (at 1 pipe = 418 litres), is to allow the reader to form an impression of the ebb and flow of exports over the course of two hundred years. However, where production is concerned, as Dr Vieira does not indicate the various sources from which he has obtained his figures, I have retained my original estimates (for which I do give sources). This is for two reasons: firstly, because I have no basis on which to choose between Dr Vieira's figures and my own; and secondly, to retain the integrity of the original text, in which such data are frequently taken from manuscript sources which are themselves of interest.

Most of the features in the first edition survive, albeit in a revised form, but I should particularly like to draw the attention of readers to the information about spelling and other conventions given at the end of the preface to the first edition, which are again followed here.

With regret, I have to note the deaths of Dieter Bohrmann (to whom the original edition was dedicated) and of John Cossart.

Dieter was, on the one hand, a Belgian industrialist, and on the other a wine producer with estates in the Douro, in Burgundy and on the Mosel. He had a marvellous palate and, every bit as much as his port, he adored his old madeiras, of which he had a fantastic collection. He generously organized a subsidy to make the publication of the original edition of this book possible, and for that, as well as for many other acts of generosity, I shall always be in his debt. John Cossart, whom I first met when preparing this book, became a personal friend. It was always a pleasure to have dinner with him on my visits to Madeira and when he came to London. His sudden death was a blow not only to his friends but to the madeira wine trade, and he is greatly missed.

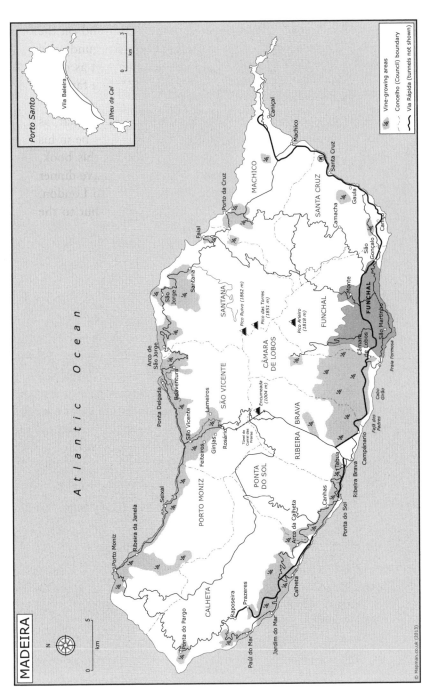

Map 1: Madeira island.

INTRODUCTION

Madeira (meaning 'wood' in Portuguese) is the largest island in a small archipelago of the same name in the Atlantic Ocean. This Portuguese possession is situated on the parallel 33°N—which puts it on roughly the same latitude as Casablanca and Bermuda—and is 796 km west of the coast of north Africa. The island is 57 km long (east-west) and, at its broadest, 23 km wide (north-south), with a total area of 736.8 square km. This makes it comparable in size to Rhodes or Minorca.

Porto Santo, the only other populated island of the archipelago, is 36 km north-east of Madeira and is much smaller, being 12 km long by 7 km wide. The remaining islands consist of two groups, the Desertas and the Selvagems, which are now designated as bird sanctuaries.

Madeira rarely fails to charm its visitors. It has an equable sub-tropical climate, year-round sunshine and is justly famous for its profusion of flowers. The island is also renowned for its spectacular scenery, ranging from alpine splendour at its mountainous centre and spectacular northern cliffs, to a desolate central plateau reminiscent of Dartmoor and pine forests reminiscent of Scotland. Madeira was once the exclusive destination of the wealthy, who came by sea, either for health reasons or simply for relaxation, but since 1965 air travel has made it accessible to a wider range of visitors and tourism has become its principal economic activity. Funchal, the capital, was until recently the main focus of tourist development, and the rest of the island still preserved much of its tranquil simplicity. But now that we have entered the twenty-first century the pace of change has accelerated sharply, and many consider that Madeira has already lost some of the atmosphere of time-forgotten remoteness which was at one time thought to be its principal attraction.

Madeira's reputation as a destination for travellers goes back to the late eighteenth century, but the fame of its wine goes back even further, to the late fifteenth century, not long after the island was colonized by Portugal. For centuries the production of wine was its principal activity, and one might say that the history of the wine and of the island are to that extent the same.

PART I

THE HISTORY OF THE WINE

1

EARLY HISTORY

Discovery, colonization and land tenure

According to what was for long the accepted story, Porto Santo was 'accidentally' discovered in 1418 by João Gonçalves Zarco, Bartolomeu Perestrelo and Tristão Vaz Teixeira, who were all in the service of Prince Henry the Navigator, the Portuguese Infante. Two years later, in 1420, Zarco and Teixeira 'ventured' 36 km beyond Porto Santo to investigate a dense, dark cloud on the horizon, and thereby discovered Madeira. A more romantic story gives the credit to an Englishman, Robert Machin, cast ashore on the island whilst eloping with a fellow countryman's wife!

The truth seems to be much more prosaic. Madeira and Porto Santo appear named as such, often with the Desertas and the Selvagems too, in numerous fourteenth-century maps, such as the Medici Atlas (1351), the chart attributed to the Pizzigani brothers (1367), the Catalan planisphere of Abraam Cresques (1375), the Solleri chart (1385) and the Pinelli chart (1390). Thus, according to recent informed historical opinion,[1] there appears to be no doubt that Madeira was discovered, nobody knows by whom, well before 1420. It was shortly after 1420—the official date is given as 1425— that the colonization of Madeira and Porto Santo started. Prince Henry appears to have taken the initiative in this, and official authorization was given to Zarco on 1 November 1430 by Prince

Henry's father, King João I, to divide up and allot the lands of the archipelago for settlement.

The settling of the islands was in fact in the hands of the three 'discoverers', who became captains of the areas (captaincies—*capitanias*) they administered. Teixeira became captain of Machico and the north east of the island; Perestrelo became captain of Porto Santo; and Zarco was appointed captain of Funchal and the south west of the island (Caniço in the south and Porto Moniz in the north marked the boundary between the two Madeiran captaincies). Each of the captains leased land to others according to a system of *sesmaria*, under which the grantees—mainly aristocrats, wealthy foreign venturers and the occasional bourgeoisie—had to undertake to develop the land productively within a specified period during which they paid no rent, but after which they entered into full possession of it. The obligations of *sesmaria* were usually discharged by importing large numbers of African and Arab slaves. This system lasted until 1501, after which land could only be acquired by purchase, leasehold, inheritance or dowry, and this tended to concentrate property ownership in the hands of the aristocracy, rich foreigners (as much through marriage as purchase) and bourgeoisie who had prospered during the initial period of development.

These began to consolidate their position by establishing entails (*morgados*), which ensured the inheritance of land and property on the basis of primogeniture. This was the foundation on which the most powerful families on the island amassed and maintained their fortunes, and at one stage it was estimated that two-thirds of the land of the entire archipelago was held in entail under the *morgado* system.[2] Although modified from time to time, this remained the real basis of land tenure until it was abolished in 1863,[3] but its effects persisted even after this, and were only finally removed as one of the results of the 1974 revolution.[4]

On to this structure of land tenure was grafted a system of tenancy called *contrato de colonia* (colonial contract), whereby the landlord owned the land but the tenant owned any improvements he had made which added value to the land, including a house if he built one. The landlord would provide or share with the tenant the costs of working the land, and in return would receive a proportion, generally a half, of the value of the crops produced. The contract passed from generation to generation, and in practice the system proved to be remarkably stable. It still exists. However, the right of the tenant to buy the freehold of his land was established in 1976. This has not only greatly reduced the number of surviving colonial contracts, but has finally undermined what remained of the system of *morgados*.

Early development and trade

The first colonists were members of the Portuguese nobility who brought with them labourers and artisans mainly from northern Portugal.[5] Wealthy and entrepreneurial adventurers from other parts of Europe (Italians, Flemish, French and Castilians—and a single Scotsman by the name of Drummond, who was a nephew of King Robert III and cousin to James I) soon followed, encouraged by special privileges designed to exploit their connections with potential export destinations. The island was covered with dense forest and the centres of population were established in areas close to the south coast, first at Machico, then at Funchal, gradually spreading westwards along the south coast. The forest had to be burned to provide arable land, and initially subsistence crops of grain and vines were planted, with sugar cane—planted speculatively for the first time beyond the European mainland—as a potential export. The rough terrain was adapted for agriculture by terracing the slopes of hills, and by 1461 a system of *levadas*, or irrigation channels, which has been consistently extended into our own day, had been constructed.[6] Spring water from the central heights of the island is diverted into collecting channels which are fed, through successive stages, into increasingly larger and more important channels, often carved out of the living rock and routed through tunnels. The *levadas* descend in altitude by very gradual degrees, and eventually provide water for crops (and drinking).

Farming prospered, and we know that Madeira was already exporting sugar, grain, wine and timber to the Portuguese mainland, to African markets, and to the Gulf of Guinea by 1461.[7] The land, enriched by the burning of the forests, was incredibly fertile. Sugar cane found new markets in northern Europe and the Mediterranean, and by 1466 it had become the principal crop, to the detriment of grain, which then had to be imported. Production grew with amazing and accelerating rapidity from the middle of the fifteenth century until it peaked in 1506, and brought correspondingly increased levels of prosperity to the settlers.

The first wine

We do not know for certain which vines were first planted, but it seems reasonable to suppose that the first settlers, amongst them many from the Minho and other parts of northern Portugal, brought with them the varieties already established in the areas from which they came. One reason for so thinking is that the traditional method of cultivation in Madeira, using trellises to support the vines, is remarkably similar to that still used in the Minho for *vinho verde*. Both in northern Portugal and in Madeira until earlier in this century, an alternative method of support was to grow vines up trees and, indeed, occasional survivals of this tradition could still be found until quite recently. It seems likely, therefore, that the settlers at first grew for their own consumption what they had been used to back home.

Nor do we know for certain when many of the grape varieties which came to be associated with madeira, like Sercial, Verdelho, Boal, Terrantez and Bastardo, first made their appearance. Fairly early on, however, Malvasia was introduced to the island. Alvise da Mosto, a Venetian navigator who visited Madeira around 1450, published an account of his voyages in 1507. His report is interesting: 'Really very good wines are produced here for a new colony, and they are so plentiful that there are sufficient for those on the island and they even ship them abroad. Amongst the vines the Lord [Prince Henry] ordered the planting of plots of Malvasias, which he sent for from Candia, and which are doing very well. And the country being so good and fertile, the vines almost produce more grapes than leaves, and the bunches are very large, of the length of two, three and, I venture to say, even of four palms, which is the most beautiful thing in the world to see. Black grapes without pips are here hanging on pergolas in complete perfection.'[8]

It is remarkable that wine was already being exported within about twenty-five years of the establishment of the colony, and the productivity of the vines is astonishing. It is implied that there are several varieties, though Malvasia is singled out—the only specific variety to be accorded special mention during this period. We are evidently concerned here with Malvasia Cândida, Cândida being a corruption of Candia, the capital of Crete (also known as Heraklion). Prince Henry may well have planted this variety speculatively (like the sugar) as a potential export because, it is said, he wished to compete with the wines from the eastern Mediterranean, of which Venice had at the time a virtual monopoly. Whether the cuttings came specially from Crete is, perhaps, another matter. It is thought that the vine had already been established in Portugal before it came to Madeira,[9] so this may simply be a colourful embellishment.

How extensive the export of wine was at this time we have no means of telling. Although sugar clearly remained the dominant commodity throughout the century, wine exports probably grew as the vineyards themselves increased in number. We do know, however, that in 1461 some islanders petitioned for exemption from taxes on their exports of wine, sugar, wood and cereals; and in 1485 the island Council imposed another tax on wine exports to meet its revenue needs.[10] As the century neared its end, however, the most significant event for the future export of madeira was certainly the discovery of America by Christopher Columbus, who had himself stayed in Funchal for some time in 1478 while negotiating a purchase of sugar, and who later married the daughter of Bartolomeu Perestrelo, the first captain of Porto Santo. His house in Porto Santo is open as a museum.

The sixteenth century

By 1514 the population had reached 5,000—not including the slave population, which some thought was large enough to constitute a risk to security. Meanwhile, Funchal prospered and had been raised to the status of a city in 1508. The customs house had been founded in 1477,[11] and banking and money-lending flourished. Despite the problems of communication between the centres of population— the only link was by sea—an elaborate customs and fiscal system operated. There were eight parishes on the south coast and one on the north. A new society, with the same social stratification as that of the mainland, had been created.

The position of foreign merchants, whose community was dominated by Italians, had been equivocal in the second half of the previous century. The strong competition, especially with regard to sugar, which they offered to native merchants led to restrictions being placed on their residential status and their trading rights. Slowly their situation was regularized, and by a decree of 22 March 1498 foreigners were again permitted to establish permanent residence on the island.[12] Giovanni Baptista Lomelino, whose descendants were to found an important madeira shipping firm, arrived in Madeira in 1476.[13] At the beginning of the sixteenth century even more Italians settled on the island. A list of the 173 most important families on the island at this period includes fifty-six of foreign origin.[14] It was not, however, until the end of the century that we can record the first English merchant, Robert Willoughby, who arrived about 1590. He was known to the Portuguese as Velovi.

Amongst the new Italian settlers was Simão Acciaioly, who arrived in 1515. He is credited with having introduced Malvasia Babosa, another variety of the grape, which now seems to be virtually extinct on the island. The Madeiran Acciaiolys were a branch of the powerful Florentine Acciaioli (as the name was originally spelled), noted bankers and the builders of the Castello di Montegufoni, famous as the Italian home of the English writer and essayist Sir Osbert Sitwell. The last members of the Acciaioly family have now left Madeira, but Oscar Acciaioly, who died in 1979, was a madeira shipper who specialized in the Scandinavian market.

Between 1502 and 1503 sugar production was almost double that of the previous year,[15] but after 1506 it began to diminish. This was the start of a long decline caused by over-production, soil exhaustion, pests and plant disease, the increasing cost and scarcity of slaves, and finally, towards the end of the century, the *coup de grâce*—cheaper competition from Brazil. Faced with these crises, many cane fields were converted to vineyards, and wine, finding new markets in the Americas and West Indies, increasingly became the island's main export. This development could not have occurred had Madeira not found itself a convenient staging post on the sea route between Europe and the New World. By 1532 wine from Madeira was being imported into France,[16] and by 1537 it had reached England.[17]

We have two specific references to Malvazia during the century. In 1530 Madeira was visited by another Venetian, Giulio Landi, who comments in his *La Descrittione de l'isola de la Madera*, published in 1574, that Madeira 'produces a large amount of wine of all sorts; but for the most part they are big wines, and white, and similar to the Roman *greco*.[18] It also produces Malvazia, but not yet in much quantity; and it is reputed to be better than that from Candia. And because those on the island are not used to drinking wine, they sell it to merchants; who then take it to Iberia and to other northern countries.'[19] Landi appears to indicate that, just as wine was overtaking sugar as the island's principal export, its celebrity was also increasing.

Another Italian traveller, Pompeo Arditi, visited Madeira somewhat later, in 1567. In his *Viaggio all'isola di Madera e alle Azzore*, published in Florence only in 1934, he wrote: 'The whole island makes a large quantity of wines which are considered most excellent and very similar to the *Malvasia* from Candia'.[20] Compared with Landi's comment about the Malvazia being 'not yet in much quantity', Arditi's phrase 'large quantity' might suggest that its production had greatly increased in the intervening thirty-five years. It may have done, but it is important to put this in the context of Landi's remark about wine 'of all sorts', mainly white, and of Malvazia. Malvasia Cândida never was, then or later, the principal grape variety in Madeira in a quantitative sense. As we shall see, commentators from the sixteenth century onwards remarked as often on the small production and scarcity of Malvazia as they did on its excellence. The scarcity of genuine Malvasia Cândida today is only an intensification of a situation which has always existed. We must not be blinded by this emphasis to the fact that the majority of the wine produced was made from other varieties, even if we have no clear idea of what they were, and that this was the main export. As a third visitor named Lopez briefly remarks in 1588: 'wine groweth in great abundance in Madeira, yea, and in my opinion the best in the world, whereof they carry abroad great store into divers countries, especially into England'.[21] At this time Tenerife—one of the Canary Islands—had conditions of wine production and commercial activity similar to Madeira. Indeed, a striking similarity between the two islands continued until the end of the nineteenth century. We may, perhaps, hope to throw some light on the other kinds of wine being produced in Madeira by looking at the situation in Tenerife.

In the first half of the sixteenth century, just as the grape varieties in Madeira appear to have had their origin in northern Portugal, so Tenerife had plantations of white varieties common to the south of Spain. Torrontés had the largest presence, followed by Listrán, Vejeriego and some Verdello (Verdelho).[22] Red wines were not popular or exportable, so there were only small amounts of Negra Molle and Tinto Mollar purely for local use.[23] In addition, Malvasia found its way to Tenerife from Madeira, doubtless a consequence of the large influx of Portuguese settlers shortly after the Spanish conquest of the island in 1494.

From these white varieties a number of different wines were produced.[24] Most important, at least initially, was a single variety, Torrontés. This was an export wine, the variety having been found suitable for making a relatively stable dry wine with a pleasant bouquet that had the important property of being unlikely to turn sour or vinegary. Secondly, there were wines that were mixtures of other white varieties, probably more often naturally occurring rather than manufactured blends, a consequence of mixed plantations that had to be harvested without differentiation of the varieties. These 'mixed' varieties could include Torrontés but never Malvazia, which—because the character of the grape was considered incompatible with the other varieties being grown—was used to make a totally different type of single wine, sweet rather than dry, suave rather than powerful and alcoholic. Malvazia, also a wine for export, remained overshadowed in commercial importance by Torrontés. At this time, therefore, Tenerife produced three types of wine: two single varietal wines and a mixture of varieties. The 'mixed' wine was called *de toda uva* ('from every grape') or *de todo vidueño* ('from every variety'), and later more simply *vino de vidueño*, indicating wine made from a number of varieties with similar characteristics.[25] 'Vidonho' is the Portuguese equivalent of 'Vidueño'. In English the term is Vidonia. While I know of no evidence that Madeira had any favoured single varietal wine other than Malvazia at this time, it does appear that what were referred to as Vidonhos in Madeira, as in Tenerife, were (probably mixed) plantings of white varieties. Bear in mind, however, that it is highly improbable that any Torrontés, a Spanish grape variety, was being grown in Madeira.

The vineyards

By the end of the century Madeira had a physiognomy remarkably like today's. Twenty-six more parishes had been created, but only seven of them were on the north coast.[26] The population of Funchal had swelled to around 10,000, while Santa Cruz and Machico had 4,000 and 3,000 inhabitants respectively.[27] Even the disposition of the vineyards, which is known to us from a chronicle called *As Saudades da Terra* by Gaspar Fructuoso (published only in 1873), is not so very different from that of the present.[28]

Fructuoso, who died in 1591 in the Azores, where he had lived for many years, wrote his chronicle towards the end of his life. The information he gives us about the vineyards, which is interwoven with a topographical description of the island, probably relates to a period at least ten years earlier—say, around 1580. Not only is it rich in detail, but he also even discusses the quality of the various wines. Yet however interesting his account is to the specialist, to quote it extensively would be wearisome to the reader unfamiliar with the island—although virtually all the rivers and places mentioned by Fructuoso are readily identifiable by the same names today.

The tour starts in the east and goes westwards along the south coast of the island (see the map on p. 14). Between Machico and Funchal, Fructuoso mentions the following locations of vineyards:

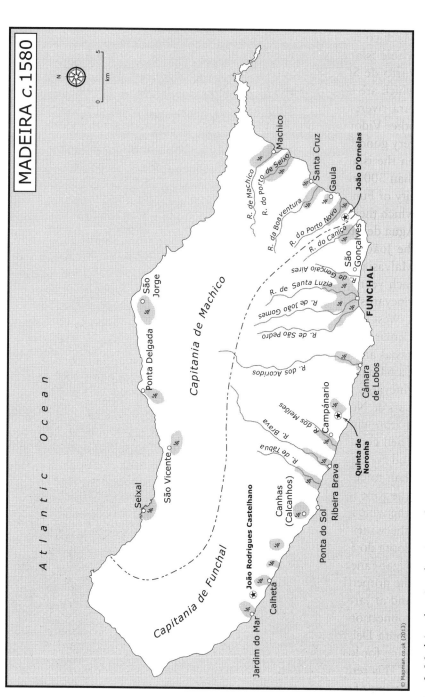

Map 2: Madeira showing the vineyards circa 1580 according to Fructuoso, including small vine-growing properties mentioned by him.

Machico itself (where 'they say that the wine is the worst in the whole island, and as such very little is loaded [exported]'); the Porto de Seixo river (with 'many Malvasia vines and Vidonhos which are better than those of Machico'); Santa Cruz; the Boaventura river; Gaula (with 'many vineyards of Malvasias and many other Vidonhos'); the Porto Novo river ('the wines from which are very good for loading, and where there are fine Malvasias, the best on the island, and other Vidonhos from which they make more than 300 pipes of wine each year'); and Caniço. In and around the city of Funchal, Fructuoso specifies the Santa Luzia river[29] ('above which they make 400 pipes each year of extremely good wine'); the Água de Mel river; the Church of Nossa Senhora de Calhau beside the João Gomes river ('above which there are many vineyards of Malvasias and Vidonhos from which they make 200 pipes of wine each year'); and the São João river ('above which there are many vineyards which give more than 200 pipes of good wine each year').

West of Funchal, Fructuoso notes the Acorridos river, just east of Câmara de Lobos ('above which there are many vineyards of Malvasias and good Vidonhos'); Câmara de Lobos; and 'a league from Câmara de Lobos is the quinta of Luís de Noronha [which] has few vineyards, being on high ground, but along the seaboard the same Luís de Noronha has a *fajã* with a large orchard and very valuable mature vines which give 40 to 50 pipes of Malvazia every year'.[30] Then come Campanário (which has 'grazing grounds, and wheat and rye crops, because the hill-folk are more given to rearing cattle than to cultivating vines'); the Melões river; Ribeira Brava (where 'the wine is not as good as it is at Funchal'); the Tábua river (where 'the wine is similar to that of Ribeira Brava'); Ponta do Sol (where 'the wines are not as good as those of Funchal'); and, north of Ponta do Sol, Calcanhos.[31] Further west the main crop seems to be sugar cane, though Fructuoso makes a passing mention of vines at the property of João Rodrigues Castelhano a league from Calheta, and at Jardim do Mar. On the north coast, vines are mentioned in connection with Seixal, São Vicente (where they are plentiful), and Ponta Delgada. Only São Jorge 'has many vines producing good wine for loading'.[32]

This remarkable and detailed account not only gives us a clear picture of the extent of the vineyards, but also enables us to make a calculation of the amount of wine produced. Simply adding the specific amounts mentioned by Fructuoso gives us a total of 1,150 pipes, most of which we must assume to have been exported. To this has to be added the production of the other areas he mentions. If we assume that this was at least half as much again, we arrive at a figure in excess of 1,700 pipes. Given that another historian has estimated that the average amount of wine exported each year in the first decade of the seventeenth century was 2,000 pipes,[33] and assuming that in the final twenty years of the fifteenth century there may have been some expansion of the vineyard area to meet growing export demand, this figure does not seem too implausible.

The character of the wine

What was the madeira of this period actually like? In terms of taste, the distinction between Vidonho and Malvazia was broadly that the former was a dry wine while the latter was sweet. But how sweet was the Malvazia? Because we are used to thinking of it as the sweetest of all madeiras, the idea that it may once have been much drier initially strikes us as ludicrous. We must remember, however, that at this time the modern technique of stopping the fermentation of the wine by adding alcohol, thereby preserving some of its natural sugar, was not employed in Madeira, so fermentation would be allowed to come to a natural end.

So far as I know, right down to the end of the seventeenth century, Malvazia is never described by those who mention it as a sweet wine: they always call it a rich wine. It is conceivable, therefore, that Malvazia had a perceived sweetness arising from the intense fruit character of the grape, rather as some dry Muscats can seem to be sweet, or as a Gewürztraminer can be rich. This view has as a representative Noël Cossart, who states that 'the Malmsey of that time was unfortified, and probably fermented right out'.[34] However, even if the Malvazia was fermented out, the grapes, which (according to some)[35] may have been left to become semi-raisins, would probably have had a sufficiently high sugar concentration to leave some residual sugar in the wine. Such a wine would not have been entirely stable, giving rise to the risk of secondary fermentations, and, as we shall see in the next chapter, there do appear to have been problems of this sort with Malvazia. Croft, in 1787, goes so far as to call it 'an unfermented wine' which 'would not stand [keep] in the English climate without passing the line, or undergoing a long sea voyage'.[36] These references to semi-raisins and unfermented wine are intriguingly reminiscent of the techniques for making Tokaji, by which shrivelled raisins, left to press against each other under their own weight, produce a barely fermented syrup with an extremely high sugar content (called *esszencia*), which is later added to fermented wines to make them sweeter. Following these hints, however, is entirely speculative and not grounded on any other documentation. What we can be sure of is that, however much Malvazia was fermented out, it was a rich wine, probably quite sweet (and maybe very sweet). It was favourably compared with wines traded from the east through Venice, which are usually accepted as having been sweet, and it may therefore be presumed to have had a similar character. In Madeiran viniculture of the period Malvazia stood in sharp contrast to Vidonho, which was undoubtedly a dry wine.

The wine of Madeira had to compete in a market dominated by sack from Spain and the Canaries, and authorities differ about whether sack was a sweet or a dry wine. Julian Jeffs, for example, asserts that 'sack was always classified as a sweet wine'.[37] He points out that methods of sweetening wines after fermentation had 'long been known' and claims that Elizabethan sack was 'certainly fortified'. However, apart from the hints mentioned above, there appear to be no specific references in contemporary accounts of the production of madeira to post-fermentation sweetening. Nor is there reason to believe that it was ever fortified at this date, though this would certainly have helped to stabilize it as a sweet wine. Indeed, the fact that none of the commentators allude to such practices until the eighteenth century seems to be a sufficient reason for ruling them out.

My own view coincides with that of André Simon, who states the matter succinctly: 'There is no doubt that, originally, the word *Seck*, pronounced and soon after spelt *Sack*, was only applied to the drier wines shipped from the south of Spain; but at the close of the

17

sixteenth and during the seventeenth century it became a generic name for all wines more or less similar, in taste and colour, to those of Jerez, whether they were actually shipped from Port St Mary, or any other Spanish or Portuguese port, or even from the Canaries and Madeira.'[38] Henderson, in his *History of Ancient and Modern Wines* published in 1824, adds a relevant observation. He says that the wines called *Sack* 'probably first came into favour in consequence of their possessing greater strength and durability, and being more free from acidity, than the white wines of France and Germany; and owed their distinctive appellation to that peculiar sub-astringent taste which characterizes all wines prepared with gypsum'.[39] Gypsum (hydrous calcium sulphate), generally known at the time as *gesso*, was commonly used to make wines of the type classified as sack. The earliest appearance of the word in English recorded by the OED—in 1598—relates to wine: 'Gesso when it is first put into the wine maketh it bitter'. Henderson points out that 'the Spaniards had borrowed from the Greeks the practice of adding gypsum to the must, which they afterwards improved upon ... as to be able to excel all other nations in the manufacture of dry wines'.[40] He adds that 'burnt gypsum ... occasions a rapid fermentation and imparts a harsh dry taste to the wine'.[41] Savary des Bruslons, in his *Dictionnaire du Commerce* published in 1723, remarks that old madeiras are better 'than in their first year, because of a bitter and hot taste which only dissipates with time'.[42] Gypsum has, of course, always played a part in the making of sherry; and, anticipating a little, gypsum is frequently mentioned between the seventeenth and nineteenth centuries in connection with the fermentation of madeira.[43] The use of gypsum in making madeira (and at times as a clarifying agent) therefore appears to have been standard practice for several hundred years. It is no longer used as a matter of course, but is still used from time to time.[44]

Gypsum was also employed in winemaking in Tenerife in the sixteenth century, where its use was probably confined (because of expense) to the production of Torrontés intended for export. Added during fermentation, it maintained acidity during fermentation, lessened the risk of the wine developing acetic characteristics, and clarified it. It was later removed with other wine dregs by racking the wine. This process also helped to conserve the wine, hence its importance for the export trade.[45] Instability remained for many years the biggest problem for shippers exporting their wines. In Tenerife, the grapes from irrigated vineyards produced less alcoholic musts and made light wines that were more exposed to the development of wine faults.[46] In Madeira, where irrigation of vineyards was the norm, the same problems must have existed.

Madeira wine in the sixteenth century clearly had much in common with that of Tenerife and almost certainly had a similar character. My contention, following Simon and Henderson's opinion that sack was predominantly a dry wine, is that the bulk of the wine made in Madeira was Vidonho (or Vidonia, as it came to be called), and that Vidonho was a type of sack. It was certainly dry, probably rather astringent when young, rather alcoholic and warming, and more often heavy and coarse rather than suave. Malvazia, on the other hand, although more celebrated, was a relatively small part of the production. It was a rich, sweetish and probably fruity wine, unstable and to that extent problematic.

2

MADEIRA COMES OF AGE

The seventeenth century

This is the century during which the export of madeira, already quite buoyant, really took off, and Madeira was able to reap the benefit which its mid-Atlantic position bestowed, linking it as a staging post to such a large number of destinations. Thus, it was ideally placed to take advantage of trade winds favouring the Caribbean (West Indies), Brazil—to which exports are recorded as early as 1572[1]—the American eastern seabord and even Canada to the west, linking them with European ports as far north as Scandinavia and into the Mediterranean. Portugal also had possessions in Africa like Angola, and trade with these colonies started very early on—wine was exported to Cape Verde regularly from as early as 1649.[2] However, although the East India Company was founded in 1600, it took another hundred years before India started to become a big player amongst the island's export destinations. Without these trade links madeira wine could never have become an important export commodity. Indeed, had the island found itself situated just as far distant from continental Europe and Africa but in a part of the Atlantic where traders had no reason to go, it is clear that the impetus to develop into a wine-producing island would have been considerably less, or might not have existed at all. It is surprising, perhaps, to realize how diverse these trade links had become so soon after the island's discovery.

Only from the middle of the seventeenth century do we begin to have (incomplete) customs house records of the duty-paid exports of wine from the island. The Funchal customs registers for 1650 indicate that 2,405 pipes[3] of wine paid duty; those for the first nine months of 1682 give a total of 3,410 (or, in annual terms, 4,546 pipes); in 1699 a total of 5,483 pipes was recorded.[4] However, since Portuguese ships enjoyed the privilege of shipping duty-free, these totals must be considerably less than the amounts actually exported, which again must be less than the amount of wine actually made. Duncan, in his book on seventeenth-century Atlantic trade, attempts to extrapolate from these and other sporadic reports about the activities of Portuguese shipping to speculative global totals for annual exports, such as 3,500 pipes for 1650 and 6,500 pipes for 1699.[5] These, in my view, have to be taken with extreme caution. Shipping must have been considerably disrupted during the Anglo-Portuguese naval war of June–December 1650, and it is impossible to know how this is reflected in the customs house figures for that year. Nor do we know whether there was a large or small harvest, always a crucial factor. Hence the duty-paid total for this year cannot plausibly be used, in conjunction with other arbitrary assumptions, to estimate the normal year-upon-year average for the middle of the century.[6]

We do, as it happens, have two independent estimates of production for this period, both astonishingly high. Christopher Jeaffreson, a young Englishman travelling to his estate in St Christopher's (St Kitt's) in 1676, reports that 'some years twenty-five thousand pipes of wine' are produced.[7] In 1689 the traveller John Ovington tells us that 'Twenty Thousand Pipes of Wine, by a modest Computation, may be reckoned the Annual Increase of the Grapes ... Eight Thousand are thought to be drunk upon the Island, three or four are wasted in Leekage, and the remainder is Transported, most of it to the *West Indies*, especially to *Barbadoes*, where it is drunk more liberally than other *European* Wines'.[8] Subtracting the amounts for local consumption and ullage gives us 8,000–9,000 pipes for export, which does not seem to be modest at all. In fact, I find it unbelievably high. So, as we cannot assess Ovington's accuracy, the most we can say with confidence is that by the end of the seventeenth century exports of wine had grown to something well in excess of 6,000 pipes, and that this must represent something like a threefold expansion of trade over the course of the century.

It is interesting to note commentators' remarks on the small amount of wine consumed on the island and on the sobriety of its inhabitants. Landi gives us one explanation: 'Amongst them the drinking of wine, old men apart, is a shameful thing; especially for the young men and the women. The reason is that they believe that those women who drink wine must be of little honesty. The young men abstain from drinking wine so as not to offend the ladies, to whom the smell of wine is displeasing.'[9] A century later, John Ovington provides a more intriguing speculation: 'The Venereal Excesses to which they are strangely addicted, with the immoderate heat of the place, would be apt to put Nature under various disorders. Therefore Men of the greatest Consequence and Fortune, (whether it be that Sobriety might render them more Spruce and Amorous for the Exercise of Love, or that they are bred up in an Antipathy to that gross and scandalous Vice of Drunkenness,) seldom exceed the allowable bounds of Drinking.'[10]

The British commercial presence in Madeira, initiated by Robert Willoughby in the 1590s, started slowly. Of the eighteen foreign merchants registered in the customs house records for 1620, only three were British. During the middle of the century, from 1638 until 1682, the principal merchant (amongst foreigners and Portuguese alike) was Richard Pickford, and from this period until the end of the century another fifteen names were added to the British contingent.[11] The 1687 customs register records about eighty names, but according to Duncan, the most important import-export business was confined to about thirty of them, of which eight or nine might be said to have been both wealthy and powerful. Of these thirty merchants, about two dozen were foreign and just short of half were British. One of them, John Carter, became the first British consul in 1658, but the most famous of the British merchants—on account of the fact that a large section of his business correspondence has been published—is William Bolton, who arrived in Madeira in 1676.[12] These merchants were prosperous and enjoyed a luxurious lifestyle. Ovington says they 'imitate the

English way of Living in their City and Country Houses; and wearied with the Town, divert themselves in their Rural Plantations' where he discovered 'the Hills were all cover'd with Vines, and the Valleys with ripe Grapes, which yielded us a fragrant smell from the fruitful Vineyards whither soever we turn'd our Eyes'.[13]

The influx of the British appears to have been closely connected with the development of colonial markets in America and also with trading concessions made to British merchants. From 1580 until 1640 Portugal was under the domination of Spain, whose kings had also been the kings of Portugal. During this period English and Dutch trade prospered at the expense of Portuguese trade, and many of Portugal's overseas possessions changed hands. The conclusion of the brief Anglo-Portuguese war in 1650 brought about a 'favoured nation' treaty in 1654, by means of which King João IV, to limit further territorial aggrandisement at Portugal's expense, accorded concessions to British merchants resident in Portugal and Madeira. The British Factory, an association of British merchants, was probably started about 1658. The trading position of these merchants was further reinforced in 1663—after the restoration of the monarchy in Britain and the marriage of Charles II to Catherine of Braganza—when, under the Staple Act, Madeira and the Azores were exempted from the prohibition in the 1660 Navigation Act against the export of any goods to English colonies except in English ships directly from English ports.[14] This concession gave the British merchants in Madeira a virtual monopoly of the trade with the West Indies and the American plantations, and compensated for the fact that Brazil, which had hitherto been the most important market for madeira, declined in importance from this date onwards.

These traders were effectively general brokers whose prosperity depended upon the importation of all manner of goods as much as it did on the export of wine. Indeed, if Bolton is representative, they did not warehouse the wine they exported, but obtained it from 'the natives' as required in settlement of credit for imported goods already supplied:[15] 'Nor, indeed, would it be any Prudence in us to buy before hand, not knowing how or when any ships may come, and the Keepeing of wine is very chargeable: it quickly makes them very deare.'[16]

As the markets in the Indies and Americas opened up, a triangular trade between Madeira, the New World and Britain or continental Europe became general, including the trans-shipment of goods from the British and Portuguese colonies back to Europe. Thus English textiles, pickled herring, butter and cheese, American wheat and cereal crops, Newfoundland and New England salt fish, Portuguese olive oil, spices, cheese and sausages—together with a huge assortment of raw materials such as metals, ship's chandlery, materials for defence, household articles and furniture—were all imported. On the export side, wine was far and away the most important commodity, amounting to perhaps as much as 95 per cent of the total. Without Madeira's location on so many trading routes this would simply have been impossible.

The wine

During the seventeenth century we find the wine being classified in various ways. At the beginning of the century, for example, the price paid to growers for their ordinary wine was fixed in October each year, after the harvest, by the council. In 1625 the price paid to growers made a distinction between the grapes grown on the middle slopes and upwards (*meias terras para cima*) and those grown on the middle slopes and downwards (*meias terras para baixo*), the price of the latter being 20 per cent higher than that of the former. Devaluation of the currency, however, reduced this differential to less than 8 per cent by 1667.[17]

In 1650 the customs house distinguished between *vinhos melhores* (better quality wines) and *vinhos mais baixos* (lower quality wines). To what extent this mirrored the previous distinction is not clear. The former were shipped mainly to the Portuguese mainland and to Brazil, and had a (customs) estimated value of 8 réis per pipe.[18] The latter went to Barbados and English plantations, having an estimated value of 6 réis per pipe. Duties reflected this differential, being 888 milréis and 666 milréis per pipe respectively.[19] In 1667, however, this duty differential vanished, and by 1670 the distinction between the two markets had also vanished. Indeed, more and more of the better wines began to find their way to

America. The prices realized by merchants generally seem to have run 20–40 per cent ahead of the customs house estimates. In the 1670s the prices were depressed, but from 1682 until the end of the century the increased trade with British colonial markets gave them a considerable boost. Thus in this period ordinary wine increased in price by 50 per cent, and Malvazia by 71.5 per cent.

Malvazia, as much because of its rarity as its quality, always commanded a higher price than the ordinary wines. In 1650, while the better-quality wines were estimated at 8 réis by the customs, Malvazia was estimated at 9 réis. Of the 2,405 pipes of wine exported in 1650, 1,540 pipes were better-quality wines, 778 pipes were of the lower quality, and only 87 pipes were Malvazia—that is, 3.6 per cent of the total quantity and 5–6 per cent of the total value. This may be a rogue figure, however, if the production of Malvazia in 1650 was abnormally low; in 1699, Bolton loaded 158 pipes of Malvazia in one day, which is over 80 per cent more than the recorded total of shipments for 1650.[20] Even making allowance for the growth of the vineyards in the half century since 1650, this seems an extraordinary difference.

The Bolton letters yield a miscellany of information, apart from giving us a graphic picture of the vicissitudes of a merchant's life (including the risk of summary arrest and deportation). He indicates, for example, that one shipment of 100 pipes of wine came, 'except some Pipes that are always forced upon us by the Governours of this Place', from a single vineyard.[21] This comment seems to indicate that there was something like a quota system in existence to ensure that some wines (perhaps inferior ones) eventually got shipped. But it also indicates that there were already some very large single vineyards in existence. Assuming a fairly large yield of 15 tons per hectare, a pipe capacity of 418 litres, and assuming that no more than 10 per cent of the shipment consisted of the pipes forced on Bolton, then at 850 litres of wine per ton this would give us a single vineyard with an area of more than 15 hectares—half as big again as the largest single vineyard on the island today.

Bolton refers frequently to *old wines*. These, however, were not generally much older than the previous vintage. They seem to have been slightly more expensive than *new wines*—that is, the wines of the current vintage, made in September and October, racked in January and on sale by Easter. The market price for wine was established on a supply and demand basis only after the arrival of 'the Jamaica Fleet' in April each year. Until then the wine producers held off declaring a price. If there were a lot of old wines available, this would hold down the price of the new wines. Generally, despite the higher price, the old wines would be loaded in preference to the new wines, whose sale would be proportional to the unsatisfied demand for old wines, and the scarcity of either would drive up the price as the year progressed. This picture could be modified in the light of the quality of successive vintages. Sometimes Bolton describes the new wines as being 'Green and Small', but even when he says 'tis the generall Opinion that ye new wines will be very good, the best that has bin for some years', he adds that they are not the clients' first choice: 'The old wines are drawing to a Conclusion. Should ships come dropping in as they doe, shall soone be forced to load ye New.'[22]

Bolton makes three references to Vidonia. He says that the grapes are vintaged before the Malvazias and susceptible to rain prior to picking.[23] Amongst the other wines mentioned by Bolton are 'white wines' and 'tent' or 'tinto'. There are more than a dozen references to the former, which obviously formed a staple part of the trade. My surmise is that these white wines are in fact the Vidonias referred to under a more generic name. 'Tent' or 'tinto', which was probably not yet made from Tinta Negra, was a red wine used to give colour to white wines. Occasionally Bolton would ship a pipe of Tent with other wines so that the recipient could improve or adjust the colour on delivery. Once he ships a pipe 'to assist ye Poor french wines'.[24]

The character of the wine

Towards the end of the century we have reports on the wine from Sir Hans Sloane, who visited the island in 1687, and the previously cited John Ovington, who visited in 1689. What they say accords well with what we learn from Bolton, except that the Vidonias are never mentioned as such.

Sloane reports that 'the greatest part of this Island is at present planted with Vines, the Soil being very proper, for it is rocky and steep; they keep their Vines very low with Pruning, in that agreeing with the Culture of the Vines in *France*, as also in that these Wines grow on the same Soil with those most esteemed there, as the *Hermitage* Wines, which grow on the rocky steep Hills on the sides of the *Rhosne*. The Grapes are of three sorts, the White, Red and great Muscadine, or *Malvasia;* of which three the first are most plentiful, for out of the White is made the greatest quantity of Wine, which is made Red by the addition of some Tinto, or very Red Wine made out of the Red Grapes, which gives it a deeper Tincture than that of *Champagne*, and helps it to preserve it self much better. It is sufficiently known that White-Wines, generally speaking, perish very soon, and that Red ones are much easier preserved, the deeper their Tincture be ... The Virgin Wine, or that made of the Juice running of the Husks immediately without standing or pressure, is soon ready to drink, fine, and very soon perish'd, the Husk impregnating the Wine with something equivalent to Hops in Beer ... The *Malvasia* or Wine made from the Muscadine Grape, does not keep, but Pricks very soon, and so is made in very small quantities. The great quantity of Wine here made, is that of the White mixt with a little Tinto, which has one very particular and odd Property, that the more 'tis expos'd to the Sun-beams and heat the better it is, and instead of putting it in a cool Cellar they expose it to the Sun. It seems to those unaccustomed to it to have a very unpleasant Tast, though something like Sherry, to which Wine it comes near in Strength and other Properties. It is Exported in vast quantities to all the *West-India* Plantations, and now of late to the *East;* no sort of Wine agreeing with those hot Places like this.'[25]

Ovington tells us that 'the main product of the Island is Grapes, brought hither first from *Candy*, of which there are three or four kinds, whereof they make their Wine. One is coloured like Champaign, of little esteem; another is more strong and pale as white wine; the third sort is rich and delicious, called Malmsey; the fourth is *Tento*, equalling Tent in colour but far inferior in Taste; it is never drunk unless in other Wines, with which it is mixt to give them a Tincture, and to preserve them. And for fermenting and feeding them, they bruise and bake a certain Stone, called Jess, of which nine or ten pounds are thrown into each Pipe. The *Madeira* Wine has in it this peculiar Excellence, of being meliorated by the heat of the Sun, when it is prick'd, if the Bunghole being open'd 'tis expos'd to the Air. The product of the vine is equally divided between the Proprietor and him that gathers and presses the Grapes; and yet for the most part the Merchant is Thriving and Rich, whilst the Grape-gatherer imploy'd by him, is but Poor. Among the Merchants the *Jesuits* are none of the meanest, who everywhere contend for precedence in Fortune, as well as in place; and have here secured the Monopoly of *Malmsey*.'[26]

Sloane and Ovington are remarkably unanimous in what they say, though there are subtle differences. Both agree on classifying the wine into three types. Firstly the red, which is poor in quality, is mixed with white wine as a colorant and preservative, and (according to Ovington) is never drunk on its own. Secondly the white, which constitutes the bulk of the export wine, is tinted to a colour (darker than champagne)—at that time a still, pale-coloured wine with 'a rosy tinge'—and becomes better with heat. According to Sloane it tastes rather like sherry and is an acquired taste. Ovington tells us that a smaller quantity is not mixed with red and is stronger and paler, like a white wine. This, one has to presume, is the Vidonia. Thirdly the Malvazia, which Ovington describes as 'rich and delicious'; Sloane says it keeps badly, turns sharp, and is therefore not made in large quantities.

The light red wine, classified by Bolton as being of the 'comon sorts',[27] constituted the bulk of the exports. From the resemblance of its taste to sherry it is clear that it must have been slightly oxidized, and in this respect may already have had something in common with modern madeira. It was almost certainly a dry wine. André Simon, somewhat surprisingly, states that 'a smaller quantity of ordinary beverage *White Wine* was made from the *Verdelho* grape',[28] without indicating his grounds for so doing. Perhaps he is alluding to Ovington's stronger, paler white wine, but as he regarded Vidonia as a sweet wine, he would not presumably have identified this wine with Vidonia. As far as I am aware, however, there is no direct evidence to show that *Verdelho* had reached the island by this time, though this is possible and even probable.

As for the Malvazia, Sloane's comment that it does not keep contrasts unexpectedly with the comments they both make about madeira's capacity to benefit from heat, and with what we gather about its ageing potential from Bolton. It may suggest that, as a sweet wine, it had the instability of a wine which had not been completely fermented.[29] Bolton indicates that there were problems from time to time, but not solely confined to the Malvazia. Thus in 1705 he reports that 'the last Vintage ... was small and we find a great many of the wines are turned sower, which makes the Natives on the High Ropes, not Knowing what to Demand for them'.[30] Because Sloane's comment is out of line with the other information we have, he may have been misinformed or may have misunderstood what he was told. Sloane does not comment on the quality of Malvazia, which may not be surprising in the light of what he does say. It is more surprising that Ovington does not comment either.

It is clear from what both have to say that heating madeira in the sun had already become a fairly common practice, although *vinho do sol* is a term which does not crop up until 1730.[31] The wine's response to heat had two aspects. First, it had the ability to withstand high temperatures, not in itself easy to explain, which is what made it, with the Azorean Pico-Faial,[32] so popular in the West Indies and the American plantations. Secondly, it actually *improved* with heat, and being stowed in holds with extremely high temperatures while being transported to tropical and semi-tropical destinations was found to improve its quality. Some even believed that the rolling movement of the ships played a part in the process. This discovery led to the practice of shipping wine back to Madeira from the West Indies for the express purpose of improving it, and we learn from Bolton that such 'back-loading' was becoming quite common at this time.[33] Here was the start of *vinho da roda* ('return wine'), also called *tornaviagem* ('round trip'), which in the next century became a specific type of madeira sold as a luxury item at elevated prices. Once again the island's mid-ocean position exercised a direct formative influence on the character of the wine—one which would in time be developed further, although it was to be another hundred years before heating the wine became part of an industrialized production process.

Ovington's mention of 'Jess' refers to the use of gesso (or gypsum) in fermenting the wine, which was discussed in the previous chapter. Bolton tells us that he made 'some white wines without Jesso which our W.B. order'd us to gett made, but not haveing heard how they prov'd, did not think it convenient to Run the Risque of makeing any more this Yeare'.[34] The use of gypsum was obviously commonplace.

It is noteworthy that by this time Malvazia was closely associated with the Jesuits. A Jesuit College was first established in Funchal in 1569. The Jesuits thereafter established a number of houses around the island, and were supported by charity, bequests and by farming the lands they came to own. The largest of these properties was Quinta Grande—'large farm'—west of Cabo Girão, an area still in existence today. It had originally belonged to descendants of Zarco, who transferred parcels of land to the Jesuits by gift and by sale, eventually making it one of the largest single properties on the island. The Jesuits continued to run Quinta Grande until 1759, when the order was expelled from Portugal and its possessions confiscated by the Marquês de Pombal. Quinta Grande was then sold by auction to João Francisco de Freitas Esmeraldo for 140,000 cruzados (56,000 réis). The quinta was always a large vine-growing area and included the famous Fajã dos Padres, the best and most celebrated Malvasia vineyard in Madeira.[35] Ovington, in common with later travellers, claims that the Jesuits controlled the entire production of Malvazia on the island, but there is no conclusive evidence that this was ever so.

By the end of the seventeenth century Madeira was poised for a further expansion of its trade, capitalizing on the unparalleled advantage of the many trading routes it enjoyed. It produced a wine which the world was to want more and more—in such quantities that production could not keep up with demand, and adulteration and falsification were to become almost the norm and very nearly its downfall.

3

THE EIGHTEENTH CENTURY

The development of trade

The privileges of British merchants were generally consolidated by the Methuen Treaty of 1703, whereby Portuguese wines imported into England paid a third less duty than, for example, French wines, and English woollen textiles (the single most important British import into Madeira) were admitted into Portugal duty-free. The merchants of Oporto, however, benefited from this treaty much more than those in Madeira, for despite this concession relatively little madeira was imported into England until much later in the eighteenth century, and the concession regarding woollens was almost immediately limited when in 1712 the Portuguese government imposed restrictions on trade with Brazil. The main destinations of exports of madeira continued to be the West Indies, North America and, increasingly, the East Indies (including non-British possessions like Pondicherry, Bengal and Surat).[1] Exports to Europe were of secondary importance.

Details of production and export volumes remain patchy and unreliable throughout the century, with regular annual figures available only after 1776–7.[2] From the scant information before this it is almost impossible to judge any trends. John Atkins, visiting the island in 1721, tells us that 'their vintage is in *September* and *October* and make about 25,000 pipes'[3]—the same total given by

Jeaffreson forty-five years earlier. The export total of 8,000 pipes for 1765[4] is similar to the figure given by Ovington for 1689. Cossart asserts that 'up to 1745 annual shipments averaged 7,000 pipes'.[5] All this suggests, perhaps, a rather stagnant level of production. Sporadic figures for the last quarter of the century[6] indicate that exports doubled over that period. America was still the prime market by a long way. Even during the War of Independence (1777–82), exports to America never dropped below 58 per cent, and twice exceeded 80 per cent, of all the wine exported from the island.[7]

These figures are misleading, however, if taken to indicate continuing and even increasing prosperity. Foreign wars in the second half of the century brought about a drop in the price of wine to under half of what it had been, and because Madeira had virtually a monoculture economy based on wine and was dependent on imports for three-quarters of its cereals, this drop produced serious social consequences. At this time most of the cereals required by Madeira were imported from North America. In 1757 the cereal crop had failed and in some places the peasants had had to sustain themselves by eating roots, fruit and broom (genista) flowers.[8] Later, the War of Independence further reduced the amount of cereals available for import, and the fall in the price of wine meant that only half the previous imports of cereals could be paid for out of wine revenue. The problem was exacerbated by a steep rise in the population during the second half of the century: from 51,343 in 1754 to 79,773 in 1797 (reaching 84,364 in 1803). Even before famine became manifest, the misery of large parts of the population, who were without work or the means of subsistence, had led to an attempted uprising in 1767, and in 1773 the peasants who held land by *contrato de colonia* had petitioned the king (unsuccessfully) for a fairer division of the profits from their work.[9]

Helpful visitors furnish us with their estimates of total production. They are fairly consistent, although curiously the alleged totals drop just as export volumes increase. These range from 30,000 to 35,000 pipes (10,000 being exported to Britain and her colonies) in 1768;[10] 28,000 pipes (8,000 for the island, the rest exported mainly to the West Indies) in 1772;[11] about 30,000 pipes (13,000 exported and the rest made into brandy for Brazil) in 1777;[12] between 15,000 and 25,000 pipes (up to 15,000 pipes being exported) in 1792;[13] and 25,000 pipes in 1797.[14]

We do, on the other hand, have production figures for 1787.[15] The north produced 8,198 pipes and the south 6,833 pipes, giving a grand total of 15,031 pipes.[16] This is far from the heady 25,000 pipes mentioned by Atkins in 1721, though it does seem plausible when compared with a known export total of 10,819 pipes for 1788. It also shows that the north was considerably the larger producer of wine. As the wine from the north always had the reputation of being considerably lower in quality than that from the south, it is no wonder that this was to lead to difficulties.

Fraud and increased regulation

The global demand for madeira during the whole of the eighteenth century was greater than could be supplied from the best wines of the island alone. This led to two sorts of fraudulent practice, which were current for most of the century: the adulteration of wines on the island, and the passing off as genuine madeira of wines from other sources. The incidence of both frauds increased as trade expanded towards the end of the century, and both contributed to the slump in sales early in the following century. This situation was a constant preoccupation of the authorities and merchants for the next two centuries and led to ever-increasing regulation of the trade.

On 23 December 1724 the Funchal Senate received a petition signed by thirty-eight merchants who, dismayed by the way that good wine was being adulterated with inferior wine from the north of the island, asked for a ban on wine produced in the north being brought to the south. This would have effectively prevented its being exported since Funchal was the only port of embarkation. No action was taken until 9 January 1737, when in response to a petition by a merchant called Francisco Teodoro, the Senate imposed just such a restriction.[17] With no official outlet except local consumption, one wonders what the authorities expected would become of the wine from the north. Doubtless much of it was distilled into spirit. But over the next thirty years, as ways of evading the law were found, the situation deteriorated further. In 1768 the authorities were forced to take action to regulate the wine trade in a more extensive way than ever before. Two official posts were created—a Juiz de Fóra and a Presidente dos Risiduos—whose role was to prevent fraudulent practices. Then, on 11 March 1768, the Governor issued an edict which confirmed the embargo on moving wine from the north of the island to the south until after the end of May each year, and expressly forbade the mixing of wines from the two parts of the island, thereby making a simple demarcation between the two areas. Moreover, a distinction was made between the inferior wine made in the upper (northern) parts of the parishes on the south coast and the better quality wine (suitable for export) made closer to the sea in the lower parts of the same parishes, implying a secondary demarcation between north and south within the southern parishes. Most importantly, the thirteen articles of the edict classified the wine into three distinct qualities based on the markets for which it was destined.[18]

This remarkable document cannot fail to remind one of the Pombaline demarcation of the port-producing area of the Douro eleven years earlier, in 1757, which may well have inspired it—even if the demarcation in Madeira had neither the influence nor the permanence of its port counterpart. The classification of the wines is similar to that of the Douro, which also corresponded with the market to which the wine was destined. Unlike the Douro classification, on the other hand, no fixed prices were set for each kind of wine. There were three categories: (1) wines of the best quality intended for export to all destinations except Brazil; (2) wines of medium quality, only to be exported to Brazil or sold for the consumption of ships' crews; and (3) wine for consumption in taverns.

At the same time as the demarcation took place in the Douro, the Marquês de Pombal, partly to regulate the market and partly to limit the monopoly of English merchants, set up (in 1757) a Portuguese monopoly company called the Companhia Geral da Agricultura das Vinhas do Alto Douro. This may have inspired a move to set up a Companhia Vinícola in Madeira. On 6 May 1774 the Funchal municipal council considered a report on the advantages of such a company, but nothing appears to have come of it.

The provisions of the 1768 edict continued in force for some time. Although the threefold categorization of quality seems in practice to have been jettisoned by the end of the century, a statement by the Governor on 21 January 1821 indicates that the demarcation between wines from the north and south still held: 'The wines of Madeira have a prompt sale in Brazil, wine from the south selling at from 130 to 140 milréis a pipe, and that from the north at 50 to 60 milréis.'[19] Despite the measures which had been taken, however, wine from the north continued to find its way on to the export market. On 16 August 1785[20] further restrictions were imposed. Wine made in the north could only be moved under a local magistrate's licence, as could the wines of Ponta do Sol, Calheta and Arco and Estreito da Calheta, which it was 'absolutely prohibited' to move into parishes eastwards of them. On 16 August 1786 there was a further and more elaborate edict on adulteration and fraud, repeating the prohibition on mixing wine from the north and south within the southern parishes, with severe penalties for offenders.[21] New forms of fraud proliferated. A ruse which the growers in the north employed to make their wines look like the tinto wines of the south was to colour them with the juice of black cherries (just as elderberries were being used at the same time in the Douro to give colour to inferior port). On 27 February 1788 the Governor ordered that all black cherry trees should be grafted with red cherries (which were unsuitable for colouring the wine) or be uprooted. Anyone caught planting a black cherry tree was subject to a fine of 6,000 réis.[22] The town council had occasion to refer to this malpractice again as late as 1819.[23]

On 20 September 1710 a prohibition on the importation of foreign wines and spirits was imposed, with the aim of stopping the adulteration of madeira with inferior foreign products.[24] The idea was not only to safeguard the reputation of madeira in foreign markets, but also to keep the price high. Despite this, inferior wine was imported into Funchal from the Canaries and the Azores, then mixed with madeira and re-exported. Less easy to control was the converse of this form of fraud, whereby madeira was imported into the Canaries and other places to be mixed with the cheaper local wines and later passed off in foreign (mainly Asian) markets as genuine madeira. During the eighteenth century a wide range of (unsuccessful) controls on the size, design and marking of casks was imposed by the authorities to combat this abuse.[25] The Funchal Archive contains a list of the ships engaged in taking madeira to Tenerife for adulteration between 1784 and 1787,[26] which can only have been possible through the connivance of unscrupulous merchants. John Barrow, visiting Madeira in 1792, marvelled that 'although it is supposed that the quantity consumed in Great Britain, under the name of Madeira, is, on the least calculation, equal to the whole quantity that is exported from the island, or more than three times what is actually imported, yet it is well known that a variety of mixtures pass for Madeira, some of which are compounded of wines that never grew on the island, as those of Teneriffe, Lisbon and Xeres'.[27] Vidonia from Tenerife was about a third the cost of madeira[28] and became known as 'mock madeira'.[29] Another measure to exclude foreign wines and spirits was passed on 27 January 1789.[30]

The British influence

The British merchants dominated the commercial scene in Funchal throughout the century, acting through their commercial association, the British Factory, under the guidance of the consul. At a meeting held on 26 October 1722, twelve merchants were present. In 1771 the Factory consisted of a consul, vice-consul and twenty-two merchants, from which ten were selected to direct the business of the factory in conjunction with the consul.[31] Shortly afterwards there seems to have been an influx of traders, for between 1786 and 1790 we find thirty-five separate British firms and twenty-one individuals listed as shippers.[32] The British Factory existed until 1838, and was financed by a levy, sanctioned in 1717, on goods imported from England and on wine shipped by its members. These funds were applied to projects of benefit to its members and to the British community.

In the middle of the eighteenth century we begin to encounter names which are still to be found in the trade, the oldest firms still existing (even if in transmuted form) dating from this time.[33] Amongst these are John Leacock, Francis Newton and Thomas Gordon. Relations between the British community and their Portuguese hosts were certainly difficult for much of the time. Strains appeared when downturns in the wine trade, on which the island economy depended, brought extensive privation and misery to the peasant population. The virtual monopoly of the wine trade enjoyed by the British made them extremely powerful. When in 1722 relief had to be granted to wine producers by reducing the 10 per cent tax—the *décima*—which had long been levied on new wine, the official decree did not mince its words: 'By reason of lack of commerce on the said island and of poverty, most of its population are in a miserable state because ... either they sell their wines to the English or they ship them to Brazil, and they get little profit from whichever of these courses they take, because the English want to wring them from them (by extortion) for very inferior prices'.[34]

Staunton, writing at the end of the century, indicates that British merchants were not averse to profitable sharp practices. He instances the commonly practised fraud of 'salt water invoices', whereby the prices paid for goods in England were increased after shipment so that even higher prices could be asked for them when they were sold on to the native Madeirans, the 'only sufferers from this ruse.[35]

Despite the many social difficulties which the island experienced during this period, the eighteenth century is notable in the history of madeira for two technical developments which permanently changed its character: fortification and *estufagem* (from the Portuguese word *estufa*, meaning 'stove', 'hot-house' and green-house'). The adoption of the second practice by the merchants also brought them closer to being wine merchants in a modern sense, because instead of merely broking wine, as was common at the beginning of the century, merchants had to acquire wine in order to heat it, and then had to store it afterwards.

Fortification

We do not know for certain when the practice of fortification first began. Experiments in distilling in Madeira took place around the turn of the century, so the possibility of fortification dates from this time. Cossart mentions that a Portuguese book on viticulture published in 1720 recommended the addition of brandy to wine in order to improve it, but it is probable that the Madeira merchants learned of the advantages of fortification as a means of stabilizing wine for export from Oporto, where the practice became general around 1730,[36] or even from Spain, where it had been used for much longer. What can be asserted with confidence is that most firms appear to have been fortifying their wine by the middle of the century. Writing in October 1753, Francis Newton who had hitherto prided himself that his wines were 'fresh and full flavoured unlike the ones laced with Brandy', was constrained to admit that I really impute the complaints I have had of wines to my not putting a bucket or two of brandy in each pipe as other houses do'.[37] In 1756 Michael Nowlan, an associate of John Leacock, received advice from London: 'Some Gentlemen here that are knowing in the Wine Trade assure me that if a couple of gallons of fine clear Brandy was put into each pipe of our best Wines 'twill improve them greatly. I believe that some of the Houses in Madeira use this method ... I observe that their Madeiras drunk here in gentlemen's houses are fine pale amber colour nothing tending to a reddish.'[38] It may be that the fortification of the wine was something of a trade secret, because we find in 1771 one of the anonymous chroniclers of Cook's first voyage round the world declaring that 'it is commonly reported that no distilled spirit is added to these wines, but I have been well assured of the contrary, and have seen the spirit used for that purpose'.[39]

It is clear from Nowlan's remark about the wine's pale amber colour that, with the start of fortification, madeira came closer to the drink we know today. Croft describes it as having 'a kernelly taste like a walnut'.[40] However, unfortified 'madeira burgundy' continued to be made for much of the next century, and fortification was not yet used to check the fermentation of the wine. It was simply an addition of spirit to the wine immediately prior to shipping, intended originally to ensure that the wine reached its destination in sound condition. According to calculations made by Noël Cossart, the wine resulting from this kind of rough and ready fortification would have had an alcoholic strength of about 15 per cent by volume.[41]

Estufagem

If fortification was common by the middle of the eighteenth century, the process of *estufagem* began only at the end of the century. However, as we know from Sloane, there was a general awareness at least as early as 1687 that the wine benefited from the heat of the sun. Croft, writing in 1787, tells us that 'in England they put [the wines] in stoves or hot-houses for the sun; in America they keep them in cisterns on the tops of the houses'.[42] The term *vinho do sol* (sun wine) was already current in the 1730s, and in the eighteenth century storehouses were built with glass roofs so that the wine could benefit from sunshine.[43] Heat was reckoned the most important element of the beneficial effect of sending madeira on long sea voyages. Many old houses in Funchal have, behind their shutters, shelves built into the sides of the window recesses, looking for all the world like small cupboards (of which the shutters are the doors). These were expressly for storing bottles of wine so that they might benefit from the heat of the sun shining in at the windows. So there is ample evidence that the wine was deliberately subjected to heat long before the invention of *estufas* enabled this to be done on a commercial scale. Jullien even reports, as late as 1816, another curious method of heating the wine, which is 'to plunge the bottles, well corked, in a trench filled with hot horse-dung, and in six months or a year the maturity, &c. of a voyage is gained'.[44] This extraordinary and commercially rather impractical procedure is confirmed by Redding—although he may have lifted the information from Jullien's book.

The first recorded *estufa* was built in Funchal in 1794 by a merchant called Pantaleão Fernandes, who 'having already observed that wine is much improved by being kept in warm places, principally by being placed in the sun, heated a store containing wine from the last vintage with little stoves both night and day, and obtained an encouraging result'.[45] The invention was hailed as a way of imparting the characteristics of maturity to the wine without having to wait for it to age naturally, and as a means of achieving the effect of a *vinho da roda* without a comparable expenditure of time and money. In no time at all other merchants were building their own *estufas*.

One such was John Leacock, who explained his plans in August 1800: 'We are erecting an *Estufa* & hope to have it furnished in two or three weeks. We shall stand in need of two common *Thermometers, good* but the *least* expensive, in order that we may regulate the heat; we therefore beg you will send out a couple very carefully packed. We hope this new Mode of treating Wine will answer, but we have never yet heard whether any remarks have been made by the Correspondents of those who ship it—they are now common & all the Houses use *Estufas*—several of them have built them, & others put their Wine into hired *Estufas*, where they pay 5mooo p. pipe[46] for 3 Months stewing. We are not yet *perfectly* satisfied of all the Effects produced by the Application of Heat to the Wine, but think that in general they keep too fierce a degree of Heat, which keeps the Wine constantly boiling, and renders it rather insipid & weak. We are of Opinion that a more Moderate Temperature will succeed better, & shall prolong the Period to *Six* instead of Three Months as we see. However the great test will be, how it is approved by those who drink it after a Voyage. Certainly to those who are not good Judges, the new Wine with three Months *Estufa* imitates Wine of 4 or 5 Years old, & we dont think that the deception will be easily discovered—however the Secret will be soon known abroad & may perhaps prejudice the character of Madeira Wine.'[47]

The adoption of this new process appears to have quickly got out of hand. At first the wines seem to have been heated to extremely high temperatures, resulting in disagreeable tastes of toasting or baking quite uncharacteristic of wines slowly aged in cask or sent on a sea voyage. It appears that some merchants like John Leacock mistakenly thought that *estufas* might make poor wines more acceptable to the market. 'We shall endeavour by our new Process to improve the *cheap* Wines in such a manner that they will answer for almost any quality, after being mixed with other good Wines. We have no doubt by what we have heard and seen that the Porto do Cruz [*sic*] Wine of good quality made up with the best Wine of a good vintage & prepared in the *Estufa* may be shipped off for *particular* ...'[48]

The impetus for making the greatest possible use of the new invention was quite simply the necessity of finding sufficient wine to satisfy the rapid upturn in trade as the century ended. England, which had remained a minor importer of madeira for most of the century, suddenly became an important market. This is partly explained by the return home of British nationals after the American War of Independence, and by the difficulty of trade with France after the 1789 Revolution and the outbreak of war in 1793, which led to tax discrimination against French wines.

It was also due to the simple fact that over the second half of the century madeira had become increasingly fashionable as a drink. Christie's, the London auctioneers, began selling madeira at auction in 1766, and madeira figured largely in the trade-orientated wine sales that began to take place in the 1780s. Edmund Penning-Rowsell, who has made a special study of them, points out that 'in the late 18th century the most fashionable wine in Britain was certainly madeira, and to be "fine" the prerequisite was that it had been on a long sea voyage or kept in the Tropics'.[49] Indeed, *vinho da roda* began to occupy an increasingly important place in such sales, being known as East Indies and West Indies Madeira. Sometimes the wine remained abroad for a number of years, and this could more than double its price because connoisseurs of madeira were prepared to pay for the mellowness resulting from the voyage.

Viticulture

The reports of travellers and official documents tell us interesting things not only about the wine, but about vine cultivation too. A guidebook published anonymously by John Adam in 1801 explains that 'the vine is generally propagated from cuttings, as the preferable mode of culture, rather than from seed. In former times it was planted with the plough, to a depth pretty much the same as that which the vine is now planted in France, being a depth of 12 or 18 inches. But at this first period the soil must have been richer ... The case however now is very different, from the poverty of the soil, and the frequent droughts. Hence it is found necessary to plant the vine to the depth of from 3 to 6 feet. It being protected from the hard ground at the bottom of the trench, by a quantity of loose earth placed underneath.'[50] James Cook, writing with the condescension typical of many English visitors, tells us that 'the inhabitants have made so little improvement in knowledge or art, that they have but very lately [1768] brought all the fruit of a vineyard to be of one sort, by engrafting their vines ... Wherever there is ignorance there is prejudice [and] it was therefore with great difficulty that the people of Madeira were persuaded to engraft their vines, and some of them still obstinately refuse to adopt the practice, though a whole vintage is very often spoiled by the number of bad grapes which are mixed in the vat, and which they will not throw out, because they increase the quantity of the wine.'[51]

Cook's dim view of the islanders seems to have been shared by the authorities, who in 1783 told the natives of Porto Santo that the degeneration of their vineyards resulted from their 'inertia, the tenacity and obstinacy with which they clung to their old prejudices ... and the hope which they had to a greater or lesser degree that nothing could throw them into the fatal abyss of hunger'.[52] Instructions were given to the Director and Inspector of Agriculture in Porto Santo about where to site vineyards and the proper grapes to plant. 'The varieties for everyone must be Verdelho, Boal or Tinta, and not Listrão, as is for the greater part planted; for its grapes, tasty though they are for eating, are not suited for wine.'[53] One visitor states that 'the island produces six kinds of grapes, viz. the Malmsey, two black, and three white kinds'.[54] Adam, on the other hand, lists twenty-six varieties (including Malvasia, Boal, Verdelho, Sercial, Bastardo and Terrantez) but agrees with the report on Porto Santo in saying that if the number were reduced 'to the Negro Mole, the Verdelha, and the Bual, the wines would certainly be of much better quality'.[55]

Here is a description of a typical vineyard: 'One or more walks, about a yard or two wide, intersect each vineyard, and are included by stone walls two feet high. Along these walks, which are arched over by lathes about seven feet high, they erect wooden pillars at regular distances, to support a lattice-work of bamboos, which slopes down from both sides of the walk, till it is only a foot and a half or two feet high, in which elevation it extends over the whole vineyard. The vines are in this manner supported from the ground, and the people have room to root out the weeds which spring up between them. In the season of the vintage they creep under this lattice-work, cut off the grapes, and lay them into baskets: some bunches of these grapes I saw, which weighed six pounds and upwards.'[56] A description of a vineyard today would be little different.

A contemporary description of the vintage would also have been quite up-to-date until about forty years ago. 'The vintage in Madeira begins early in September—the process of making wine is extremely simple. The grapes immediately when cut are put into the press, which is a machine of great simplicity in its construction, and not unlike the instrument used in England in the making of cyder. It consists of the *Paixa*, or reservoir [normally called the *lagar*], with the Fuzo, or spindle, and the *Vara*, or lever. The paixa is of a square or oblong square figure, made of the plank of chesnut [sic] tree, about two feet thick, and supported on three large beams. The vara, or lever, goes across the reservoir, which extending nine or ten feet beyond the paixa, is connected at its furthest extremity, where there is a female screw, with the fuzo, or spindle. The upper end of the fuzo is a male screw, while its lever end is fastened by means of an iron spindle to a large stone, the size of which is proportionate to that of the press. When the grapes intended to be prest are all cut and placed in the reservoir, three, four, or more labourers enter that part of the machine, and with their feet tread the grapes so long as any juice can be expressed from them. The juice is allowed to run into a vessel under this *paixa*, through a hole at its middle, or at one corner, over which is generally placed a small basket by way of a sieve, in order to prevent any of the husks, seeds, or stalks from escaping. After this first pressure, or treading, the mashed grapes are collected into one heap, which being surrounded by a cord in close circles, and having boards and pieces of wood laid about it, is then placed under the lever, which is forthwith sunk upon it, and allowed to remain in this position till the liquor ceases to flow. It is then raised, the boards and cords are taken off, and the mass being broken in pieces by tools something like hoes, is made to undergo a second treading or pressure, and again also subjected the operation of the lever. This process is even repeated a third time, with a view to obtaining a further quantity of wine from the grape, and lastly, a fourth time, for the purpose of obtaining the *Aqua hé* [*sic*]. In this fourth or last time however the mass when broken up is as dry as a piece of chip, and therefore previous to treading it, it is necessary to add to it a quantity of water ... The mass for procuring *Aqua hé* is generally put under pressure in the evening and allowed to remain in this situation till next morning, when the *Aqua hé* is drawn off, and put into casks for immediate use.'[57] *Agua pé* is a weakly alcoholic drink made by adding water to the *bagaço* or pressed grapes, and served to the labourers.

Towards the end of the century, the authorities did all in their power to improve the quality of the wines. A detailed regimen for the vintage was issued by the Governor on 12 August 1784 to combat the too-early and unselective picking of grapes.'[58] This included the setting of dates in each parish before which the vintage might not begin (1 October in the case of Malvasia); the requirement to obtain permission from the Inspector General of Agriculture of each district before starting the vintage; the appointment of inspectors to ensure that only appropriate *lagars* were used; and the imposition of confiscations and prison sentences for infringements of the rules. These measures worked only imperfectly, and they were clarified and tightened up on 16 August 1786.[59] An order dated 18 October 1792 forbade the cultivation of corn, barley or potatoes as intercalated plants in vineyards.[60] Later, between November 1794 and March 1795, doubtless as a response to the recent growth in trade, more than 176,000 vines were planted in Câmara de Lobos alone.[61]

The wine

Malvazia remained a prestigious product, although available only in small quantities. In 1704 Bolton reports that 'all that was made in the Island does not exceed 80 to 100 p^s; they will be dearer by much than those the Last year, there being so few and every body's Eyes upon them'.[62] Croft-Cooke reports a shipper writing in 1757: 'As regards the Malmsey, the whole Island produces only about 50 pipes annually'.[63] Staunton, however, suggests that the average annual production is 500 pipes.[64] This is probably a wild exaggeration, because Malvazia's rarity is attested by the fact that, according to merchants' ledgers of the time, it was generally shipped in quarter-pipe or hogshead quantities.

Wines were made from other single grape varieties, as a few surviving bottles of Boal, Terrantez, Moscatel and Sercial attest, but contemporary prices suggest that such wines were of a rarity equal to, or even greater than, that of Malvazia. The so-called Rainwater madeira also made its first appearance in the second half of the eighteenth century. Designed for the American market, it was a delicate Verdelho. Amongst various competing explanations of the origin of the name, Cossart's account of the 'discovery' of Rainwater by Francis Newton provides at least a certain cynical amusement. If he is to be believed, some pipes of Verdelho awaiting export were accidentally left unbunged on a rainy night, but were nevertheless shipped and found favour in Virginia. Thereafter, a special water-diluted blend was made up to satisfy the demand for the new style.[65] The main emphasis in wine-making was on producing 'madeira', which was a generic wine into which a wide assortment of grape varieties found their way, just as (until comparatively recently, at any rate) was the case with port. That the wines were a mixture is implied by a sentence from a letter by Jackie Leacock in 1793, quoted by Croft-Cooke: '[Mr. Snell's wines] are perfectly pale smooth and nutty flavoured as being mostly *Boyal* and *Verdelho*, and have no Tinge from the red Grape'.[66]

During most of the eighteenth century this wine was sold according to its destination, though in the last quarter of the century categorization became much more elaborate than in the classification of 1768. The names for generic madeiras, which survived into the twentieth century, originated from the wine auctions held at the London docks in the 1760s.[67] In the Invoices Book for 1794 of Newton, Gordon & Murdoch (the firm that eventually became Cossart Gordon), the following list of shipping prices is noted:

Malmsey	£63
Particular	£34
London Market	£30
India	£28
New York	£26
Cargo	£23[68]

The invoices refer to Fine Old Wine, London Particular Wine, Old Particular Wine, New York Wine, Particular Wine, India Market Wine, Cream Malmsey, Fine Old Malmsey and Fine Burgundy Coloured Wine. There is no mention of any grape variety other than Malvasia, but in the early nineteenth century Sercial and Tinta commanded the same prices as Malvazia.

On the other hand, the Purchase Book for the same period shows acquisitions of wine for each vintage as one of the following: Malvazia; wine from the north; wine from the south; or wine from a specifically named place (such as Campanário, São Martinho, etc.). The quantity of Malvazia purchased was minute, amounting to no more than some half-dozen entries amongst several hundred.

One market for madeira, singled out in the edict of 1768, deserves special mention before we leave the eighteenth century: ships' crews. Madeira was found to have health-giving properties for sailors deprived of fresh food for long periods afloat, and was carried for this purpose by Anson in 1740 and by Commodore Byron. Captain Cook also loaded 'ten tuns of wine' for his first world voyage in 1768. Some writers (Croft-Cooke,[69] Cossart,[70] Lemps[71] and others relying on Cossart) have erroneously reported that Cook took on board 3,032 gallons of wine. Cossart, whom I believe to be the original source of this misinformation, worked this out to be a ration of 200 bottles per man for a voyage of some 900 days. However, all this is quite untrue and stems from a misreading of Hawkesworth, who actually wrote 'we took in … 3,032 gallons of *water*, and ten tuns of wine' (my italics).[73] It is regrettable that this mistake appears without editorial comment in the second edition of Cossart's book.

On the other hand, in 1785 Lapérouse, having had the intention of loading thirty pipes of madeira on to each of his ships, jibbed at the cost and wrote to his superiors from Madeira on 16 August 1785 that 'the information which I have had about the price of the madeira wine appropriate for crews makes me determined to set sail immediately for Tenerife where I will procure the same quality of wine'. Lapérouse himself, however, was happy to accept a gift of a hundred bottles of Malvazia from a Mr Johnston, an associate of Francis Newton.[74]

4

THE NINETEENTH CENTURY I

The unpopular British

The new century saw an ever greater involvement of the British in the development of Madeira. During the Napoleonic wars there were two occupations of the island by the British army, largely to protect British interests by preventing a French invasion. The first, in 1801, lasted until the beginning of the following year. The second occupation was a much longer and more serious affair, lasting from Christmas Eve 1807 until October 1814. Both added to the growing anti-British sentiment on the island. Drunken soldiers involved in incidents such as church desecration did little to endear the British to the locals, and many suspected a devious British plan of out-and-out colonization. British merchants kept themselves apart, and they struck visitors to the island as aloof and petty. 'There is not that good feeling amongst the English which there should be; arising I apprehend, from all of them being dealers in the same article, wine.'[1]

During the War of the Two Brothers (1825–34), which deter-mined the Portuguese succession, dissension amongst the British was extreme. 'Private society was completely destroyed; discord pervaded every family ... the rancour and bitterness of party spirit evinced by these individuals surpast almost any thing of the descrip-tion witnessed by me, even in England.'[2] In 1849 'factionalism became a way of island life'.[3] Only two philanthropic merchants, Robert Page and Joseph Phelps, appear to have enjoyed any popularity with the Portuguese. Page alone amongst the British opposed both occupations of the island; he was cordially disliked by his fellow British merchants.[4]

At the opening of the nineteenth century there were a score of important British merchants and about half that number of Portuguese. A slightly later but noteworthy addition to the British contingent was John Blandy. He came to the island first in 1808 as an invalid seeking employment as an accountant,[5] went home in 1810 to get married, and returned to Madeira to become a merchant in 1811. Only a few of these merchants—the oldest established and most powerful—actually belonged to the Factory House. In 1811, for example, despite the ever-growing number of British merchants, the British Factory consisted of only ten firms. An entry in the notebook of one of its members records under 5 November 1817: 'There was a Meeting today of the Members of the Old Establishment/or Factory; which keeps itself distinct, from the general Commercial Body.'[6] This division in the ranks of the British caused much resentment, and in 1812 the Factory House levy which had been imposed on all British merchants' exports was abolished under pressure from the junior merchants, and its property was administered by the British residents in general.[7] Of the firms then trading, only the names of Blandy's, Leacock and Gordon have survived into the twenty-first century. The firm of Condell, Innes & Co (later to become Duncan, Innes, Lewis & Co), however, is also noteworthy because one of its members—Mr Innes, perhaps—kept the notebook from which we have just quoted, into which he meticulously copied a great deal of information concerning his firm and the wine trade generally. It covers the period 1789 to 1820, and provides an unparalleled insight into the workings of a merchant's firm at the turn of the century.[8]

Boom and bust

In business terms—despite the continuing worries about fraudulent madeira and the misuse of *estufas*—the nineteenth century opened in an optimistic way with exports, according to Biddle, totalling 16,981 pipes in 1800 and not falling below 11,011 pipes a year during the first decade.[9] Biddle unfortunately gives us no information about the years 1812–19, but with the help of the Condell Innes Notebook we can fill in some of the blanks.[10] From the report of a British Factory meeting dated 15 January 1815, we learn that 'the General Shipments last year exceeded 18,500 pipes by the Custom House Books, a larger quantity than for Several years past: about 12,000 of which were by British Vessels'.[11] A further undated note tells us: 'NB. Shipped in 1815—13,500 Pipes in British Vessels—2,500 Do in Portuguese Vessels—16,000 Pipes'.[12] It is evident, therefore, that exports remained very high until 1815.

This boom, which was due to the Napoleonic wars, was short-lived. Whereas 1811, 1812 and 1813 had all been productive years, there followed a series of disastrously short vintages: 1814 was less than half of that for 1813 and 1815, at about 6,000 pipes, was again less than half the previous year. 'Exports of wine must for Some time be very limited, for a most Substantial Reason, it has not been produced: If one fourth is taken from the whole produce of last year [1815] as consumed on the Island & unfit for Shipping, there will remain only about 4,000 pipes of New Wine for Exportation. The Stock of Old wines was in General comparatively very Low.'[13] With poor vintages, booming exports, diminishing stocks and rising prices, and a post-war depression looming, disaster was inevitable.

As before, when considering wine production and export totals during this century, considerable caution is necessary. Competing figures abound, and it is difficult to know which to believe. Most are only guesstimates. For the five years after 1815 the Condell Innes Notebook provides us with the following figures.[14] 1816: production 'about 10,000 pipes'. 1817: production 'about Ten thousand pipes, with this advantage that mostly the whole will be fit for Shipping'. 1817: 'the general Shipments by the Commerce here, for 1817, was only about 8,000 Pipes'. 1818: 'the general shipments for the Year … amounted to about 21,000 pipes. The produce of the last Vintage is estimated at from 18 to 21,000 pipes, but the *First Quality very limited*'. 1819: the vintage 'very productive' and 'very Superior' after a season 'the finest we remember for upwards of 30 years'. No figure is given for exports, but the comment for 1820 is relevant: 'The shipments of the Factory House last year [1820] were 6263 pipes, which is about 500 pipes more than the preceding [year]. The rest of the Commerce may be about one third more.'[15]

From these figures we can see that exports dropped significantly after 1815, and that even when better vintages came along they fell far short of the records established during the war years. The consequences to Madeira were grave: misery and near-starvation for the vast majority of the island's inhabitants. 'While the war lasted the ports of France and Spain were closed, good and bad wine found a ready market, the island of Madeira flourished, and Madeira and Portugal alone exported their fortified wines ... but once peace had been made the ports opened, and with this the export of Spanish and French wines increased while the number of consumers diminished enormously.'[16] Things were not about to get any better, and thus began a slow decay of the fortunes of madeira wine which has not, even today, really been reversed.

Disaster looms

During the first half of the nineteenth century the use of *estufas* and the reputation of madeira abroad were continuing concerns. No sooner had *estufas* become established at the end of the previous century than their use was banned by an edict of the Governor dated 23 August 1802, on the grounds that the good reputation of madeira was already suffering from the misuse of *estufas*, that there was a fire risk in Funchal and that smoke and coal fumes were affecting the health of those living near the *estufas*. Protest led to the lifting of the ban on 7 May 1803, largely because of the following economic argument: 'The shippers are obliged to store superlative wines in quantities corresponding to the orders which they are accustomed to receive annually, and to assign them a period of time of at least four years, such that the shipper who exports 300 pipes of old wine each year, finds himself needing to have a reserve of not less than 1,000 to 1,500 pipes lying stagnant and dead in his lodges;

and his commerce suffers from these tied-up funds, because with only part of them he could embark on new adventures and speculations, which would legally augment his fortune, put his establishment on a more solid base, and would certainly benefit the public and augment the Royal taxes so much more.'[17]

Relief was temporary, for the ban was reimposed on 6 November 1803, only to be rescinded yet again on 7 May 1804. The plain fact was that *estufas* were necessary to enable the trade to meet the growing demand for madeira. It seems clear that initially the wines were generally overheated for short periods, producing harsh results. Interestingly, Condell & Innes stood out against the trend. 'We are one of the few Houses on the Island, who have never made any use of the Stew fired Wine, or what has been in the Estufa; a mode of forcing it by fire, to have the appearance of being much Older than it realy is; & our opinion is, that it will, after undergoing that operation, rather go back than Improve, however it may deceive at first Sight.'[18] *Estufas*, however, provided new opportunities to impose taxes. By 1828 there was an annual tax of 1,920 réis per pipe on *estufas*.[19] A municipal commission on *estufas* was set up in 1834, and in the same year, by a decree of 23 July, a monthly tax was imposed on each pipe undergoing *estufagem*—a strong incentive to opt for short and sharp, instead of long and gentle, heating and a further burden on the over-taxed trade.

As far as fraudulent madeira was concerned, the efforts to stem this trade came much too late. The deceptions became increasingly sophisticated, with *estufas*, for example, being set up in the Azores, the Canaries and even in the Cape of Good Hope.[20] A law of 22 July 1801 yet again banned the importation of wine from the Azores. It was occasioned by the activities of a Madeiran merchant called Domingos d'Oliveira Junior, who had a base in Faial (in the Azores) from which he plied mock madeira. He had evaded the previously imposed anti-fraud regulations by such ruses as taking coopers from Funchal to Faial to make imitation madeira casks; and when he had attempted to import Faial wine into Madeira in 1800, and had been stopped by the authorities, he had even tried to get the royal court in Lisbon to override their decision. These 'sordid projects by a non-patriot' backfired, but advertisements had to be placed in English, American and Asian newspapers to counteract the bad publicity. Foreign authorities were urged to be vigilant in checking the papers of ships importing alleged madeira into their countries.[21] The next quarter century saw the council many times struggling to enforce anti-fraud measures and trying to persuade the Crown to support them, but without lasting success. By 1836 Cape Madeira, Sicily Madeira, Faial Madeira and Tenerife Madeira were being advertised daily in London.[22]

During this period the emphasis quickly shifted from the importation of Azorean wine to the importation of brandy (from Brazil) and of gin. The authorities became alarmed over two matters: the general health of the population, which they believed suffered greatly from 'the immoderate and disgraceful use' of spirits, and the question that arose after 1820 of how to deal with over-production and how to dispose of excess wine. Thus we find an edict of 21 March 1814 reinstating the ban enacted in 1789 on the sale in taverns by any persons 'of whatever rank, quality or condition they may be' of 'ardent spirits or any other spirituous drink which is not produced in this island'.[23] The solution favoured by the authorities was, briefly, to exclude from the island all foreign spirits, except the French brandy needed to fortify the wine (whose entry had been permitted since 1760),[24] and to direct the surplus wines into local taverns.

Smuggling was rampant, and apparently connived at by the customs authorities themselves. Holman [1827] reports that during his visit 300 cases of gin were smuggled ashore and stored in a cave near Prior Bay, a little west of Funchal. The following day two lovers on an excursion to Câmara de Lobos took shelter in the cave and later reported what they had discovered there to the Customs, hoping for a reward. 'The Custom-house people, who were probably already aware of the circumstance, did not appear to be very anxious to interfere, and told the disappointed informers that they might take a few cases for themselves, and say nothing more about the matter.'[25]

The main villains, however, were perceived to be the British merchants, who took advantage of permission from the customs house (controlled from continental Portugal) to import foreign spirits in defiance of the town council's wishes. The taxes were punitive, and the Royal exchequer was glad to have them. In 1816, for example, the council complained that they had carried out 'a duplicitous importation of foreign spirits by paying the fines which were imposed on them by the edict of this Council of 21 March 1814 ... an abuse which can alone be avoided if the Junta of the Royal Estates allows only the importation of French brandy for the making of our wines and totally prohibits the clearance of all other drinks made outside the island, as is ordained in the royal proclamation 22 July 1801.[26] The crown failed to respond to this appeal.

At the same time, while pleading that the council's attempted embargo on the importation of foreign spirits was an infringement of free trade, the British merchants further alienated the authorities by delaying their purchases of new wine for up to three years,[27] thereby putting producers, especially the tenant farmers, in an impossible position. 'Our commerce is absolutely inactive; the English take our wines prisoner, with the following effects: the money of the agrarian workers is completely in their power for long periods, because payment has to be dragged out of them; and to increase still further their domination and commercial ascendancy, they manage to leave a large excess of wine in our hands only so that it will later pass into their hands at the prices they desire.'[28]

The denunciations of the British merchants to the Crown by the town council became increasingly shrill as their conduct had graver and graver consequences for the island's economy, with references to 'the odious and intolerable projects of the [British] consul and other negotiants who only cherish goals of sordid self interest',[29] and 'the evils which stem from this system of egoism which predominates in the British community [which] will end in the total ruin of our agriculture (which is already so much run down), since the English wish for nothing more than to increase our poverty and keep us in eternal dependence on them'.[30]

Doubtless the merchants had their own problems. With trade stagnant and warehouses full, it was natural that they should stop buying and try to drive prices down. There was, as the town council suspected, something of a conspiracy on the part of the British merchants: 'There was a Meeting today [5 November 1817] of the Members of the Old Establishment/or Factory ... to endeavour to fall on some means, to bring down the prices which the planters, & others aspire at.'[31] But an anonymous commentator found their efforts inept: 'This high price is occasioned by the want of unanimity among the English merchants, or indeed a want of good faith towards each other, for they appear occasionally to rouse from their lethargy, meet at their consul's, and agree to give only certain prices for the wines at the press; but, immediately after, each outbids the other, and the wine jobber laughs in his sleeve, and profits by their folly.'[32]

However, there were other problems for which the British were not responsible. Post-war recession hit hard. Exports to the United States dropped dramatically. In 1827 an American wrote that 'we imported 355,837 gallons annually for more than twenty years, which amount has now sunk to 16,483'[33]—this despite a reduction in American duties on madeira in 1822 (355,837 gallons amounts to some 3,235 pipes and 16,483 gallons to about 150 pipes). Nor did the post-Napoleonic fashion for madeira in England sustain itself for very long. By 1841, imports into England, which had been close to 6,000 pipes in 1815, had sunk to a derisory 800 pipes.[34] But most of all, there were the difficulties Portugal itself put in the way of the islanders. There was a prohibition on the import of madeira into Brazil (the natural destination for the inferior produce of the north), so surplus stocks of wine could not be disposed of there—something which affected the native Madeiran merchants more than it did the British. Secondly, there were high taxes on exports and property, and taxes to maintain the state. There was still a 'temporary' tax first imposed in 1641 to defray wartime expenses. Worst of all, however, there was a tax, rising to 15 per cent by 1843, on the import of the island's staple, corn. The state arranged everything to help itself and nothing to help Madeira. A letter dated 18 May 1822 to the *Patriota Funchalese* put the point succinctly: 'Obliged to be consumers of certain goods produced by Portugal, with which we have no commercial relationship, whilst we can receive equivalent goods from other nations with whom we do do business with our wines (and cheaper), puts us, as Mr De Pradt has sagely remarked, in a state of war with the Metropolis, which forces us thus solely to its own advantage.'[35] The supplications for help, like the denunciations of the British, became increasingly urgent but fell on deaf ears. 'The lessening of taxes is a matter your Majesty should consider. Without doubt they are overwhelmingly damaging to the island of Madeira in present circumstances, and almost impossible to pay, which people certainly could do when your Majesty deigns to privilege them by favouring the export of their wines … How are the inhabitants to pay if there is nobody to buy what they produce? … How are the proprietors and merchants to pay if their wines remain stuck in their stores without any outlet? … Your Majesty would weep with sorrow if he could see with his own eyes the efforts and pains which the inhabitants of the south of Madeira suffer in making a pipe of wine … Their prosperity is that pipe of wine; if they cannot sell it they die in misery.'[36]

This was in 1821; but by 1824 the picture was even grimmer. Although bulk imports of French brandy had been stopped by a regulation of 31 July 1822,[37] bottled French brandy was still permitted and around 3,000 pipes of ardent spirits from various foreign sources were being imported. There were some 40,000 pipes of old wine remaining in the hands of the growers.[38] The council even presumed to lecture the crown on its lack of wisdom and responsibility: 'The true interests of the royal exchequer are those which result in national happiness and prosperity, and those which oppose the general good are always disgraceful';[39] 'It is not impartial justice for your Majesty to promote the advantages of one part of the nation with the ruin and misery of the other part'.[40] The lack of help from the Crown inevitably made the islanders feel that discrimination against Madeira was unfair. They were right: it was. Nor was it an exaggeration when the council advised that 'it might be necessary, in order that they should not die of hunger, that his Majesty should command the dispersal of two-thirds of the population to the interior of Brazil'.[41] Before many years had elapsed, emigration was indeed to become the only alternative to starvation.

It would be impossible to guess at the desperation of the social situation just from looking at export totals. Between 1820 and 1825 they averaged over 13,000 pipes a year, which compares quite favourably with the record average of 15,722 pipes a year for the first decade of the century.[42] Indeed, such figures were to become remarkable in retrospect, because after 1825 the figure of 10,000 pipes a year was never again equalled during the century. So, were the town council exaggerating from a desire to reduce taxes so that they could try to recapture the boom? Perhaps it would have been against human nature not to do so, but dire poverty there undoubtedly was. It cannot have been an entirely pleasant place for invalids and visitors to come to. 'Bands of sturdy beggars, almost in a state of nudity, greet the traveller on his arrival, exposing to view ghastly wounds, and thrusting themselves upon his notice with an eagerness and ferocity not only revolting but appalling.'[43]

Wine shippers had to apply themselves to commerce afresh. If trade would not come to the island, then it had to be sought out. Peter Cossart, a young member of Newton and Murdoch (later to become Cossart Gordon), was therefore sent on a visit to England and America to drum up business. He left Madeira on 14 July 1833, not to return until 15 May 1835. We gather his frame of mind from an entry in his journal for 23 July 1833: 'Letters from Madeira—all quiet there to 2nd inst, business very dull—fear our trade has seen its best days. Nor do I calculate on much if any improvement.' In under a year his sales campaign had taken him the length and breadth of America. 5 May 1834: 'I have now set foot in all the four & twenty States and in two out of the three territories (and very few, even Americans, can say as much) besides Upper & Lower Canada & New Brunswick'.[44] The only time he found any madeira worth mentioning was in Savannah, where at the Quoit Club 'the wine, which is furnished by said Members in turn, was excellent being N & M [Newton and Murdoch]' and at the Mayor's, where he was given 'good wine of our own Sending'.

During the quarter-century up to 1850 exports dropped to an average of 7,649 pipes a year, or about 60 per cent of the average for the previous period. As the writers of petitions to the throne never ceased to point out—and as we too must always bear in mind—Madeira was virtually a wine monoculture, dependent on its exports to buy three-quarters of its food (and other) supplies; so that, during this period, the profits on the export of an average of fewer than 10,000 pipes had to support a population of considerably more than 100,000—with the proprietors and merchants getting proportionately more of these profits than the peasants. Thus, the situation of the vast majority of the islanders, already fairly desperate by 1825, grew steadily worse, and was not improved by the uncertainties of the War of the Two Brothers, which began in that year and lasted until 1834. The one positive and lasting achievement of this decade was the founding in 1836 of the Associação Commercial do Funchal, the outcome of the deliberations of a commission of five (which included John Shortridge and Joseph Phelps) which the Governor had set up the previous year. It immediately provided the trade with a single voice to represent its interests, and the Association has had a continuous existence (though somewhat transformed) to the present day.[45]

While the council continued to petition the crown for reduced taxes, denunciations of an increasingly revolutionary kind appeared in local papers. In 1841 a remarkable and lengthy liberal 'catechism' appeared in O Defensor, calling for wise constitutional laws on the British model. There was a perceived risk of a peasant uprising. Emigration had always taken place in times of misery,[46] and it is estimated that between 1835 and 1855 around 40,000 people emigrated from Madeira to Demerara and the British East Indies (only half of them with passports).[47] The exodus really got going in the 1840s, with 4,045 in 1841, 4,945 in 1846 and 4,720 in 1847. In the autumn of 1846 the potato crop,[48] the staple of the peasant diet, failed. This coincided with another notable decrease in the price of wine. Relief supplies arrived from abroad, and public subscriptions in the United States, Britain, Ireland (astonishingly, in view of its own similar problem), Germany and Russia raised quite large sums. By 25 May 1847, merchants and farmers had themselves raised a 32,500 milréis food fund; but there was no food to buy, and some of the money financed public works. Taxes on corn were reduced to 25 réis, but not abolished. Of this sad country in 1849 Dean Peachcock of Ely wrote that he had 'nowhere seen, not even in the worst parts of Ireland, more intense misery than among the people of this island. A stranger is assaulted, whenever he appears near these destitute and overpeopled districts, with crowds of mendicants, whose emaciated and diseased appearance shows too plainly that their food is insufficient and unwholesome.'[49]

This is the background against which wine was being produced as the first half of the century came to an end. An article in the *Correio da Madeira* for 1 June 1850 catalogued the taxes then current on wine, and showed that wine from the north was taxed at between 70 and 80 per cent, and wine from the south at between 30 and 40 per cent, of its value as must.[50] How, the article asked, was it possible for wine so burdened to compete on the international market? How, indeed? Yet calamitous as the situation must then have seemed, its gravity paled into insignificance by comparison with what happened when the first of two vine plagues, *oïdium*, made its appearance in February 1851. Its impact is graphically illustrated by comparing two editions of Robert White's *Madeira, Its Climate and Scenery*. The first, published in 1851, portrays a flourishing culture of the vine; in the second, published in 1857, the section on wine has been entirely transcribed into the past tense! For the writer madeira wine was already a thing of the past, a fact of history.

The first crisis

Oïdium Tuckeri, known in Madeira as *mangra* but now better known as *uncinula necator* or as powdery mildew, was originally identified in the United States in 1834. In Europe, it was first detected in England in 1845, in Mr Tucker's garden in Margate. It is a fungal disease which first attacks the leaves—causing white patches which eventually rot and wither—and then covers the grapes with white powder and causes lesions, after which the vine itself succumbs. It is thought to have been brought to Madeira by a French plant salesman who sold vines brought from an *oïdium*-infected part of France. The disease spread quickly, and by the following year, 1852, it was evident in all parts of the island, though the west was comparatively unaffected. After that it seemed unstoppable. First to be attacked were vines grown in corridor formation, then those on trellises, and lastly *vinhas da pé*, where the vines had little or no support. Isabela, the American variety, proved to be most resistant by far to the disease; Verdelho and Tinta varieties such as Tinta Negra were attacked with less ferocity than those, like

Boal and Malvasia, with higher sugar levels. Just occasionally, for some inexplicable reason, a single vineyard would remain defiantly untouched. In the whole of the Funchal area the only example was the Quinta das Maravilhas, which belonged to Miss Norton, an English lady resident on the island. The 'Quinta of Marvels' must indeed have seemed well named.

There was then no known cure, and over the next three years the producers and merchants could only stand by and watch as their vineyards were systematically destroyed. The devastation was not just immense, it was complete. According to Silva and Meneses,[51] wine production, which had been averaging only 11,956 pipes a year up to 1851, plummeted to 1,913 pipes in 1852, 717 pipes in 1853 and a mere 143 pipes in 1854.[52] In 1855 production was only 36 pipes.[53] This represents a drop in production of 99.7 per cent over four years. A total wipe-out, and for the island virtually total economic ruin. The annual loss to the proprietors and growers was estimated at upwards of £230,000 sterling.[54] The cost to the island's economy was very slightly offset by the revenue from invalids and visitors, estimated at £30,000–£40,000 per year,[55] but this did not directly help the wine trade.

The impact on the already fragile economy of the island was cataclysmic. It was the culmination of years of decline and, as one commentator put it, 'the disease of the vines must not be accused of ruining the viticultors in Madeira; this ruin was imminent, the disease only hastening a crisis which was already very near'.[56] As already noted, mass emigration rocketed. Even the least prosperous of the British wine merchants gave up and left the island.[57] On 22 November 1852 the Governor nominated a commission to solicit help from abroad, and subscriptions were opened in various countries. For the second time within a decade Madeira had to throw itself on the mercy of international aid. A shipload of food and clothing was sent from London, and a total of 37,000 milréis was collected. Schemes to employ the poor were also set in motion, but labour for 300 men for six months building (but not completing) the first major road on the island, the Estrada Monumental which connects Funchal with Câmara de Lobos, was a pitifully inadequate response to the magnitude of the disaster. Another response, however, though doubtless thought eccentric at the time, was later to develop into a significant ingredient of a more diversified island economy. Elizabeth Phelps, the daughter of Joseph Phelps, a partner of Phelps, Page & Co. and noted philanthropist, introduced embroidery as a cottage industry amongst the womenfolk of the unemployed workers on the company's vineyards. The project prospered. Within twenty years, more than a thousand women were employed on embroidery, and in 1862 a British firm was established on the island to handle exports. By 1923, more than 70,000 people were employed in the industry.[58] In the late 1990s embroidery outperformed wine as an export industry but, currently, with only eight registered firms, it is almost struggling to survive.

The gravity of the wine crisis was not at first realized. Newspaper correspondence assumed that the disease would run its course and things would return to normal. Amid exhortations from the Governor to trust in God's bountifulness, the more thoughtful of the populace saw the *mangra* as a warning of the dangers of a monoculture, and they advocated more diversity in agriculture: more sugar cane, coffee, tropical fruit. On 29 July 1853 an agronomist named João de Andrade Côrvo arrived in Funchal. He had been sent to observe the situation by the Royal Academy of Sciences in Lisbon, to which he presented a long report on his findings in February 1854.[59] He had nothing to say, however, about what might be done to counter the disease. On 18 April 1854 the Governor issued a decree setting up a Commission, but it too seems to have been of little help.

In 1852, most of the grapes that had been attacked were jettisoned on the grounds that the value of the wine would not justify the expense of making it. By 1853, however, the shortage of wine for ordinary consumption on the island, coupled with the rising price of ever-scarcer *aguardente*—the importation of brandy was still prohibited—induced some proprietors to make a wine from grapes in such an advanced state of decomposition that even a person 'wretchedly consumed with hunger would hesitate to touch'.[60] The must was diluted, and had the colour of muddy water and the smell characteristic of *mangra*, 'which is easier to recognize than to describe: a repugnant and sick smell, somewhat akin to that of cleaning copper with a light acid'.[61] After a short, quiet fermentation and clarification it produced a liquid to which it would be difficult to give the name 'wine', with a detestable smell and an insupportable, bitter taste of the parasite fungus. It was considered, however, that drinking this 'wine' presented no risk to the health of the people!

Happily for the poor people there were alternatives. Wine was made from pears, oranges and sugar cane; there was some beer; but, most importantly, there was non-alcoholic ginger beer, first made by João Caetano about 1851. Nevertheless, when the fall in municipal income in 1854 led to new taxes on alcoholic drinks, ginger beer was also taxed—but only at half the rate of real beer, so it became the staple drink of the populace.[62]

After the all-time low of 1855, production figures for the rest of the decade slowly increased: 87 pipes in 1856; 101 pipes in 1857; 184 pipes in 1858; and 151 in 1859. Again, export figures give no clue to what was happening in the vineyards, for they remained surprisingly buoyant during the 1850s, never dropping below 1,000 pipes a year until 1862 (although not rising above 1,000 pipes a year again until 1870).[63] These figures were initially made possible by using reserve stocks, but over an eight-year period (1852–59), during which exports exceeded production by some 12,000 pipes, these became almost exhausted. Moreover, the current levels of production did not provide for internal consumption or for distillation into brandy. Other solutions had to be found.

The obvious solution was to import wine from abroad and re-export it as madeira—precisely the same abuse which everyone had struggled to prevent at the start of the century. The pressure to do this started in March 1857, when a project to import wine from Lisbon was advanced by António Correia Herédia. This met with popular acclaim, but nothing happened. The idea was floated in parliament in 1860. A Ordem was the only newspaper in Funchal to oppose the idea, on the same grounds—that it would damage the future integrity of the wine—that had been argued sixty years earlier. This argument, supported by the town council and the Associação Commercial, carried the day and, despite later attempts to remove it, the ban remained in place.[64] So help was not forthcoming from this quarter.

The merchants remaining on the island—particularly Blandy, it seems—were astute enough to buy up the stocks of departing merchants at knock-down prices. As the stocks diminished the price rose, according to Vizetelly, from £25 to £75 a pipe for the lowest qualities.[65] Many of the shippers adopted the *solera* system, sometimes called fractional blending, as a means of eking out their stocks of old vintages. More recently, old soleras have been seen as a not-quite-fraudulent way of selling young wine under old dates, but it does seem that they answered the need of the moment to conserve stocks and maintain quality.

Mr Tucker became famous not just because he was the first person in Europe to be visited by *oïdium*, he was also responsible for finding the best means of combating it, and after 1854 sulphur dusting became the universally recognized means of controlling the fungus. However, it took a long time for the vineyards to recover. Large areas of vines were dead, and because of shortages of suitable cuttings, they often had to be replaced with stock imported from mainland Portugal. This brought new varieties such as Arinto to the island, and Isabela, being virtually immune to *oïdium*, had an understandable appeal to growers.

Many vineyards, however, were not replanted. Although sugar was again being cultivated in Madeira at the beginning of the nineteenth century, the quantities were insignificant until the *oïdium* disaster, which gave an impetus to the diversification of Madeiran agriculture and led to considerable replanting with canes instead of vines. A regenerated sugar industry in Madeira flourished for more than a century, making it once more an important element in the island's economy.[66]

Slowly, things got better for the wine trade, if not for the general population. In 1856, as if things were not bad enough, there was a serious outbreak of cholera. It is estimated that out of a population of 105,000 at least 10,000 died. It was once more a matter of subscriptions and shiploads of relief supplies. The efforts of the British community on this occasion earned the thanks not only of the Governor, but of the Portuguese king.[67]

An event of importance to Madeira occurred in 1861, when all the taxes which had so grievously afflicted the island throughout the century were abolished. It may sound as if the islanders' prayers had at last been answered. A law of 11 September stated that, as from 1 January 1863, Madeira would pay the same taxes as continental Portugal. It proved to be a mixed blessing, and soon the cry was that taxes devised for the mainland were often wholly inappropriate to the circumstances of the island. Another legal event of lasting significance to the wine trade, even if its effects took time to manifest themselves, occurred in 1863. The same António Correia Herédia mentioned above began to campaign in February 1849 for the abolition of *morgados* (the institution of property entail)[68] which had existed in Madeira since the fifteenth century. Many enlightened people felt that it inhibited agricultural progress. The opposition from the landowners was immense, and they managed to block this reform. However, a law was passed on 11 May 1863 which abolished entails throughout Portugal. Thereafter, these large properties were gradually broken up as from generation to generation they passed into wider ownership.

During the period of retrenchment in the 1860s, even if exports diminished, production stabilized and increased slightly. The quality of the vintages was consistent and on the whole encouraging. As the decade ended, although still rather small, production of about 16,000 pipes was again being achieved.[69] The outbreak of the American Civil War in 1861 brought exports to America to a virtual standstill, but the winding-up of the East India Company after the Indian Mutiny in 1857 was compensated for by an increase in exports to the subcontinent to supply military messes and clubs, and this built up steadily into the next century. Against this, the opening of the Suez Canal in 1869 meant that ships bound for the east no longer called at Madeira. Russia, to which exports had slowly started as far back as 1793, had from the 1830s become a major market, and exports to Russia competed in size with those to Britain until the end of the century.[70] Stocks began increasing once more, and by the end of the decade there was a collective sigh of relief that the worst was over and that the trade had managed to come through the crisis. Madeira wine was not to become, as had once been feared, a thing of the past.

5

THE NINETEENTH CENTURY II

The second crisis

Phylloxera (*Phylloxera vastatrix*) was first identified in Madeira in 1872. It is a vine louse which attacks the roots of European vines and is endemic in America, where some varieties of vine are immune to it—no one yet fully understands why. Like *oïdium*, the first time it was detected in Europe was in England, this time at Hammersmith in 1863. During the 1860s phylloxera had devastated European vineyards, and there must have been a fear that it would sneak into Madeira, as *oïdium* had done. But no thought seems to have been given to taking precautions, and ironically the plague appears to have arrived with some sprigs of Isabela, imported because of the variety's *oïdium*-resistant properties. It took more than ten years to come to terms with phylloxera, and in Madeira as elsewhere, confusion, ignorance, misunderstanding and panic contributed almost as much to the length and ill-effects of the plague as the vine louse itself.

It was an international rather than a local problem, and required international co-operation to solve it. Many remedies were tried. Between 1872 and 1876 some 1,044 suggested treatments were assessed at the School of Agriculture at Montpellier in France. A few retarded the progress of the devastation, but the most effective measure in practice was the injection into the roots of a carbon bisulphide solution. The value of this treatment, although apparent to many vineyard proprietors, was unaccountably not recognized at Montpellier, though it was taken seriously by the International Phylloxera Congress which met at Bordeaux in 1881. The competing solution—grafting a vine shoot of a European variety on to the roots of a resistant American variety—eventually suggested itself when empirical observation made it clear that some American vines in European vineyards survived phylloxera while all native varieties succumbed. Grafting had been gaining support in France since 1880, and it eventually established itself as the best, and so far the only wholly effective, way of dealing with phylloxera.[1]

When a Comissão Anti-filoxérica was set up in December 1882 (ten years after the louse was first detected), it was not yet entirely clear that grafting was the proper solution to the problem, and the Commission simply endorsed and actively promoted the alternative, ultimately inadequate, solution of sulphide injections. Even after there was a consensus that the way forward was by grafting, it took considerable trial and error to discover the most suitable root stocks: not only because some American root stocks (such as *Labrusca*) are not particularly resistant to phylloxera, but because some which are do not suit all types of soil. The growers in Madeira, therefore, were in no worse a position than anyone else: everyone had to do what he could for himself.

The way in which phylloxera attacked the vines was not so immediately dramatic as the onslaught of *oïdium*, and nothing like as severe as it was in the Douro or in France. Henry Vizetelly, visiting the island in 1877, five years after the blight began, remarked on its slow spread, 'having confined its ravages … to a comparatively small area,[2] and he was able to find many vineyards which were apparently quite unaffected. The main damage was at Câmara de Lobos, where phylloxera destroyed nearly all the vines and reduced production from 3,000 to a mere 100 pipes. On the other hand, at Estreito de Câmara de Lobos, to the north, phylloxera had only attacked the vines on the lower slopes. At Quinta Grande, to the west, the vines were but slightly affected and promised to give a very fair yield. Further west still, Campanário was 'untouched at present'. In Funchal and in surrounding villages there were symptoms of phylloxera: at São João many vines had been seriously affected; at Santo António there was some phylloxera side by side with healthy vineyards; whereas at São Martinho the attack had been slight. East of Funchal, Caniço and Machico were not seriously affected, while at Santa Cruz there were no signs of blight at all. Thus the worst problems seem at this time to have been confined to a relatively small area, albeit the most important in terms of quality. Phylloxera spread slowly in the north. For example, it took until 1883 to reach the Visconde de Val Pariso's vineyards at Porto Moniz on the north-western tip of the island. By this time, however, the situation elsewhere had deteriorated to the point that only 20 per cent—about 500 hectares—of the vineyards in production at the outset of the attack were still yielding: their production of some 3,500 pipes, however, compares very favourably with the miserable totals of the mid-1850s. Vizetelly, the most knowledgeable of nineteenth-century commentators, gives us an interesting account of his visit. The overall impression he conveys is, contrary to what might be expected, not one of desperate crisis. Efforts were being made to defeat phylloxera, but life and trade were otherwise going on as usual.

Thomas Slapp Leacock, a grandson of the first member of the family to come to Madeira, appears to have been in the forefront of those experimenting with ways of curing the problem. He owned a vineyard at São João, and there, as early as 1873, he found that periodic painting of the roots of the vine with a solution of resin and turpentine in hot water, described by Vizetelly as 'a kind of varnish', effectively retarded the progress of decay. It was, however, thought by other proprietors to be too expensive a treatment for general use. Leacock's son John was a member of the Comissão Anti-filoxérica, which met between December 1882 and 7 November 1883. It decided to establish a treatment post and a nursery of American vines, and a property of about one hectare in São João was acquired for that purpose. A ban that had been imposed on the importation of American vines in the wake of *oïdium* was lifted. A team of three started carrying out anti-phylloxera treatment with sulphide injections in February 1883. The results were thought auspicious.[3] An official district inspector called Almeida e Brito was appointed in June and was put in charge of the operation.

Two nurseries were established in Funchal, one at Ribeirinho and the other at Torreão, and by 1883 some 60,000 vines had been distributed. At first Riparia, Jacquet, Herbemont, Rupestris, Solonis, Taylor, Clinton, Elsimbro and York Madeira were all cultivated. Later Cunningham, Viala, Elvira, Othelo, Cinerea, Black Pearl and Gaston Bazile were added. Experience showed that Riparia, Herbemont, Cunningham and particularly Jacquet were best suited to conditions on the island, and they became the preferred root stocks for grafting. Not all were grafted, however, and it is in this period that the predominance of American vines in Madeiran viticulture for more than a century began. Nor were all the former vineyards replanted. Vizetelly mentions several times that he found sugar cane had been planted in place of dead vines, especially in Câmara de Lobos. However, although some of these vineyards, like those of the Torre Bella estate, reverted to vines, there was a net loss of vineyards across the island.

Fortunately, the island had had relatively large stocks of wine when phylloxera arrived—Vizetelly estimated them at 30,000 pipes in 1877—and exports, having managed to rise above 1,000 pipes a year in 1870, actually increased to over 2,000 a year for the rest of the decade. Thereafter they mounted steadily, from just over 3,000 pipes a year in 1880 to just over 5,000 pipes a year by the end of the 1880s.[4] Some markets were lost. According to the Conde de Canaval, the imports of madeira into the States in 1882 amounted to only 48 litres, or a little less than an eighth of a pipe—a figure which makes one blink.[5] There were few casualties amongst the shippers this time. Of the fifteen British merchants listed by Cossart for 1855, thirteen were still active in the 1870s and 1880s, and there were sixteen Portuguese firms (of which three—Henriques & Henriques, Justino's, and Borges—are still in existence today).

The effect of phylloxera on the Madeiran population at large was also less dramatic than that of *oïdium*. A certain amount of emigration continued, but the numbers leaving Madeira fell far short of those seen during the *oïdium* period. The Sandwich Islands, better known today as Hawaii, became a favourite destination after 1878, and Portuguese colonies in Africa, such as Angola and Lourenço Marques, became popular after 1884. Another cottage industry, wickerwork, grew in importance. It had started in a small way at Camacha around 1812, but expanded greatly during the 1870s. Today, as a result of competition from the east, it has all but disappeared.

A period of consolidation followed the upheavals of the 1870s and 1880s. The Conde de Canavial, a prominent wine expert, began campaigning in 1879 for the foundation of a commercial society of growers to protect their interests, but it took more than twenty years before such an association came into being, in 1900. However, a Commission to Assist Farming (Comissão de Auxílio á Lavoura) was set up in 1888, led by a crown commissioner named Manoel de Moraes who had been sent to study the state of the vineyards and to distribute free American vines. From this we must suppose that the number of American vines continued to grow. Production went up to about 8,000 pipes in 1895 and reached 9,200 pipes in 1900.[6] Exports remained buoyant, hovering between 5,077 and 6,346 pipes during the first part of the 1890s.[7] With returning prosperity the price of madeira again fell and island stocks rose again. During the vine plagues of the second half of the century, madeira had lost markets to sherry and malaga, which could be sold at a fraction of its cost. At the same time, Tarragona, the Midi in France and Hamburg all cashed in on the production of counterfeit madeira. This spectre, which had haunted Madeira for more than a century, was at last laid to rest when, in June 1900, John E. Blandy finally won a protracted legal case in France against a Spanish firm which had shipped 500 pipes of imitation madeira to Le Havre. 'Madeira' thereafter established itself as a term which could only be properly applied to the produce of the island, and this was reflected in an Anglo-Portuguese treaty signed in 1914.[8]

Viticulture and the wine

Finally, we must review the development of viticulture, winemaking and the wine itself through the nineteenth century. The vines grown in the north, according to Holman [1827], were all of white varieties, whilst those in the south were chiefly red. Low trellises continued to be the predominant method of training vines, and were recognized as giving the best fruit. Only exceptionally, as at Lea-cock's São João vineyards, were vines trained in rows along hori-zontal wires.[9] After *oïdium*, the growing of vines on chestnut trees in the north was progressively replaced by the trellises of the south. Vineyards were situated as high as 700 m in Estreito de Câmara de Lobos, 670 m in Camacha and 520 m at Monte, north-east of Funchal, but it was recognized that the best wine generally came from vineyards no higher than 150 m.[10] Before phylloxera, propa-gation was either by the traditional method already described,[11] whereby cuttings or rooted vines were planted in trenches, or by grafting, which as we have seen[12] was also used in the eighteenth century. Bowdich [1823] says that when the latter method is used, 'they prefer the *verdelho* of the north, when forming a plantation in the southern part of the island, as it improves considerably from the better soil, climate and aspect: on this they engraft any other variety they may wish: the grapes yield no wine until the fourth year'.[13] Vineyards were watered three times, if possible, when the summer was dry or the vines were young, but growers were aware that although irrigation might improve the quantity, it would reduce the quality of their grapes. Animal manure, used by some, was shunned by others because they thought it affected the flavour of the grapes. Instead, they grew lupins in the January of every second year, cutting them down and turning them into the soil after the rains which are common at the end of April.

The best time to prune the vines was disputed—between January (unusual), February (normal) or the middle of March (late)—but depended on predicting from the weather when flowering would occur. The best method was also debated—long or short pruning—as was its effect on the life of the vine. Many vines were healthy and productive for only ten to fifteen years, and this was blamed on inappropriate pruning, which had not been adjusted to the variety and circumstances of the individual vines. Small vineyards generally had a mixture of varieties, white and red, and only in larger vine-yards was it possible to harvest grapes of a single variety.[14] Yields varied. It was common to remove some leaves and expose the grapes to the sun to assist in their ripening. Bowdich calculated that four pipes of must an acre (almost ten per hectare) were possible in the most favourable conditions, but that one pipe was the average across the island. Growing vegetables under vine trellises was common, and grass abounded. All writers mention the depredations caused by lizards and rats, which never touched Sercial but fell upon Tinta Negra with a vengeance. According to White [1851], 20 per cent of the harvest was generally lost in this way:[15] Harcourt [1851] puts the losses at 10 per cent.[16] Woe betide the farmer who harvested after his neighbours—which may be the explanation for the premature picking which so upset the authorities from time to time.

References to about forty named grape varieties abound, though some are synonyms of others.[17] Several writers, from Adam onwards, claimed that Verdelho, Tinta Negra and Boal were the best varieties for making generic madeira, the latter two giving flavour to the former. Verdelho was, according to Holman [1827], the chief grape variety grown in the north. According to Vizetelly [1877], Verdelho constituted two-thirds of the vines on the island,[18] while Taylor [1882] put the proportion as high as three-quarters.[19]

As we have seen, the number of American vines increased progressively in the last quarter of the century, and new varieties were imported from mainland Portugal to replace dead vines. Most of the new varieties do not appear, as far as one can tell, to have had a lasting presence on the island.

To reinforce the legislation of 1784 preventing the harvesting of unripe grapes, in 1819 three inspectors were appointed for each parish,[20] and growers had to obtain their permission before starting the vintage. The distinction in quality between wines of the north and south remained important throughout the century. There were three categories of quality (reflecting the height above sea level of the vines) for grapes in each council area, and prices, which were set by local councils, varied widely. The following table, showing the average prices in 1851 at Câmara de Lobos in the south and Santana in the north, illustrates the extremities of this range:[21]

	Average price of wine	
	In Câmara de Lobos	*In Santana*
1st quality	4,320 réis	1,780 réis
2nd quality	3,440 réis	1,580 réis
3rd quality	2,500 réis	1,600 réis [*sic*]

The British Factory had continued to try to control prices by coordinated buying until its abolition in 1838, and as late as 1885 Johnson reports that many shippers still bought their must in advance of the harvest. Methods of vinification do not appear to have changed very much during the century. Descriptions of the vintage are all very similar, although White [1851] tells us that 'the grapes, when gathered, are "escolhido," or picked [i.e. selected]; those of an inferior quality being generally reserved by themselves'.[22] Vizetelly [1877] mentions that at Leacock's São João vineyard 'the grapes would be picked at no less than eight different times, only the perfectly ripe bunches being gathered on each occasion'.[23] All varieties except Tinta Negra were fermented off their skins, Tinta being macerated to increase the colour. Whereas it was common to press the grapes two or three times after treading, Tinta Negra was pressed only once. Sometimes the pressings would be kept separate from the trodden wine, at other times added to it. Fermentation took place in open-topped vats (*bica aberta*) and lasted from six to eight weeks, sometimes longer for rich wines, unless checked. Until about the middle of the century, gypsum was added to the wine made from grapes grown in the south to clarify it, but apparently not to the wine from the north.[24] After the violent fermentation had subsided (10–12 days), gypsum would be added and the wine stirred twice a day until the carbonic acid gas stopped. It was then racked, usually in January. Subsequently, clarification was carried out using egg whites or blood.

Until the middle of the century it was usual to fortify the wine only when it was being prepared for shipping. However, Thudichum and Dupré [1872] report a more elaborate process: 'The must is mostly mixed with brandy at once, stated to be from half a gallon to a gallon to the Portuguese pipe. After the first fermentation is over, the wine is racked from the gross leas, and again mixed with a similar quantity of brandy. After about three weeks, it is racked a second time, fined, and a gallon of brandy is again added. When the wine has become bright, it is racked for the last time, and placed in large barrels for ripening. This process requires about six years. Before exportation each pipe receives another gallon of spirit.'[25] Fortification was with French brandy until 1822, when its importation other than in bottles was forbidden. Thereafter, distilled spirit from the north of the island and Porto Santo was used.

After the vintage the wine was transported to the shippers' lodges. When possible this was done in cask, drawn in ox carts from the suburbs of Funchal, or brought by sea from further afield, the half-filled casks often being floated out to boats propelled by men swimming behind them. Once safely on board they were then topped up. From the interior of the island the wine was moved to the shippers' lodges in Funchal by processions of *borracheiros*, so named because they carried on their shoulders, steadied by a strap round their foreheads, containers of wine (*borrachos*) made from goat skins which still retained the rudimentary form of the animal. The weight of a full goat skin was about 50 kg. A file of *borracheiros* might contain forty or fifty men, and they would sing as they marched along. The almost complete lack of roads made this method of transport general. Wise shippers took precautions. 'One of the merchant's clerks attends at the *lagar* to see that the operation of crushing is properly carried out. He ascertains the specific gravity of the juice as it comes from the press, and the must is again tested on its arrival at the store, so as to prevent the carriers tampering with it on the way.'[26]

Vinho da roda or *tornaviagem* madeira, continued to be produced until well into the twentieth century.[27] It became common in the United States to name the wine after the ship in which it had been transported or the country in which it had been matured, or occasionally after the family which owned it.[28] Even today, some of these wines still surface from time to time.[29] *Estufas* remained contentious throughout the period, but their use was widespread—although Vizetelly [1877] notes that two firms, Welsh and Donaldson, did not use them.[30] At the beginning of the century, when fortification was done prior to shipping, the wine was heated without brandy; later, when fortification became part of the wine-making process, it was heated after the addition of brandy, and this was acknowledged to give a better final product.[31] It was also generally agreed that prolonged slow heating at low temperatures gave the best results. In 1847 there were 39 *estufas* in Funchal alone.[32] Some were run by shippers, who would rent space to other shippers who had no *estufas* of their own. There were also public *estufas*, where according to Bowdich [1823] the wine was all but boiled. Later *estufas* were elaborate and sophisticated. Vizetelly [1877] visited both *estufas do sol* and *estufas* with artificial heating. Some firms, such as Krohn Bros, and Henriques and Lawton, had both. Vizetelly gives a detailed description of one of the latter: 'The Estufa stores of Messrs. Cossart, Gordon, & Co. comprise a block of buildings of two stories, divided into four distinct compartments. In the first of these common wines are subjected to a temperature of 140 deg. Fahrenheit—derived from flues, heated with anthracite coal—for the space of three months. In the next compartment wines of an intermediate quality are heated up to 130 deg. for a period of four and a half months; while the third is set apart for superior wines, heated variously from 110 to 120 deg. for the term of six months. The fourth compartment, known as the "Calor," possesses no flues, but derives its heat, varying from 90 to 100 deg., exclusively from the compartments adjacent; and here only high-class wines are placed.'[33] This store could deal with 1,600 pipes at a time. Evaporation led to the loss of 10 to 15 per cent of the wine. Leakage of casks was an undesirable effect of the heating, and this had to be monitored night and day.

The main problem was that, owing to the expansion of the wine when heated, the casks which contained it could not be completely sealed, and the combination of extremely high temperatures and contact with the air caused a most disagreeable over-oxidization and the production of acetic properties. An improvement on this situation was advocated by the Conde de Canavial who, impressed by the work of Pasteur, invented a new method which he put into operation in 1889 and which briefly found favour. The idea was to raise the temperature of the wine rapidly to pasteurizing heat—as high as 80°C—by passing it through a sort of *bain marie*, and then to let it cool slowly in sealed containers, out of contact with the air. This killed off bacteria and any remaining ferments, and preserved the balsamic qualities of the wine without risk of the baked, over-oxidized characteristics imparted by conventional *estufas*.[34] The disadvantage of pasteurization is that it makes the wine into an inert substance, incapable of further development, and is therefore unsuitable for a wine intended for even a brief period of evolution. The enthusiasm for pasteurizing madeira soon passed. It was followed by the development of *cubas de calor*, vats at first made of wood, and then of concrete, that were heated by means of internal spiral tubes containing hot water. By varying the heat of the water the temperature of the wine could be controlled. Technically, the early *cubas de calor* were undoubtedly an improvement, though not all the problems associated with *estufagem* were removed. Such *cubas* have not entirely died out, but those with the most modern technology have *estufas* made of stainless steel. These are well insulated and are heated by means of thermal lagging (often called 'jackets') which incorporate a means of heating. Inside, they have an expansion space and they can be hermetically sealed.

I cannot leave the subject of *estufas* without repeating a delightfully zany story which first appears in White [1841], is later repeated by Wortley [1854], and casts a new light on the notion of fraudulent wines. Speaking of the wines which, after *estufagem*, take on a 'dry and smoky flavour, which can never be entirely eradicated', White tells us that 'this class of wines is shipped annually, in large quantities, to Hamburg, where it undergoes a process which changes its character to that of Hock, under which name a large portion of it finds its way into the English market'.[35] The mind boggles at the idea. Is it possible, perhaps, that Mr White got his story a little mixed up—or could the Germans really have been so fiendishly clever?

In the nineteenth century, as now, the vast majority of the production was of generic madeira, with a base of Verdelho and Tinta Negra, but according to several writers frequently containing Boal, Bastardo and Terrantez. Whereas generic madeira had, at the start of the nineteenth century, been marketed as a wine of a particular vintage, after phylloxera it was 'nearly always a blended wine, and very seldom a vintage wine, the main object of the merchant being to keep up continuously, as far as possible, the same character and type in the different qualities'.[36] It was mostly fermented dry, and sweetening was added as required to cheaper blends after fermentation by using a variety of additives, as explained later in this book.[37] According to Thudichum and Dupré [1872], better wine had to be kept for ten years in wood, followed by ten years in bottle, to be at its best.

Malvazia continued to be made in minute quantities, and apparently in different types and qualities. The best quality remained that made from Malvasia Cândida, and the Fajã dos Padres is continually cited as its *locus classicus*. Inferior kinds were made from Malvasia Babosa and Malvasia Roxa, and a generic Malvazia 'requiring burnt sugar, &c. to give it a sweeter flavour' was also produced.[38] Even a Green Malmsey, 'bearing some resemblance to Frontignan', is mentioned.[39] In 1825 we hear for the first time of the fermentation of Malvazia being 'checked earlier than that of other wines, to increase its sweetness'.[40] At the start of the century, Sercial, with a production limited to less than 50 pipes a year,[41] emerged as the real connoisseur's wine. Boal was equally scarce and expensive, but seemed to some commentators not to merit the cost. Terrantez was 'held in some estimation when old'.[42] By the middle of the century there was a fairly large selection of single-variety wines.[43] Tinta, as a wine, seems to have remained a comparative (and costly) rarity. Although originally the name for a white wine tinted with the juice of red grapes, it subsequently became an unfortified beverage wine made from Tinta Negra. It was said to be at its best from two to three years old; thereafter it lost colour, and after twenty years tasted like any other madeira. This kind of Tinta continued to be made long after it became standard practice to fortify other sorts of madeira, but eventually, after *oïdium*, it was treated like the others. Several writers say that not much was made because of the limited foreign demand for it.[44] It is quite difficult to imagine what unfortified Tinta was like. Universally described as astringent, it was suggested by some that, when young, it was like burgundy, and by others that it was like Hermitage; that it made an acceptable substitute for port (the importation of which was forbidden) for the British in Funchal; and that it was good for making sangria! Johnson [1885] warns the reader to distinguish Tinta, made from Tinta Negra, from Tinto, the name for any common red wine— which, according to Thudichum and Dupré [1872], was deficient both in quality and quantity.

Vinho palete is what the Portuguese call Rainwater; it was made from Verdelho clarified with charcoal, which 'destroys the rich colour, and in a great measure destroys the body and fine flavour of the wine'.[45] From time to time a number of curiosities were produced: Negrinha, a rich red wine or cordial made from Maroto grapes dried in the sun on the roofs of houses;[46] Nun's Wine, a commercialized *vinho surdo*;[47] Vizetelly mentions White Madeira, a Verdelho with 4 per cent added alcohol, shipped under that name to Russia.[48] Towards the end of the century *vinho quinado* was developed mainly for the Portuguese African colonies, and this remained in production until just after World War Two.[49] Finally, something called *vinho verde* (literally 'green wine'), also called 'refuse wine', was produced from unripe grapes and those of inferior varieties.[50] Most was doubtless distilled into brandy.

Inevitably, during the wine plagues the quality of madeira must have been even more variable than usual. In 1882 João da Camara Leme spoke openly of 'all the artificial wines made on this island in imitation of madeira wine'.[51] The making of madeira from ungrafted American vines, or 'direct producers' as they are called locally, must have become increasingly widespread. Desperate situations breed desperate solutions. And so a tradition of making madeira from direct producers, which lasted until the entry of Portugal into the EU, became established. It was, without doubt, the least desirable development in wine-making of the entire nineteenth century.

6

THE TWENTIETH CENTURY AND BEYOND

Changing markets and the German 'threat'

The nineteenth century in Madeira was a period of drama and despair. By comparison, the history of the twentieth century was relatively prosaic but finally, in my view, gave grounds for optimism. Exports up to World War One rose to over 7,000 pipes a year, and at first remained buoyant, despite events: in 1916, with a striking 11,375 pipes, they exceeded 10,000 pipes for the first time since 1825.[1] During this period, however, the price of madeira slowly fell, and markets during the first two decades of the century changed radically. Although Britain had remained a principal market up until the end of the century, the popularity of madeira there began to decline. Imports, which had averaged 2,204 pipes between 1884 and 1893, dipped to 1,650 pipes between 1894 and 1903 and, at 810 pipes, reached less than half that figure between 1904 and 1913.[2] Russia's imports at the opening of the century were only marginally higher, and they were to cease abruptly in 1917 with the Revolution—as reflected in the total export figure for that year of 3,035 pipes, the lowest since the start of the century. The beginning of prohibition in 1920 meant that the American market was lost until 1934, by which time the era of cocktails had arrived and thoughts of madeira were a thing of the past. On the other hand, France and Germany became growing markets. From an annual average of 1,017 pipes during the period 1884–93, exports to France increased slightly to 1,472 pipes during the period 1904–13. But it was the German market which showed the most spectacular growth: from an annual average of 578 pipes in the first period, exports doubled to 1,161 pipes during the period 1894–1903, and almost doubled again to an average of 2,109 pipes in the period leading up to the war. This was more than two and a half times the quantity being taken by Britain, and was accompanied by a growing German interest in Madeira.

This interest had been increasing throughout the 1880s and 1890s. Germans had effectively taken over the burgeoning embroidery industry, German shipping had taken an ever greater share of freight and the number of German tourists had also been rising. Considerable efforts were made to establish a commercial footing on the island, with hotels to rival Reid's and even a German wine company. Customs concessions and various monopolies threatening British interests (including the expropriation of British property such as Reid's Hotel) were agreed to in return for piping water from the mountains to the edge of Funchal. The Funchalese authorities supported the German initiative, and traditional anti-British feeling quickly turned into popular enthusiasm for all things German. What had threatened to escalate into a diplomatic incident ended in farce. The Portuguese withdrew the concessions when the scheme was revealed as cover for a fraudulent plan to open gambling casinos (then illegal in Madeira) and make Funchal into a sort of Monte Carlo. The joke was that although William Reid had protested loudly that competition from casinos would completely ruin his hotel business, he had himself hired out the Quinta Pavão, which he had purchased to test the expropriation threat, to a gambling syndicate.[3]

In spite of everything, a treaty between Germany and Portugal was signed in 1910, but those German business enterprises which remained in Madeira disappeared in 1916, when Portugal joined the allies in World War One and German property was confiscated (the low exports of wine in 1917 and 1918 were largely due to the threat of German submarines). The reputation of the British suffered further. Had not the defence of their commercial interests deprived Funchal of a free water supply? A leaflet referring to the 'Usurpers of Madeira', which was sent to all British firms in October 1911, threatened to blow up their buildings. It turned out to be a hoax, but is nonetheless indicative of popular sentiment.[4] During the war, when the poverty of the masses once more increased, many of the British were again perceived as indifferent. For example, in 1916—when wine exports were the highest for over ninety years—the British Foreign Secretary received the following report from a resident, himself British: 'It sounds queer for Mr Blandy to say that the mail and other boats not calling makes no difference to the prosperity of the island. The poor boatmen and coalmen are starving, there is no wickerwork being exported or embroidery ... the poverty is terrible, soup kitchens cannot keep up with the needs of the hungry.'[5] The struggle against hunger remained a stark reality for many of the population during the first half of the century, and increases in the prices of flour and bread caused serious rioting in 1921 and 1931.[6]

Developing control of the trade

The twentieth century saw considerable evolution in the way the production and marketing of Madeira were regulated. A law of 18 September 1908—in parallel with Oporto, Carcavellos and Setubal—revoked all previous legislation and introduced more stringent regulations to control the manufacture and sale of madeira. In 1909 a Comissão de Viticultura was set up with the following objectives: to control the entry of wines and spirits into the region; to make a register of the properties producing fortified wine; to compile production statistics for each council area, including where possible the name and address of the recipients of the wine; to issue certificates of origin to growers or shippers who required them. The Commission consisted of two growers from each of five councils in the south, and one from Porto Santo, Machico and three councils in the north. Although in Oporto a *Grémio* (Guild) of exporters was set up to regulate their activities, in Funchal customs officials were made responsible for keeping a register of exporters of madeira, and for listing the quantity and verifying the quality of all existing stocks of madeira in growers' and shippers' hands. The plantation of new vineyards was suspended for six months to allow another commission to investigate what future controls would be desirable. New experimental stations were authorized. A further thirty-six articles covered miscellaneous points. The regulations as applied to Madeira were promulgated on 11 March 1909. Although much transformed by the passage of time, these regulations remained the basis for the control of the trade throughout the century.[7]

It must have been a heart-stopping moment when, in 1912, another vine plague made its appearance on the island: mildew (*Plasmopara viticola*). Although this caused damage enough, the remedy was at hand. Downy mildew (to distinguish it from *oïdium*, or powdery mildew) had wrought havoc throughout French vineyards as early as 1882, and a cure in the form of the copper sulphate-based spray called Bordeaux Mixture was already available.

A charter for the madeira wine industry was proposed in November 1913 but not approved; this was followed by another charter in 1915, which met with universal opposition but was nevertheless imposed. Finally, in January 1924 the Ministry of Agriculture set up a commission to advise on what alterations should be made to the 1913 charter to establish the most rigorous control of wine and avoidance of adulterations.[8] This had become necessary because, although the foreign competition from false madeiras had virtually ceased, the poor quality of madeiras made from ungrafted American stock was again undermining the wine's reputation. These vines, with their good colour, high productivity and comparatively easier maintenance, were continuing to replace traditional vines.[9] According to Noël Cossart, only 20 per cent of the vintage came from grafted European vines.[10]

In 1900 the Associação Vinícola da Madeira was founded, with an annual council subsidy of 100 milréis. It was the realization of a project first conceived in 1774, but sadly it did not last long. On 12 July 1909, prompted by the continuing drop in the price of madeira on the international market, there was a meeting to discuss the founding of another wine association or even of a commercial wine company. Despite the good will of many proprietors nothing came of this either.[11] In 1913, however, a different sort of wine association did come into being, and this profoundly influenced the subsequent history of the trade.

On 9 August 1913 Wm. Hinton & Sons joined with Welsh and Cunha—itself the amalgamation of two nineteenth-century companies—and Henriques, Camara & Cia. These were reconstituted as a new limited company called the Madeira Wine Association. This was the prelude to a complicated series of amalgamations which continued intermittently for the next twenty-seven years, during which all the British firms and many of the Portuguese firms joined forces—to a total of twenty-eight exporting companies—under the umbrella of the Madeira Wine Association, which was eventually to become the dominant commercial force in the wine trade. No further changes took place, however, during the next twelve years.

The inter-war years

Immediately after World War One, in 1919, a new export record of just short of 20,000 pipes was established, but this heady total was not to be maintained or ever again matched. It may have reflected the general lack of wine resulting from the war, but it is worth noting that Sweden alone imported 7,734 pipes—38.7 per cent of the total. After a couple of lean years, reminiscent of the latter stages of the war, export levels climbed to over 11,000 pipes a year in 1923 and apart from dipping in 1926 and 1927, oscillated between this figure and 9,500 pipes a year until 1931.[12] Prices also increased sharply during the decade. It is perhaps remarkable that exports performed so well, given the loss of the Russian and American markets and the depletion of the important German market. However, Sweden and Denmark, which had imported only a little madeira just before the war, became the nucleus of the emerging Scandinavian market, which continued to grow steadily up until the outbreak of World War Two. The French and British markets remained steady, with small oscillations.[13]

On 17 June 1925 a new company was founded, the Madeira Wine Association (1925) Limitada. Its shareholders were the original Madeira Wine Association (with its three founding member companies), Blandy Bros & Co, Leacock & Co, and Thomas Mullins. Mullins was not himself a shipper, but became the efficient and highly respected manager of the new company, of which he was a shareholder. No further changes took place until 1934, when on 9 May a third company, simply called (like the original company) the Madeira Wine Association Limitada, came into being. The latter, which had a capital of £85,000, resulted from the amalgamation of the companies which made up the second company with Power Drury & Co. and a proportion of the shares of T. T. da Camara Lomelino Lda. Each firm joining the Madeira Wine Association maintained a separate legal identity, but became a shareholder in the Association. As each shipping company joined, then and later, it brought with it its business premises, its stocks of wines, etc., which then became the property of the Madeira Wine Association. The companies ceased, however, to have a separate trading identity. Their brands were produced in conformity with established styles, but were blended from the common stocks of the Association by its chief blender. The Association continued to trade under the companies' names through their existing agents, but in organizational terms it was just one big company which maintained the image, for commercial reasons, of being a collection of several separately functioning smaller companies. Only stocks of old wines (vintage and solera), while they lasted, maintained their identity as the wines of the shipper who had brought them into the Association. Subsequently other firms joined the Association, and there were seventeen associates by the end of the decade.[14]

In common with other wine markets, exports of madeira suffered from the slump of the early 1930s, but gradually recovered to their late 1920s level by 1939, only to be struck again rather badly by the outbreak of World War Two.[15] In general terms, the best wines went to Scandinavia and the worst to France.[16]

The period immediately before World War Two saw important changes in the way madeira was marketed. The names by which it had been known—such as 'London Particular' and 'Old East India'—which often reflected the market for which it had been destined, were largely, if not completely, abandoned. They survived longest on the American and Scandinavian markets. Elsewhere they were replaced by branded blends such as Blandy's Duke of Clarence Malmsey,[17] Cossart Gordon's Good Companion Bual and Lomelino's Henry the Navigator Sercial. The use of varietal names for these brands did not mean that the contents of the bottle had been vintaged from them: it simply indicated a wine in the style associated with that variety. Thus Sercial indicated a dry wine, Verdelho a medium dry wine, Boal a medium sweet wine[18] and Malmsey (Malvazia) a sweet wine. This misuse of varietal names, which had started in the late nineteenth century in the wake of phylloxera and the proliferation of ungrafted American vines, now became general. A decrease in the production of the four classic varieties between the wars acted as a catalyst. As Noël Cossart explains: 'At first my company did not agree with the practice of using the names of special growths (grape names) on blends, but in the end we had to go along with the rest. My father's cousin, Sidney Cossart, who was in the London house at the time, would spit with fury when he saw a comparatively modestly-priced madeira labelled Malmsey.'[19] While vintage wines and soleras continued to be what they purported to be, commercial blends for current drinking were almost exclusively made from hybrid vines (for the cheapest end of the market) and from Tinta Negra (for the better blends). By present-day standards of authenticity it was a fraudulent system, but it survived until 1990. It should also be noted that at this time almost all madeira was still exported in cask and bottled at its destination.

In 1933, the year after Salazar became prime minister, the Federação dos Viticultores do Centro e Sul de Portugal (Federation of Viticultors of the Centre and South of Portugal) was formed, and in 1937 this was reorganized and renamed the Junta Nacional do Vinho (abbreviated to JNV). It became the official government body controlling the production of wine throughout Portugal, taking over responsibility for the direction of the *Grémio* of port producers. More revised regulations were published in a law dated 12 October 1939, and in August 1940 the Junta installed a Delegation in Funchal to control wine production in Madeira.

The way in which shippers purchased wine from the growers had been changing throughout the century. After 1922 it had become common to offer different prices for must according to the variety of grape from which it had been made, the traditional varieties quite naturally commanding the highest prices. This was a natural out-come of the preponderance of musts from American varieties, and it effectively marked the end of the north-south division which had governed the purchase of wines for several centuries. Moreover, the system by which the shippers agreed the prices of musts and wines before the vintage (taking account of the size of the vintage, their export requirements and so on) survived until 1938. After this date an effort was made to stabilize prices and the free market came to an end. Tables of minimum prices were fixed by the JNV.

Climbing out of the doldrums

World War Two had a devastating effect on madeira sales, not just during the hostilities but after they had ended. Social habits changed and have continued to change, and fortified wines, although they have had periodic revivals in fashion, have declined sharply in popularity all over the world. Along with port and sherry, madeira has been the relatively helpless victim of this trend. The subsequent history of madeira, one might therefore say, can be expressed either as a fight for survival, or less bleakly as a gradual contraction and rationalization of the trade. During World War Two there were around sixty export firms registered with the Funchal customs. By 1973, when I first visited the island, that num-ber had shrunk to twenty-three; by the first publication of this book in 1997 it was down to seven.

At this point, in conformity with trade practice, we have to make the awkward transition mentioned in the preface to the second edi-tion, to talking about the volume of exports in hectolitres rather than in pipes. The reader who wishes to translate into equivalents is reminded that there are 218 litres to a pipe. Thus, 2.18 hectolitres (hL) equals 1 pipe.

Exports, which had dropped to under 10,000 hL in the first three years of World War Two, began to increase again in 1943, reaching 31,871 hL in 1947. Thereafter they dropped back to former levels until 1951, when they reached 34,471 hL, and then fell below 30,000 hL only three times before climbing to 44,145 hL in 1960.[20]

During this period—and indeed until the 1970s—Sweden and Denmark remained the foremost importers of better quality madeira, with Finland an increasingly important market, but France began to increase its imports of bulk wine for cooking to become, in volume terms, the largest foreign market for madeira. Great Britain came after Germany, the fifth market in order of volume, though still a prime customer for fine wines. British imports of madeira, although they grew steadily throughout the 1950s, were only a fraction of what they had been 150 years earlier. By comparison, the United States at this period seldom exceeded half the volume imported by England.

Annual production in the mid-1950s was around 12,000 hL. During the first five years of the decade only 26.1 per cent of the crop, on average, consisted of traditional grape varieties, and by far the greatest part of that would have been Tinta Negra. On 25 June 1957 a new law (No. 41 166) was promulgated to 'provide a more efficacious functioning [of the export of madeira] within the framework of the national economy'. Its aim was to regulate the activities of the shippers, allied to measures designed to improve the quality (and defend the genuineness) of madeira, and to stimulate a return to the growth of the grape varieties on which the excellence of madeira was based. It confirmed or revised many of the regulations which had been established in 1909 and superseded some of those imposed in 1939. Many of its provisions are still in force and are discussed later in this book.[21]

The 1957 law made reference to wine co-operatives. These, which provided smaller growers with some independence from the landowners and the shippers, now began to make an appearance. There had always been (and still is) co-operation of a good neighbourly kind where the use of *lagars* was concerned, but this now began to take on a commercial aspect. The first regional co-operative was established in Porto Santo in 1955 and started production the following year. Another was built in Câmara de Lobos in 1959 and a third, the Adega Co-operativa do Norte, was started at São Vicente in 1980. Their main function, like that of the *partidistas*, was to keep wine made during productive periods for sale when vintages were small, maintaining the price to their members and a supply to the shippers. But they were not a success. As Eduardo Pereira puts it, 'notwithstanding the convincing advantages from the agrarian, economic and social point of view, these have not yet entered into the minds and experience of viticultors'.[22] None of these co-operatives any longer exists—although a previously existing animal-feed co-operative has just entered the field of madeira production.

During the 1960s exports rose to more than 40,000 hL and remained above this level, usually quite substantially, until 1980, once even breaking through the 50,000 hL barrier with 52,128 hL in 1972.[23] Comparing decade with decade, trade was therefore, in volume terms, at its best since the start of the century. Yet it has to be said that most of these exports were of bulk wine, mainly destined for cooking and of a very poor quality. The proportion of fine wine sales was lamentably small. Standards of viticulture and vinification were still quite primitive, having changed little during the century. Living standards for the vast majority were very low. Oddly, as exports increased production went down. This was because some growers, mainly the smaller tenants, were being increasingly attracted to bananas as an alternative crop. The advantages of bananas were that they offered a year-round income, needed little maintenance and were less subject to the vagaries of the weather. For many these remain persuasive advantages. Many of the conversions of vineyards to bananas took place in the south, particularly in the Câmara de Lobos area, where the best varieties were grown. By 1970 it was clear that this trend could produce a long-term shortage of wine, and in 1972 the government introduced subsidies to encourage growers to regraft their vineyards with the classical varieties. The scheme was a modest success, and between 1973 and 1983 more than 1,125,500 vines were re-grafted free of charge. As a result the production of the classical varieties had increased by almost 150 per cent by 1980.[24]

The end of the twentieth century

The most significant events of the last quarter of the century for Madeira were, of course, the Revolution in 1974, which brought the old fascist dictatorship to an end and re-established democracy, and Portugal's entry into the EC in 1986.

Not only did the Revolution lead to constitutional and social change, it hastened the modernization of the island. This was made possible by a structural fund known as POSEIMA (*Programa* de *Opções Específicas para fazer face ao Afastamento e á Insularidade* da *Madeira e dos Açores*—Programme of Specific Options to deal with the Remoteness and Insularity of Madeira and the Azores) implemented by the European Community in 1992, whereby an initial sum in excess of 60 billion escudos (£250 million; €300 million; $400 million) was allocated to modernization of the island's infrastructure and improvement of its agriculture. Its aim was to bring Madeira's economy closer to that of the Community's more prosperous members. The government's policy was to turn Madeira into a modern holiday destination and at the same time to exploit it commercially as a free port. During the nineties and the first decade of the next century Caniçal, at the south eastern extremity of the island, was developed as an industrial free trade zone and as the site of Madeira's International Business Centre. A business and industrial park extending to 120 hectares was created, with grants and tax advantages to lure investors, and the harbour was developed into the principal cargo port of Madeira, with facilities for containers, bulk shipping and fishing. Cargo shipping at Funchal ended in 2007, and Caniçal now has a monopoly. POSEIMA was the first of a multitude of finance-based schemes to support development of the islands, many of them specifically designed to support and develop the grape and wine sectors.

Meanwhile the island was provided with a new infrastructure. The airport was remodelled and the runway extended to provide access for large aeroplanes. Work started on the construction of a *via rapida* to supplement the old, narrow and twisting roads along the south coast. This involved the provision of long tunnels and many spectacular viaducts which became a slightly intrusive feature of the landscape. The road now connects the airport at Santa Cruz with Funchal and further westwards to Ribeira Brava. When completed it will go as far as Ponta del Pargo. In Funchal construction work started in earnest. Hotel development and scores of apartment blocks have forever changed the appearance of the city, especially in the Lido area. In 1986, prior to Portugal's joining the EC, the island provided 10,492 tourist beds and recorded 319,419 visitors. By 1999 there were 22,234 beds and 830,416 visitors—an expansion of considerably over 100 per cent in some thirteen years. For many loyal foreign visitors the old world enchantment of this semi-tropical backwater where one might seek respite from the stress of modern life was thereby fatally compromised, but it meant that Madeira was now accessible not just to the comparatively affluent, but to a new kind of holidaymaker. All this had rather mixed repercussions on the wine trade. Shortly after the Revolution the government approved a system of land enfranchisement whereby tenants under the *contrato de colonia* system could purchase the freehold of their land. Many were of course in no position to do so, but those who did soon discovered that they could make a fast profit by reselling the land for non-agricultural purposes. Anyone who knew the island before the Revolution and who visited the south now would be astonished at the housing development, partly due to returning emigrants, that has taken place in the last quarter-century. This, coupled with the rapid development of infrastructure, light industrialization and tourism which are mentioned above has particularly affected classic vineyard areas such as São Martinho, to the west of Funchal, Câmara de Lobos, and large tracts of land on the south of the island where, it used to be considered, the best wine was produced. Funchal, for example, having been at one time the fourth largest *concelho* in terms of vineyard area is now eighth, just ahead of Machico, Santa Cruz and Porto Santo. Over the years land enfranchisement has resulted in a grievous loss of irreplaceable prime vineyard land.

On the positive side, POSEIMA and other similar schemes like PRODERAM gave (and continue to give) substantial help to the wine industry. Four producers benefited from agricultural subsidies which enabled them to build new wineries outside Funchal. One of these was the now defunct Silva Vinhos, the first new company to appear for over half a century. Subsidies became available for the replanting of vineyards with *Vitis vinifera* varieties and for restructuring (for example, reconverting banana plantations back into vineyards). These became important in a drive to reduce the number of direct producer vineyards and increase the production of recommended and approved varieties. Other subsidies aimed at promoting the quality of wine have become an important part of most producers' balance sheets. The growth of tourism also played an important part in promoting island sales, to the extent that Madeira itself has now become, after France, the largest single world market for madeira.

On 6 April 1979 the Delegation of the Junta Nacional do Vinho was abolished.[25] It was replaced by a new controlling body called the Instituto do Vinho da Madeira (IVM—Madeira Wine Institute), with wide-ranging responsibilities for the production on the island of wines and other alcoholic products, their marketing and export, and the import into Madeira of similar products. The Institute directly regulated all aspects of the madeira wine industry except the vineyards, which were the responsibility of a collateral branch of government, the Direcção Regional da Agricultura (Regional Directorate of Agriculture) through its sub-department the Direcção de Serviços de Produção Agrícola (Directorate of Agricultural Production Services).[26] The IVM, of course, played a major part in the tricky discussions on wine matters that preceded Portugal's entry into the EC in 1986. In some cases it voluntarily embraced or even extended EC norms—such as the rule that when a label mentions a varietal name, the wine must contain at least 85 per cent wine from that variety,[27] which was implemented on 1 January 1993 after a seven-year transition period. In 1988 the IVM, as a mark of the industry's increasing self-respect, inaugurated a trade guild, the Confraria do Vinho da Madeira.

In the 1980s exports suffered a sharp drop. This was mainly due to the fact that in 1980, under pressure from the EU, the IVM banned the use of direct producers in the making of madeira. The immediate result was a 30.5 per cent fall in the volume of exports. However, sales figures at least levelled off, averaging an annual 3,371 hL during the 1980s and 3,667 hL during the 1990s—not spectacular, but healthily steady. Nevertheless, although volumes remained fairly constant, the makeup of the market changed quite significantly. At the beginning of the period 88.74 per cent of exports were in bulk, whereas by the end of the century that figure had dropped to 68.35 per cent. This is a clear indication of the efforts that were being made to raise quality standards. France remained the most important export market in volume terms, but mainly for bulk wine of rather poor quality. Germany maintained second place, with Britain mostly in third place, with a large share of higher quality bottled wine. Belgium, an increasingly important customer, was in fourth place, while Denmark and Sweden, still important customers, moved down the league a little. Japan, however, became the second most important customer for bottled wine. USA, another big market for bottled wine, slipped in the early 1990s but by the end of the century returned to where it had been in the early 1980s. In 1980 32.8 per cent of total grape production was of *Vitis vinifera* while 67.2 per cent was from direct producers. By 1995, however, the balance had turned round, with *Vitis vinifera* varieties accounting for 54 per cent of production compared with 46 per cent from direct producers. There had therefore been some increase in the proportion of European varieties. Although in 1992 a wine writer recorded the fond hope that the direct producers might be eliminated by 1997,[28] at that rate of progress another thirty years would have been required. It is also interesting to note that during the same period the number of farmers diminished from 3,916 in 1980 to 2,284 in 1995.

The statistics provided by the IVM and IVBAM from 1990 onwards give a further breakdown of the totals for the production of *Vitis vinifera*, with sub-totals for the classical varieties. In 1990 there were only 2,791 hL of classical varieties (6.9 per cent of all *Vitis vinifera* and 3.6 per cent of total production); and in 1995 there were only 2,817 hL of classic varieties (8.6 per cent of all European varieties and 4.6 per cent of total production). The balance of the European varieties production would have been almost entirely of Tinta Negra. Although these figures also showed a welcome increase, it was a pitifully small one. Despite the slow progress of vineyard reform, with sales steady and with the island on an economic roll and no end to continued development in sight, there appeared to be grounds for considerable optimism about the future. After a rather static century in the history of madeira it was hoped that the new millenium would usher in a revival of the wine's former fortunes.

The twenty-first century

In June 2006 the IVM ceased to exist after being merged with IBTAM (*Instituto do Bordado, Tapeçarias e Artesanato da Madeira*—The Madeira Institute of Embroidery, Tapestries and Handicraft) to form IVBAM (*Instituto do Vinho, do Bordado e do Artesanato da Madeira*—The Madeira Wine, Embroidery and Handicraft Institute). Behind this move was the realization that both institutes had to deal with much the same problems—especially with promotion and development—and that duplication of resources and effort could be reduced. However, to many it looked like a demotion for madeira wine—as if losing its independent institute, and being grouped with such disparate activities as the production of embroidered tablecloths and wickerwork furniture and baskets, somehow made it an adjunct to, or a component part of tourism. It certainly was not a good move from an image point of view. The new Institute moved into the building formerly used by IBTAM, a more modern and functional, if less charmingly exotic, one than Consul Veitch's house where the IVM had had its headquarters. At the same time control of vineyards passed from the Direcção Regional da Agricultura to IVBAM, and at last supervision of wine production from grape to purchaser became the responsibility of a single entity. (The structure and functioning of IVBAM are described in more detail in Appendix 5).

The new century opened buoyantly with sales in 2000 and 2001 in excess of 4,000 hL for the first time since 1988, but dropped with a bump in 2002 to 2,818 hL. This was due to the discontinuation of bulk sales of *granel*, a one year old wine of the lowest quality which was subsequently bottled in the recipient's country, beyond the control of the Madeira authorities (bulk sales, on a considerably smaller scale, do continue, but only of modified wine which is supplied to the catering trade). However, after the blip in 2002 sales levels quickly recovered and have since averaged 3,386 hL up to and including 2012. One reason for this is the continued increase in tourist numbers as the building of new hotels and apartments has proceeded apace. By 2005 there were 29,193 beds and, with 1,011,080 visitors during the year, the million mark was passed. Sales of madeira on the island increased correspondingly, dented only by the introduction of restrictions on carrying liquids in air flight cabin bags after a terrorist incident in August 2006. This was a sizeable blow to the trade, and one might have supposed that the world economic downturn which followed the banking crisis in 2008 would have led to a further diminution of sales. However, this did not happen, and sales of 3,407 hL in 2012 prove the point. In the same way, tourist numbers have held up well despite the recession. Partly this is because the typical holidaymaker in Madeira is mainly from northern Europe and belongs to sectors of the economy that have been least affected by the downturn, and partly it is because the wish to avoid civil strife and war in other winter sun destinations like north Africa has diverted tourists to Madeira. In 2012 the number of beds available reached 30,170. This represents a large over-provision in terms of demand but, with an occupancy rate of 57 per cent over the year, Madeira fared better than either the Algarve or Lisbon and did well, with 996,423 visitors, to approach so closely the million level reached in 2005—a three-fold increase in just over a quarter of a century.

Silva Vinhos, the most recent company of shippers to be established until the present century, having been founded in 1990, ceased trading in 2002 after going bankrupt. It appears that the firm was unable to break effectively into the trade. Its wine, including what had been acquired from an older firm called Veiga França when it had gone out of business, was purchased by Justino's, and its vinification equipment was acquired by several firms. Meanwhile, in 2011, a new shipper was registered—the Adega Cooperativa do Funchal. This company made wine during the 2012 vintage but, lacking stocks of old wine, has yet to start trading. The number of registered shippers therefore remains at seven, but Artur Barros e Sousa, a long established and respected firm (which is not, however, registered as a shipper) is up for sale. The ownership of two of the shippers has changed. Henriques & Henriques and Justino's (formerly Justino Henriques) are now wholly owned by La Martiniquaise, the French giant multinational holding company with wine and spirit interests in twenty-six countries. They are, however, run independently of each other apart from sharing bottling line facilities. The balance of ownership of the Madeira Wine Company has altered, with Blandy's now owning 90 per cent of the shares and the Symington Group down to 10 per cent.

Table wine production has increased: there are now twelve registered producers, a number that has held steady for three years. In this respect the hopes of the IVM have not yet been fully realized. However, considerable progress has been made in diversifying the market for madeira with the successful launch of new categories of aged wine such as madeiras that are 20, 30 and over-40 years old, and the development of *colheitas*—also referred to as Harvest Wines: *colheita* means 'vintage' or 'harvest' in Portuguese. These are madeiras from a single vintage year which, to distinguish them from *garrafeira* or *frasqueira* wines (often referred to as vintage madeiras) are less than twenty years old at the time of bottling.

Getting rid of the direct producer vineyards, a main proccupation of the IVM in the 1990s, has lost some of its importance. The supply of grapes is now getting into balance with the needs of the shippers. Indeed, there was an excess of Tinta Negra in 2012 and the only worry now appears to be the possibility of a future shortfall of the classical varieties, something that is beginning to concern some producers.

Export markets have expanded in number: some remain modest, some have grown, most fluctuate a bit. In 2012 the pecking order was France (with a massive 11,486 hL), followed by the UK (3,554 hL), Japan (2,802 hL), Germany (2,535 hL), Belgium (2,176 hL), USA (1,603 hL), Sweden (948 hL), Switzerland (716 hL), Holland (688 hL), mainland Portugal (503 hL), Denmark (489 hL), Austria (430 hL), Canada (424 hL) and Poland (334 hL). The total number of countries importing madeira in 2012 was thirty-six. Three countries (Korea, Cyprus and Hungary) which had imported madeira up until 2011 dropped off the list. Japan's import growth has been particularly striking, with a jump of 34 per cent in 2012 compared with 2011.

On 20 February 2010, the island suffered its worst flooding catastrophe for a hundred years. After a warm and serene day a nocturnal innundation caused mudslides and flooding in various parts of the island. Roads were undermined, bridges, and even some houses were swept away and there were several deaths. Crops were ruined and some vineyards—although, mercifully, not too many—were damaged. In Funchal the water swept down the hill-side, carrying with it huge boulders and rocks (some of them said to be detritus left from the construction of tunnels for the *via rapida*). The three rivers that run through the centre of the city, which normally act as storm drains, were unable to cope, got blocked, and caused considerable flooding of low-lying areas. Even the main street, the Avenida Arriaga, was awash. Two shippers were particularly affected. Pereira D'Oliveira's *adega* in the Rua Visconde de Anadia and Barbeito's wine shop, Diogo's, in the Avenida Arriaga were flooded, with the loss of a considerable amount of stock. Flooding of basement shops and car parks and damage to buildings adjacent to the torrents of water were extensive. Amongst many buildings affected were the former IVM headquarters and the Sugar Museum, which is yet to reopen. Meanwhile, re-development of the area south of the market where two of the rivers issue into Funchal Bay, coupled with a scheme to provide an extension of the marina and a bathing beach in front of the Old Town, is slowly continuing.

Other events of relevance to madeira which have occurred since the turn of the century will be dealt with in more detail in Part II of the book.

PART II

VITICULTURE AND THE WINE

7

THE SOIL AND THE GRAPES

The soil

The soil in Madeira is of volcanic origin, consisting mainly of basalt, trachytes and trachydolerites, tufa, scoria (clinker) and conglomerates. Over time, the volcanic rock disintegrates under the erosion of sun and rain and produces a variety of soils. In general terms, these soils are clayey, acid, rich in organic material, magnesium and iron, poor in potassium and adequate in phosphorus.

Basalt predominates at lower altitudes, and is the origin of more or less clayey dark or reddish-brown soils. Trachytes are grey or dark-grey rocks found above 300 m. Trachydolerites are lighter coloured and are found at very high altitudes. Tufa is solidified volcanic mud and occurs in two forms: *pedra mole*, which is yellow, and *cantaria de forno*, which is red. They have a variable composition. Scoria is solidified cellular lava, dark (sometimes purple) in colour, and porous in texture. Conglomerates are formed from basalt and tufa detritus.

From these basic geological types are derived various mixtures of soil, which have been classified into sub-types using regional names:

Massapez	heavy clayey earth that does not drain water and cracks when dry
Salã	a reddish clay similar to *Massapez*
Terra Grossa	a heavy mixture of clay and grit

Pedra Mole	a mixture of yellow clay and grit
Meia Terra	a red and yellow medium soil
Poeira	a fine, dusty red and yellow soil found in the highest, coldest areas
Delgada	a very gritty soil, rich in organic material
Solta	a mixture of white clay and grit, rich in organic matter
Areão	sandy soil

The best soils are gravelly (*saibro*) or positively stony (*cascalho*). Those derived from red tufa *(cantaria de forno)* are preferred, especially when they have a stony admixture of basaltic rock. *Pedra Mole* and *Massapez* are the least suitable for growing vines. As in the Douro, vines do best in what seem to the layman to be the least propitious circumstances, and in these soils they are too prolific, producing grapes with inferior sugar levels, and they age prematurely. On the other hand, when such soils contain an appreciable quantity of organic matter and small stones to facilitate drainage, their disadvantages are considerably lessened.

In general, vines are grown in *Salão* and *Terra Grossa* in the north and *Terra Grossa, Delgada* and *Solta* in the south. However, the widespread use of man-made terraces, which after construction had to be furnished with soil brought from various other locations, has frequently resulted in random mixtures of soil types. It is therefore not uncommon to find several types of soil within relatively small areas and within a single vineyard. This said, very large areas of the island provide soils which are suitable for viticulture. There is no particular soil type which is more suitable for one variety of vine than another.

The grapes of Madeira

It would give a rather misleading picture of Madeiran viticulture to concentrate solely on those varieties mainly used in the production of fortified wine: that is, the traditional varieties; the all-purpose workhorse grape, the Tinta Negra; and a few others. Astonishingly, an appreciable part of the grape production on the island is of varieties which do not find their way into authorized fortified or table wine at all.

Those which do go to make fortified wine all belong to the genus *Vitis vinifera;* that is to say, the traditional European vine varieties whose roots are vulnerable to attack by the louse *phylloxera vastatrix.* To counter this problem, it has been normal since the widespread phylloxera devastation of European vineyards in the second half of the nineteenth century to graft *Vitis vinifera* on to phylloxera-resistant American root stock. Various vines, consisting of *Vitis labrusca, Vitis riparia* and certain hybrids derived from them, were used in Madeira for this purpose in the nineteenth century.[1] However, as also happened in other countries, these vines were used not just to provide root stock for grafting purposes but were themselves extensively planted. In Madeira these American vines and hybrids are known as 'direct producers', which terminology I shall also use.

Direct producers, although common, are not now permitted to be used for the production of fortified wine, although they were extensively employed for this purpose from the end of the nineteenth century until relatively recently. From the point of view of madeira production, they are therefore no longer directly relevant. They are used in fact to make a rustic table wine called *vinho seco.*[2] Limited in 2007 to consumption only by the producer's household, an EU derogation of 13 March 2013 now permits its sale solely within the area of its production. From the point of view of the island's viticulture and economy, therefore, direct producers are something of an embarrassment, and for the last thirty years a lot of thought has gone into working out what best to do with the large amount of the vineyard space given over to their production.

Having made this point, there is no need to dwell on it. Although I shall briefly include direct producers in my survey of the grape varieties to be found in Madeira, it is those which are currently used in the production of fortified madeira that are of immediate concern here.

Vitis vinifera

The four classical and best-known types of madeira (Rainwater apart) are named after the grape varieties from which they are

List of approved grape varieties for the production of Madeira

Recommended varieties

	Recognized synonym
White	
Sercial	
Verdelho	
Malvasia Fina	Boal*
Malvasia Cândida	
Folgasão	Terrantez*
Black	
Bastardo	
Tinta da Madeira	
Tinta Negra**	
Malvasia Cândida Roxa	
Verdelho Tinto	

Authorized varieties

White

Caracol
Listrão
Malvasia Branca de São Jorge
Moscatel Graúdo
Rio Grande
Valveirinho

Black

Complexa
Deliciosa
Triunfo

---

* These are traditional Madeiran synonyms of varieties officially listed in the EU Code of Grape Varieties as Malvasia Fina and Folgasão respectively. The EU approved names are used in all EU legal documents, but the use of the synonyms is permitted locally. I shall follow local practice and use the synonyms throughout this book.

** Formerly Tinta Negra Mole, this variety is now known simply as Tinta Negra.

made: Sercial, Verdelho, Boal and Malvazia, all in current production. A further three varieties, relatively uncommon and therefore not so well known, have also been used traditionally to make single-variety madeiras. Terrantez, always very scarce, is still seen from time to time, whilst Bastardo and Moscatel, known mainly from old vintages, are hardly ever made nowadays and are to be considered almost as curiosities.

A type of madeira called Tinta (made originally from one or other of the *tinto* varieties, then subsequently from Tinta Negra) used to be produced, and old bottles of it surface occasionally; but although Tinta Negra is the variety from which by far the greatest amount of madeira is produced today, it cannot at present be sold legally under its own name. Tinta can therefore only be considered as a type of madeira in a strictly historical sense. However, although it is sold anonymously, by far the greatest amount of madeira on the market—some three quarters of the total—is made from, or contains a high proportion of Tinta Negra.

The official classification of grape varieties recognized as suitable for making madeira used to be divided into three categories: 'Noble', 'Good' and 'Authorized'.[3] The use of the term 'noble varieties' is officially discouraged nowadays, however, and the phrase 'traditional varieties' to refer to Sercial, Verdelho, Boal, Malvazia, Terrantez and Bastardo has been substituted. Even so, this phrase is not used in the present official classification, which is divided into two categories—'Recommended' and 'Authorized'—and which is shown on the page opposite. The lists give the official name of the grape variety followed by the synonym for it that is permitted for use in labelling madeira. There is a separate list of grape varieties used for making table wine: see p. 290.

The recommended varieties

The areas of cultivation given for each variety are those valid in 2012. The figures given below for degrees of sugar (potential alcohol) of each variety have been supplied by the MWC. Note, however, that the average for each harvest is in reality a very variable figure.

Sercial (16.01 ha) as it is known in Madeira—very occasionally spelt *cerceal*—is the same variety as the Portuguese mainland's

Esgano Cão or 'dog strangler', so called because of its mouth-puckering, astringent acidity. For a long time it was said to be related to the German Riesling, with which it actually has no connection at all. It can grow at the highest altitudes (from 600 to 700 m)—which makes it, with Malvasia (but for different reasons), one of the last varieties to be harvested—but on the north it grows along the coast at 150–200 m. Sercial has the reputation of being difficult to grow and thrives in only a limited number of island sites on both the north and south coasts—Porto Moniz and Seixal are reputed the best—and Jardim da Serra at Estreito de Câmara de Lobos is its *locus classicus*. Prolific in the right habitat, it is resistant to mildew and *oïdium*. Sercial provides extremely acidic musts which, in general, normally never exceed 11° sugar and are often around 9.5°. In 1998, however, bad weather conditions led to the postponement of picking, as a result of which, according to the late John Cossart, some Sercial had unheard-of levels of sugar between 15°—20°. The more I ponder this, the more I wonder if he was not mistaken. If it was indeed the case, it is perhaps a pity that the opportunity was not taken, out of interest, to vinify a sweet Sercial.

Verdelho (50.72 ha) in Madeira is different from Verdelho Branco or Gouveio, the variety of Verdelho found in mainland Portugal, but is the same variety as that found in the Azores. Verdelho was the commonest variety until phylloxera, at which time it is estimated that it comprised two-thirds of the island's vines. It was not regarded as anything more than a good variety until early last century, when it was elevated to classical status, and in the late 1990s it had the smallest presence on the island of all the classical varieties. Now, thanks to reconversion and its suitability for making table wine, it has the largest presence. Verdelho grows mainly on the north of the island, where it is suited to the harsher climatic conditions. It responds better to being grown in vineyards whose vines are close to the ground than to being trained over trellises, and prefers well-drained soils. It thrives at up to 400 m, close to the sea. The best Verdelho is currently said to come from Ponta Delgada and São Vicente. Picked during the middle of the harvest and highly acid, Verdelho gives musts with a sugar content in the range 10° to 12°, and averages 10.5°.

Boal (15.59 ha) as *Malvasia Fina* is known on the island, is a relatively uncommon variety. It grows at fairly low altitudes (100 to 300 m) on the south of the island, and at present the best seems to come from Campanário and Calheta. It is a sturdier vine than Malvasia and is relatively low-yielding. It produces dense and compact fist-sized bunches of rather small, sweet grapes with a sugar content in the range 11° to 13°, with an average of 9.5°. It also makes a good table grape.

Malvasia Cândida (area unrecorded) is, for historical reasons, the classical grape variety on Madeira, having been cultivated there since the fifteenth century. Of Greek origin, this variety, though it makes the most famous madeira of all, has never been as extensively cultivated as its celebrity might suggest. Like Terrantez, it almost became extinct. An official report in 1944 states that Malvasia Cândida 'has almost completely disappeared, one or another farmer keeping only a few as a relic of a past era'.[4] According to Cossart, the 1920 Malvazia was the last vintage to be made from the Cândida variety. However, vintages subsequent to 1920 have certainly appeared on the market, and it is clear that small parcels of Cândida vines survived through the twentieth century. Malvasia Cândida is particularly sensitive to situation and climate. It thrives only at very low altitudes (not more than 150–200 m above sea level) and in microclimates which provide sunny, sheltered locations to protect it from dampness and mildew, to which it is particularly prone. Given a good habitat, it is reasonably prolific, and is best trained on trellises. The grapes are picked when they are beginning to shrivel, and have a sugar content in the range 10° to 13°, averaging only around 10.5°. The best Malvasia, grown almost exclusively on the south of the island, currently comes from Jardim do Mar. The Fajã dos Padres, the *locus classicus* of Malvasia on the island, has a tiny private production some of which has been incorporated in Malvasia blends marketed by Barbeito. At one time, according to Cossart, Malvasia was fermented on the skins with some of its leaves,[5] but not only is this apparently no longer done, I could not find a wine-maker who had ever heard of such a thing. Statistically, IVBAM does not distinguish between Malvasia Cândida and Malvasia de São Jorge (see below). They occupy a combined area of 36.84 ha.

Terrantez (1.52 ha)—the name by which *Folgasão* is known on the island—also has a black variant *Terrantez Tinto*. Its presence in Madeira was first recorded in the eighteenth century.[6] We know that it was widely cultivated at Lamego in the Douro region of mainland Portugal as early as 1531,[7] so it may well have arrived in Madeira earlier. The grapes are sweet and the sugar content fairly high. Terrantez all but died out during the phylloxera blight. In 1921 Silva and Meneses report that it is 'cultivated on Porto Santo, but appears to be extinct or almost extinct on Madeira'.[8] Happily it is still with us and appears, if the increasing number of more recent vintages to be found is any guide, to be slowly, if uncertainly, gaining ground. It can be made in a dry, or a semisweet style (with about 1° of residual sugar). Carão de Moça figured until very recently on the list of authorized varieties, but microsatellite analysis[9] has shown it to be identical to Terrantez, which is why it has disappeared from the list!

Bastardo (1.73 ha) is the same variety that is used in the Douro to make port. It appears never to have had any definite preferred growing locale in Madeira, and like Terrantez was almost wiped out by phylloxera. It is now so scarce that very few makers can obtain a viable amount to vinify. Whenever it does get it, the MWC vinifies Bastardo with its Tinta Negra. Although its grapes are sweet, the wine is occasionally made in a dry style, and shares to some extent the bitterness characteristic of Terrantez.

Tinta Negra (260.46 ha) was until about ten years ago called Tinta Negra Mole, when it was discovered that it is biologically different from the Tinta Negra Mole found in the Algarve in continental Portugal. It is consequently known now simply as Tinta Negra in order to distinguish it from its mainland cousin. It is sometimes claimed that the variety was originally derived from crossing Burgundian Pinot Noir with Grenache,[10] but this is not so. 'Tinto' wine, as we have seen, is mentioned as far back as 1687, although I have not come across a specific mention of Tinta Negra prior to 1801,[11] when we also encounter other Tinto varieties such as Castelão, Maroto and Negrinho. Tinta Negra currently provides over 54 per cent of the grapes used in the manufacture of madeira. Until 1993 it was one of Madeira's best-kept secrets that, amongst the better qualities, most of what was sold under the names of Sercial, Verdelho, Boal and Malvazia was made from Tinta Negra. Nothing has changed since then as far as the wine itself is concerned: it is just that it is now labelled in a more honest way with an indication of style.

One of the reasons for Tinta Negra's dominance is its remarkable versatility—sometimes called chameleon-like—which enables a skilful wine-maker to use it to make madeiras which to some degree mimic the characters of the four classic varieties. Cossart states that Tinta Negra 'is unique in its ability to acquire the characteristics of the different *castas nobres* according to the height at which it is grown'.[12] This appears to imply that a wine-maker wishing to make a Sercial lookalike would have to choose Tinta Negra grown at about 600 m, whilst if he were aiming for a Malvazia lookalike, he would need to find some Tinta Negra grown at about 200 m.

There is one element of truth in Cossart's assertion, which is that the sugar content of Tinta Negra will vary somewhat with the altitude at which it is grown, which will govern the amount of sunshine and other climatic factors affecting the ripening of the grapes. So, if such a choice were to be made, it might be quite an apt one— but in practice this choice is never made. Life is too short. The wine-maker is constrained to accept the grapes as they arrive, and there is no question of sorting them into batches according to altitude of growth. Whether the Tinta Negra ends up making a dry Sercial-like style or a rich Malvazia-like style depends wholly upon the skill of the wine-maker. The chameleon-like quality of the variety is, in prosaic fact, a certain neutrality in the kind of wine it produces which accepts, fairly gracefully, the interpretation the wine-maker gives it.

Tinta Negra is grown pretty much throughout the island, but particularly in Camara de Lobos and São Vicente. Its leaves turn an intense scarlet with russet patches in autumn, making the vineyards with Tinta Negra easy to identify. I have been told that, for whatever reason, in the north Tinta Negra tends to have smaller and darker berries than in the south, where the bunches are bigger and the grapes have less colour. Some winemakers prefer Tinta Negra from the north because the vineyards there require no irrigation and receive less treatment with fertilizers. Its grapes have thin skins and their softness yields to the touch (the *Mole* in Tinta Negra Mole means 'soft'). Although a red variety, its pulp is always clear. Tinta Negra gives musts which, in general, are not very concentrated, with a potential sugar content in the range 9° to 12°, depending on where they are grown, with a low average of only 9.5°. They make good table grapes. Many shippers regard it as anomolous that this recommended variety from which so much madeira is made cannot at present be sold under its own name, but only as a style—dry, semi-dry, semi-sweet and sweet.

IVBAM itself does not discriminate between three of the ten recommended varieties in its published statistics, and because there is as yet no published *cadastro*—that is, no register of island vineyards and the varieties they contain—it is very difficult to give much useful information about them. *Tinta da Madeira* is very like Tinta Negra. Its grapes are very sweet and have a clear or lightly coloured pulp. Very little appears to be produced for wine. *Malvasia Cândida Roxa* is, at best, extremely uncommon and, according to IVBAM, is available from only 'two or three growers'. *Verdelho Tinto*, apart from its presence in IVBAM's experimental vineyards, may well be verging on extinction.[13] Only when we have a *cadastro* shall we know the precise position.

The authorized varieties

Malvasia Branca de São Jorge was neither a recommended nor an authorised variety in the late 1990s when this book first appeared, yet it was extensively used in the production of most of the wine sold as Malvazia. The official position of the IVM then was that it had been referred to the Serviços de Produção Agrícola for analysis and assessment. In 2002 it was added to the list of authorized varieties. It appears that this grape was created from parents at present unknown by Engineer José Leão Ferreira de Almeida at the Estação Agronómica Nacional at Oeiras, near Lisbon.[14] It was first cultivated in the parish of São Jorge in the *concelho* of Santana, from which it derives its name. Morphologically, Malvasia de São Jorge and Malvasia Cândida are quite different in the characteristics of their leaves, grapes and bunches. Malvasia de São Jorge has medium-sized, tight bunches of small, golden yellow and highly perfumed grapes. Like Malvasia Cândida, the must has a potential alcohol of between 10° and 13°. It has been established through microsatellite analysis that the two malvasias are entirely separate varieties. It follows that malvazia made from this variety—that is to say, well over 90 per cent of current malvazia production—is quite different from that made from Malvasia Cândida. This is not to imply that it is inferior in any way to the wine made from the Cândida variety—it is just that it is different. Anomalously, it is the only authorized variety that may be sold as a dated wine (although it is discreetly labelled 'Malvazia' instead of being given its full name). As noted above, IVBAM statistics do not currently distinguish between the two varieties. They occupy a combined 36.84 ha of vineyard area.

Complexa (34.49 ha), like Malvasia de São Jorge and Triunfo (see below), was developed by Engineer de Almeida at Oeiras. It is a tetrahybrid of João Santarém with Tintinha and Tintinha with Moscatel de Hamburgo. The Estação Agronómica Nacional is unable to provide any ampelographical details of this variety, which apparently has not been studied 'because it is a variety without importance in Portugal'! Complexa has a tougher skin than Tinta Negra and is resistant to diseases. It produces musts similar to Tinta Negra and goes into blends. There is not much agreement about its quality. Artur de Olim of Barros e Sousa prefers it to Tinta Negra: Ricardo de Freitas of Barbeito has been quoted as saying that its 'quality is extremely poor' and that 'planting Complexa has been one of the biggest errors made'.[15] It is grown mainly in São Jorge, and its quantity appears to be diminishing—which will please some people.

The remaining authorized varieties are of minor importance. They exist in IVBAM's experimental vineyards but are on the whole not significant in madeira production. *Triunfo* in Madeira is not the same as the hybrid of Chasselas Musqué and Concord produced in America in 1880, but is a cross between João Santarém and Moscatel de Hamburgo. It produces musts with a potential alcohol of up to 12.8° but low acidity. It is still rather an experimental variety and not much liked by winemakers. It and *Deliciosa* are said to 'occupy areas of some significance'[16] which nevertheless remain unquantified. *Rio Grande* appears hardly to be grown at all.

Listrão is a table grape, and in Madeira now exclusively so. It was once extensively grown in Porto Santo where, apart from the table, it was used to make a rather ordinary table wine and, by Barros e Sousa, a fortified madeira. It can achieve (for Madeira) a remarkably high sugar content of over 13°.[17] *Caracol* is, like Listrão, now principally a table grape, while *Moscatel Graúdo* is the same variety that is used to make Moscatel de Setúbal, better known as the Muscat of Alexandria (it appeared on earlier lists of authorized varieties under its synonym Moscatel de Málaga). It too is a table grape. Its grapes are large, pale green in colour and have a distinctive sweet flavour. Therein lies the main reason why it is virtually no longer made into madeira: it fetches about three times the price of the most expensive wine varieties when sold for the table, and is therefore beyond the winemaker's economic grasp. It is high in sugar and low in acidity. Most wine-makers think it makes an atypical wine. Occasional bottles of Moscatel madeira are still to be met with. When old, it has a heavy, rather treacly character—very akin, indeed, to the style of old Moscatel de Setúbal.

That leaves us with *Valveirinho*. Although it is represented in IVBAM's experimental vineyards, I have yet to find any evidence of its presence elsewhere in Madeira and conclude that it is of no practical interest. However, there are certainly other varieties that do exist. *Portalegre*, once but no longer an authorized variety, was introduced from the mainland about thirty years ago. IVBAM has no knowledge of its actual presence on the island today. Of three other non-authorized varieties known still to exist on the island— *Bastardo Preto*, *Ferral* and *Tinta de Lisboa*—not much need be said. In 1921 Bastardo Preto was said to be plentiful on Porto Santo but cultivated in Madeira only at Estreito and Jardim da Serra; Ferral was found in Funchal, Seixal and Ponta Delgada; and Tinta de Lisboa was confined to the surroundings of Funchal and reputed to be poorly esteemed as a wine grape. All three produce good table grapes and, if they survive at all, are probably currently used exclusively for that purpose.

In 1998, when the first edition of this book was published, the list of authorised varieties included, but no longer includes, *Malvasia Babosa* (the variety introduced by Simão Acciaioly) and *Tinto Negro*. Tinto Negro was apparently growing on Porto Santo in 1921, but was mistakenly thought to be extinct on Madeira.[18] Its grapes are sweet and have clear or pale violet pulp. Its must yield is high, but of indifferent quality. Both varieties still have a tenuous existence on the island.

Before going on to discuss in more detail the so-called Direct Producers, for the sake of historical completeness I wish to take a brief look at the diversity of varieties that have been part of Madeira's grape culture in the past. The discussion up to this point has revealed a sizeable number of relatively obscure secondary varieties (like Triunfo and Rio Grande) that can currently be used to make madeira in addition to the relatively well-known traditional varieties (like Verdelho and Boal) that have for centuries been at the core of madeira production. In the same way, two centuries ago, that same core was supplemented by the now totally obscure fringe varieties of their time. Mention of their names (some of them rather quaint synonyms of other varieties) nowadays mostly produces a shrug of the shoulders and a smile or a blank look.

Overleaf is a list of the secondary grape varieties appearing in writings about madeira up until the 1920s. Those marked with an asterisk are to be found in Viala and Vermorel's seven-volume *Ampélographie* (1901–1910). This was certainly the most authoritative world-wide survey of grape varieties of its day, and in certain respects has never been surpassed. Comments opposite each variety indicate what little I have been able to discover about its identity, and the likelihood according to the Madeiran viticultors whom I have consulted of its still surviving in the archipelago today (which, again, is something we shall need to wait for the *cadastro* to determine). It is interesting to note that, to judge from information in the *Elucidário Madeirense*, some now-extinct varieties appear to have survived longer in Porto Santo than in Madeira.[19] Why this might be so I am afraid I do not know.

*Alicante Branco**	Table grape; probably extinct in Madeira
Alicante Preto	Table grape. Synonym: Ferral
Arinto	Introduced after *oïdium*, this was once an approved variety
*Bagonal**	Probable synonym: Boal
Barrete de Clerigo	Synonym: Barrete de Padre
*Barrete de Padre**	Mentioned by Cossart, but probably extinct in Madeira
Barrete de Frade	Porto Santo synonym of above
Bastardo Preto	Still exists; very limited
Boal de Cheiro	Possible synonym: Maroto
Boalerdo Branco	A form of Boal?
Branquinho	Unrecognized
Bringo	Unrecognized
*Cachudo**	According to some a synonym for Boal, and to others an inferior form of Boal, probably extinct in Madeira, the synonym of which is Babosa
Cadel	Synonym: Malvasia Cândida
Carão de Dama	Synonym: Bastardo Branco
*Castelão**	A Tinto variety; probably extinct in Madeira
*Casuda**	Synonym: Casculho. Extinct in Madeira
*Chasselas**	Probably extinct in Madeira
*Corintho**	Extinct in Madeira
*Dedo de Dama**	Possible synonym: Ferral
*Fernão Pires**	Probably extinct in Madeira
*Ferral**	Still exists; very limited
Gancheira	Unrecognized
Great Muscadine	Probably a synonym for Malvasia Cândida
Lestrong Galija	An anglicized form of Listrão?
Malvasia Babosa	A little may still exist on the island
Malvasião	Synonym: Malvasia Babosa
Maroto	A poor Tinto variety. Synonym: Negro. See also under Boal de Cheiro
*Maroto Branco**	Extinct in Madeira
Moscatel de Málaga	Only as a table grape if it exists at all
Moscatel Tinto	Synonyms: Ferral, Alicante Preto
Negrete	A Tinto variety; probably extinct in Madeira
*Negrinha/Negrinho**	A Tinto variety. Possible synonym for Maroto or perhaps Castelão
Negrinho de Água de Mel	A form of Negrinho?

114

Negro	Synonym: Maroto
Palomino	Extinct in Madeira
Pergola	Unrecognized
Peringó*	Extinct in Madeira
Rio Grande	A little still exists on the island
Sabba	Unrecognized
Serilha	Unrecognized
Simão	Unrecognized white variety
Terrantez Tinto	Extinct in Madeira; mainly a table grape
Tinta da Madeira	A little may still exist on the island
Tinta de Bago Pequeno	Synonym: Negrinha
Tinta de Lisboa*	A little still exists on the island
Tinta do Padre António	Introduced after *oïdium*; probably extinct in Madeira
Tinta do Porto Santo	May still exist in Madeira
Tinta Molar	May still exist in Porto Santo
Vermejolho	A type of Malvazia with thick-skinned grapes; probably extinct in Madeira
Vidonho	See Appendix 7

The direct producers

Most, but not all, of the direct producers were introduced to Madeira following the onset of phylloxera in 1872. In that panic-filled moment any possible remedies had to be tried, and the importation of American varieties was widespread. Some have now more or less disappeared: Black Pearl, Gaston Bazile, Clinton and many others. The most common direct producers remaining are: Isabela (*Vitis labrusca*), the first to be imported and commonly known in Madeira simply as *Americano*; Jacquet, Herbemont and Cunningham, which were introduced much later and are hybrids of the American genus *Vitis aestivalis* with *Vitis vinifera*. There is also some Seibel. Direct producers, although they are no longer used in making fortified wine, account for a large vineyard area and, if for no other reason, demand some attention here.

Isabela—so named (around 1816) after Isabella Gibbs of Brooklyn, New York, in whose garden it was cultivated—is a vine notable for its resistance to *oïdium*, which made it extremely popular in Europe during the first half of the nineteenth century. It was introduced to the island from Africa, probably Algeria, in 1843,[20] eight years before *oïdium* appeared in Madeira. It is prone to mildew and black rot, however, and, not being resistant to phylloxera, was often grafted at the end of the nineteenth century. Despite this, it is planted, and survives, ungrafted in Madeira.

Isabela is the original 'mile-a-minute' vine, with a vigorous growth and rampant habit. Its tendrils can easily smother a living tree, climbing to the top, descending and remounting the same or a neighbouring tree. It requires a lot of water, hence its suitability to the north of the island. Its grapes (and hence the wine) are characterized by what is called a 'foxy' character—which distinguishes all wine made from *Vitis labrusca* grapes—and have a smell very reminiscent of *fraises de bois*. Isabela makes a light, often rather acid, deep *rosé* table wine which is known locally as *vinho americano*. It is not often bottled, but is drawn from cask when required or stored in demijohns, and it is generally used up within the year. Some people find it refreshing; I find it usually has the disagreeable overacidity which characterizes cheap Beaujolais Nouveau, although I find the wine's foxiness rather invigorating.

On 30 August, 2013 the *Jornal da Madeira* reported that the president of the Casa do Povo of Porto da Cruz is campaigning for the recognition of Vinho Americano do Porto da Cruz as an authorized label for retailing *vinho americano*, and that he also wishes to launch Isabela as a table grape. Without the blessing of IVBAM I cannot see this initiative having much success.

Jacquet (alternatively spelled *Jacquez*) is practically immune to phylloxera and was brought to Madeira for that reason. Its musts are low in quantity, low in acid, fairly high in sugar but lacking in flavour. If well made, and if the low acidity is corrected, Jacquet produces a tolerable, quite alcoholic, if somewhat rustic red wine. It does not age well, however, and although more often bottled than *vinho americano*, tends to be drunk within a year or two. Wine produced from Jacquet and other *Vitis aestivalis* hybrids is known in Madeira as *vinho seco*. There is a white variety of Jacquet, said to be similar in appearance to Terrantez, but I have never had the opportunity of tasting the wine made from it.

Herbemont and *Cunningham* are the two other main red direct producers to be found in Madeira, and they make wine which is similar to, but not as good as, Jacquet. It has been claimed of Herbemont, as of Jacquet, that it had a Madeiran origin. This is not impossible. According to Cossart, a variety known as York Madeira was taken from Madeira to Georgia in 1732,[21] and given the amount of trade between Madeira and the American colonies for 200 years, the mutual exchange of vine cuttings is by no means impossible, or even improbable.

No statistics exist for the amount of each variety, but in the 1990s red Jacquet appeared to be the most extensively planted direct producer, closely followed by Isabela, then by Cunningham and lastly by Herbemont. They are still mainly found along the north of the island, to which they are suited by reason of their robustness and general resistance to disease. This, which reduces their need for constant nurture, coupled with their productivity, endears them to lazy or absentee farmers.

The grapes from direct producers—indeed, from all American hybrids—have the common identifying feature of containing a substance called malvina (anthocyanin diglucoside), the presence of which can of course be detected by analysis. Such tests are routinely used by IVBAM to ensure that wine from direct producers is not used in the making of madeira.[22] The medical effects of malvina have been, and still are, disputed. At one time it was (wrongly) thought that prolonged exposure to malvina could lead to liver disease, and it is sometimes asserted today by Madeirans that it causes mental problems. Whatever the truth of this, under EU regulations musts from direct producers are not permitted in the manufacture of fortified madeira.

Those who remember the trade just after World War Two were not shy about admitting the use of direct producers. While the musts were quite certainly poor compared with those of *Vitis vinifera*, they could give cheaper wines a reasonable structure. Some makers, such as Peter Cossart of Henriques & Henriques, liked them for this reason. Younger members of the trade say that they do not age well; older members tend to disagree. Noël Cossart says of a 1907 Jacquet, bottled in 1926 and tasted in 1967, that 'it was a typical old madeira, although rather a heavy peasant wine'.[23] But, in any case, keeping qualities are irrelevant when it comes to making cheaper wines.

The cadastro

A *cadastro* is a register of all grape growers, with the extent of the holdings and a record of the vine varieties and the quantity of each on their properties. It is common for the administering authority of a wine region to maintain such a record. A *cadastro* for Madeira was in fact started by the Delegation of the JNV just after World War Two, but it was not kept up to date and rapidly became useless. The establishment and maintenance of a *cadastro* then became one of the sixteen specific responsibilities laid on the IVM at its formation in 1979. Little had been done to implement the formation of a *cadastro* by the time this book was first written, but moves were afoot by the director of the Direcção Regional da Agricultura to persuade the EU to finance the work involved in establishing one. Nothing, however, had yet been achieved by the time the IVM was abolished in 2006.

Part of the explanation of the delay may well have been strong opposition by members of the Associação dos Agricultores da Madeira, the professional body to which many viticultors belong. Grape growers were apt to view a *cadastro* as unnecessarily restrictive in its implications and favoured self-regulation. The IVM itself was satisfied with existing controls and, I was told, believed that the usefulness of such a register was exaggerated. However, the vagueness of the information I was given about uncommon grape varieties and, as we shall later see, about the extent of vineyards, rather persuaded me to the contrary.

It was left to IVBAM to start the establishment of a *cadastro* in 2010. In a way its hand had been forced by the promulgation of EU Regulation No. 479/2008 of 29 April, 2008, making it mandatory for member states with areas of vineyards of 500 hectares or more to maintain a *cadastro*. The project has a total value of €120,547, 85 per cent of which has been financed by the EU, the remainder being financed by the autonomous regional government. The *cadastro* is based on the information recorded on the viticultural files (*ficheiros vitivinícolas*) held by IVBAM—that is, the files on which the details of each grape-farmer's holdings are recorded. This is allied to a computer programme operated by an independent specialist contractor. As it is not yet possible to compile information through the geo-referencing of individual wine parcels, the project is proceeding indirectly by labelling and individually numbering parcels on orthophoto maps, and this information is currently being verified by visits to each vineyard parcel by IVBAM's technical staff. It is due to be completed this year.

The survey is being carried out with regard both to vineyards with plantings of *Vitis vinifera* and of direct producers, so it should eventually throw light on several interesting issues, such as: (a) the extent of plantings of the less common authorized grape varieties; (b) the extent of plantings of varieties that are not either recommended or authorized; and (c), most interesting of all in some ways, there may just possibly be rediscoveries of 'lost' grape varieties that were planted pre-*phylloxera* and which are now presumed to be extinct—although this is perhaps a little improbable, and such varieties may now exist, if they exist at all, only as individual plants in vineyards of direct producers.

8

THE VINEYARDS

In general

Let us start by putting the vineyards into perspective in relation both to the general agricultural situation on the island and to other forms of cultivation. According to the 2009 agricultural census, the total agricultural area of Madeira was then 5,383 hectares. Vines, which used to be the largest form of permanent cultivation, now, at 1,131 ha, yield that honour to horticulture and floriculture (1,209 ha), followed by potatoes (907 ha), subtropical fruit (849 ha) and other fruit (378 ha). Cereals, which in 1989 came between the last two on this list, have shrunk to a mere 88 ha, smaller even than the cultivation of nuts (104 ha). Wicker—and with it the products so characteristic of the island that used to be made from it—has all but disappeared.[1]

If we break down the census figure for vineyards of 1,131 ha we get a big surprise. In 2012 there were 1,466 grape-growers producing grapes for making wine, and the area producing *Vitis vinifera* totalled 476.06 ha (including 44 ha of table wine varieties). What, by comparison was the area of direct producer vineyards? IVBAM does not know exactly, and estimating this is not an easy task. We start from the astonishing 2009 agricultural census figure of 1,131 ha of vineyards. If we subtract from this the current area of vineyards used for making DOP madeira and DOP table wines (476 ha, in round terms), and that used for growing table grapes (4 ha, in round terms), we are left with a presumed area of direct producers of approximately 651 ha. We also have to take away from this the area of direct producer vineyards that have been restructured since 2009, which is 27.25 ha. This reduces the total area of direct producers to 624 ha (again in round terms), which is 130 per cent the size of the grape growing area that is accounted for in the production of DOP madeira, DOP table wine, and table grapes. This indicates how little progress has been made in reducing the area of direct producer vineyards. Indeed, the total amount of restructuring that has taken place since 2000 is only 128 ha (including 10.36 ha scheduled to take place in 2013).

We do have production figures for direct producer vineyards because these have to be declared to IVBAM. Here are some figures:

Date	Quantity	Percentage of total vinatge
1980	77,259 hL	67.21%
1985	36,954 hL	63.92%
1990	36,866 hL	47.81%
1995	27,812 hL	45.98%
2000	5,915 hL	9.47%
2005	1,903 hL	4.72%
2010	2,613 hL	7.63%

These statistics reveal a marked reduction. Direct producer production in 2012 was 2,710 hL, and this suggests that production has rather levelled off since 2009, the year of the census. However, the reduction in production over a thirty year period down to less than 10 per cent of total wine production is not because the area of vineyards has shrunk in the same way. So what is the explanation? I wish I knew. According to IVBAM many direct producer vineyards have been sold off for development. But most are in parts of the archipelago where no real development has taken place. Some have been abandoned, but it surely cannot be that the owners have walked away from more than 50 per cent of them. Some have been reconverted, but only a tiny amount. So what has happened? Your guess is as good as mine. In reply to an enquiry about the present area of direct producer vineyards, IVBAM's response was 'We believe that the area found in the last Agricultural General Census (RGA 2009) is close to reality'. Having noted this mystery, let us continue with a closer look at the 276.06 ha that are our main concern.

Where are the vineyards?

'The vineyards do not appear so numerous as the stranger would expect'.[2] This is as true today as it was in 1824 when Cyrus Redding visited Madeira. The visitor expecting to see fields of vines like those in continental Europe will be very disappointed. Nothing could be further from the reality. Madeira's vineyards comprise a mosaic of tiny plots. In 1989 the average vineyard area was 1,292 square m. In 2009 that figure was just short of 2,000 square m, the slight increase in average size being due partly to a diminution in the total vineyard area (the result of sales of land for building development) and partly to a certain amount of consolidation. But, although this was the average size, many plots are even smaller than the average British urban back garden, and are located in residential areas on the south of the island. The commonest situation is for the family's house to be built on the plot of land which it farms.

Climbing the road from Câmara de Lobos towards Estreito de Câmara de Lobos in the autumn, when the leaves of the Tinta Negra (the predominant variety here) have turned to scarlet and copper brown, gives one a good idea of the disposition of the vines, because at this time of year they can be more easily distinguished from the other major crop, bananas. This is a densely populated area, and the vines seem to jostle with the houses for space. Thus, although vines represent about 21 per cent of all the land in Madeira under permanent cultivation, they are scattered around the island in mostly small plots; especially during the summer, because of the all-pervasive greenness of the bananas, they are quite easy to overlook unless you are being particularly observant.

It is often helpful in wine areas to look at the past in order to understand the present. I am therefore going to examine two 'case histories'—both rather sad—which will, I think, illuminate the current vineyard situation.

The Torre Bella estate

The original distribution of land in Madeira, shortly after the discovery of the island in 1420, is described in detail in Chapter 1. The three captains granted land to influential aristocrats and most of these subsequently founded *morgados*, or strict entails, to maintain their wealth. The Torre Bella estate was one such case. Not only is it interesting in relation to the study of the vineyards, it also offers a sidelight on the relationship between British and Portuguese families in the nineteenth century.

The family is descended from João Afonso Correa, a companion of Zarco, who was Prince Henry's treasurer and who acquired a great deal of land. Fernando José Correa Brandão Bettencourt de Noronha Henriques, seventh in line of succession from João Correa, was born in 1768. A diplomat, he was successively Portuguese ambassador to Vienna, Berlin and Naples, where he died in 1821. He was certainly the largest landowner in Madeira in the eighteenth century. Diplomatic life being expensive, he decided to sell some of his estates—despite the family motto: 'We never sell, we only buy properties'! He managed to break the entail, and there was a scramble to buy what was being sold off. One property was the Quinta da Achada with its great vineyards at São Martinho, which now belongs to the Blandy family. Another was the Fajã dos Padres. As a consequence of his success as a diplomat, he was created Visconde de Torre Bella in 1812.

His son, the second Visconde (1794–1875), died without a male heir, so the estates and title were inherited by his daughter Filomena Gabriela, born in 1839. In 1857 she married Russell Manners Gordon, the grandson of the Thomas Gordon who had arrived in Madeira to become a wine merchant in 1758.[3] He was offered, and accepted, the title of Conde de Torre Bella by the Portuguese king, on condition that he changed from English to Portuguese nationality. This he did, but in consequence had to resign from Newton, Gordon, Cossart & Co., whose constitution did not permit foreign members.

The remainder of the family history can be briefly told. Russell Manners Gordon and his wife also failed to produce a male heir, and their only daughter Isabel married an Irishman called Joseph Bolger. Their only son Dermot married Phyllis Alexander, who was Scottish, and they had two daughters, Ann and Susan, both of whom married but neither of whom had children. Thus the original Portuguese family effectively became transmuted into an Irish-Scottish one, the only Portuguese blood of the present generation being that of their great-grandmother. Susan, Viscondessa and Condessa de Torre Bella, is now a widow living in the south of England, the last of the family; there are no immediate cousins.

According to one estimate, the Torre Bella estates at the time when Russell Manner Gordon married into the family comprised almost 60 per cent of the entire island. Even if this is an exaggeration, we may be sure that the Torre Bella land holdings were very large indeed. More accurately, the family estates at the time of Dermot Bolger's death in 1974 were assessed at 10.5 per cent of the island—much less than two generations previously, but still considerable. Although officially abolished, the *morgado* remained *de facto* intact because until the present generation there was only ever a single heir.

The Torre Bella estates, as one would expect, have always been diversified, and until now included a huge number of vineyards. Indeed, from the eighteenth century up to 1974 (and quite probably during the two previous centuries as well), the Correas were by far the largest wine producers on the island. In 1974, at the death of Dermot Bolger, there were vineyards at São Roque, Câmara de Lobos—where the Torre Bella (the 'beautiful tower'), traditionally said to be the site of the first vineyards on the island, used to stand—Campanário, Ribeira Brava, Arco da Calheta and Estreito da Calheta. These vineyards were, of course, farmed by tenants under the *contrato de colonia* system described in Chapter 1,[4] the wine being divided between the family and the tenants. There were *lagars* at São Roque, Torre, Campanário and Arco da Calheta. Formerly these were used to make the wine which was sold to the wine merchants—most recently to the MWA and Henriques & Henriques—though latterly, with the coming of adequate roads, the crop was sold as grapes. A certain amount of wine was also made and kept for the use of the family and its tenants, though this was but a fraction of the main crop.

Quite coincidentally, the Revolution of 1974 occurred within three months of Dermot Bolger's death, and this added considerably to the problems of sorting out his estate, especially as one of the first measures taken by the new government was a provision to enable tenants to buy out their landlord's interest.[5] Not all tenants could afford to do this, but most did, with the consequence that today the Torre Bella estate has only three or four tiny vineyards, none of any significance. The Torre hill itself, a tourist vantage point above Câmara de Lobos, has rather ugly housing on its eastern side and plenty of bananas. There are a few vineyards with Tinta Negra on its western side. By the turn of the century the vineyards of the most significant wine-producing family on the island had been entirely dispersed.

The Fajã dos Padres

The Fajã dos Padres[6] is without doubt the most celebrated of all the vineyards in Madeira. It is first mentioned at the end of the sixteenth century by Fructuoso[7] and has been constantly praised for the quality of its Malvazia—the finest on the island—by all commentators from the seventeenth century to the nineteenth. It is not only the most famous of Madeira's vineyards, it is the only famous one, equivalent in Madeira terms to Chateau d'Yquem in Sauternes.

Not the least remarkable thing about the Fajã dos Padres is its situation on the south coast of the island, at the foot of a 300 metre-high cliff to the west of the Cabo Girão. It was for centuries only accessible by sea. Only in 1984, when the present owner installed a small and precarious lift down the cliff face, did it become possible to gain direct access to the Fajã without coming by sea. Even today, its air of remoteness has not been compromised.

We first hear of Malvazia being a monopoly of the Society of Jesus from Ovington in 1689. The Jesuits, he says, have 'secured the Monopoly of *Malmsey*, of which there is but one good vineyard in the whole island, which is entirely in their possession'. This was the Fajã dos Padres. It strikes one as odd that Malvasia, which seems originally to have been the principal grape variety on the island, should have so quickly dwindled to this extent, though it perhaps explains how it came to be in such short supply.

Edward Bowdich, the first English writer to mention the Fajã by name, visited it in 1825: 'A fall of water, of one shallow, and two deep stages, descends the whole depth of the western end of the cliff, which adjoins the Fazenda dos Padres, perhaps the finest malmsey plantation in the island, and created entirely by an *avalanche* of tufa, which, falling from a height of upwards of 1,200 feet, has lodged and spread at the bottom of the cliff. The house and vineyards are only accessible by water, to those who shudder, as most persons do, at the daring route of the labourers, who ascend and descend the cliff by a succession of simple stakes driven into, and projecting from it.'[8] Nobody who sees the cliff face today can really believe it possible that anyone could go up and down in the way described by Bowdich. The usual mode of access is confirmed by John Driver in 1834: 'The best Malmsey is from the vineyards of *Fazenda dos Padres*, adjoining the western end of Cape Giram—only accessible by water, and this attended with danger'.[9] Other nineteenth-century writers who refer to the Fajã are Dillon, Isabella de França, Wortley and Vizetelly.

The Fajã became the property of the Jesuits in 1595, shortly after they had established themselves in Madeira.[10] It was part of Quinta Grande in the parish of Campanário, the most important of the Jesuits' agricultural enterprises on the island. Apart from being maintained by a permanent settlement, we also know that the Fajã was used as a retreat, and a chapel dedicated to Nossa Senhora da Conceição was already in existence there by 1626, when the Fajã was sacked by pirates. This chapel was later converted into an *adega* (which it still is), the original use of which is apparent from a holy water stoup let into one of its walls.

The Jesuit order was expelled from Portugal in 1759 and its properties auctioned off.[11] Thereafter the Fajã's history becomes somewhat confused, as much in wine terms as in a general sense. It appears to have been owned for a brief period by the Torre Bella family, but was sold again when some of the family land was sold off by the first Visconde. Subsequently it became, according to Vizetelly, the property of a family called Netto, by which time, he says, it was 'planted principally with vines of the verdelho variety'.[12] Later still it became the property of Colonel Manuel de França Dória, who 'after having grown sugar cane on his land, but without much result, went back to growing vines, which seem to be more suited to the soil of the area'.[13] Doubtless the sugar cane was planted, as elsewhere, when phylloxera—which at the time of Vizetelly's visit had not yet reached so far west—took its toll. We also learn from the *Elucidário Madeirense* that 'besides the best Malvazia wine produced on the island, Sercial and other excellent quality varieties are grown there'. It appears, therefore, that the Fajã stopped being a wholly Malvasia vineyard after about 1870, virtually stopped being a vineyard at all after phylloxera, and then became a mixed vineyard once more. The Fajã was sold in 1919 by a Captain Dória to Joaquim Carlos de Mendonça, the paternal grandfather of the wife of the present owner, Mário Eugénio Jardim Fernandes. At this time there were still vestiges of sugar cane, vines (but no Malvasia) and vegetables. Cossart's statement[14] that 1920 Malvazia was the last vintage to come from the Fajã does not therefore accord with either the information in the *Elucidário Madeirense* [1921] or what I have been told by the present proprietor.

With a seaboard of about 1,020 m and a depth towards the cliff face of about 250 m at its greatest, the Fajã has a total area of about 9 hectares. Although relatively flat, the ground rises quite steeply towards the cliff, where at one time there were stone-walled terraces. Around 1930 bananas were planted, and somewhat later the Fajã was developed as a tropical fruit farm. At the moment there are 2 ha of mangoes, 1.5 ha of bananas, 1 ha of avocado pears and smaller quantities of other tropical fruits. In all, about 6 ha are under cultivation. The effect is of a park planted with fruit trees. For the last eighteen or so years Mário Fernandes has run the Fajã as a remote, get-away-from-it-all mini-paradise. Day visitors can arrive by boat or by road, using a panoramic elevator opened in 1997 to descend the cliff face, and nine self-catering small renovated farmers' cottages welcome guests who wish to enjoy the peace and quiet for longer periods. A small restaurant and bar have been built, and bathing is possible from the stony beach.

So, from a wine point of view, is the Fajã now of purely historical interest? Not at all. In 1940 a single Malvasia Cândida vine had survived in a rocky situation, and from it clones were generated and planted at Torre by Dermot Bolger.[15] It seems unlikely that they have survived. In 1979 Engineer Fernandes, conscious of the history of the Fajã, repeated this operation from the same single vine (now gone), sending materials from it to the Gulbenkian Institute in Lisbon. The resulting clones were planted at the Fajã, grown on pergolas over a broad path. However, a small additional vineyard has been established with just over 0.4 ha of Malvazia Cândida, and a tiny 0.025 ha of Terrantez, which has been planted experimentally. The delicious 1986 Malvazia which I tasted from cask in 1997 was bottled in 2012 by arrangement with Vinhos Barbeito in an edition of 654 numbered bottles, and visitors to the Fajã may, if they are lucky, be able to sample the wine or even buy a bottle of it.

I once asked Mário Fernandes if, in view of its former glory, he had ever thought of converting the Fajã back to an exclusively Malvasia vineyard. 'Yes, I've thought of it, but I do not think the conditions are any longer suitable. Besides, the profits from tropical fruit are quicker and more secure.' Meanwhile, the visitors to the Fajã are very happy to experience the special atmosphere of remote tranquility that prevails here and, perhaps, if they are madeira lovers, to reflect—preferably with a glass in hand—on its over half of a millenium history of Malvasia production. A visit to the Fajã dos Padres for a madeira enthusiast is, after all, the nearest thing in wine terms to a holy pilgrimage.

The present situation

Whatever the advantages of the redistribution of land from the point of view of social justice, the transformations of land use in cases like the Torre Bella estate—which happens to be a particularly striking example of a general trend—have been rather disastrous from the point of view of wine. As has already been said, the period after 1974 was one of decline for wine production and export. Many of the farmers who enfranchised their land therefore decided to convert from vines to bananas, which were beginning to become more important to the island's economy and which provided an all-year-round income independent of the vagaries of bad vintages. This period also saw the start of the development boom, which accelerated with Portugal's entry into the EU, and continued until the economic downturn following the banking crisis in 2008 all but stopped further development. The increase in house construction meant that much of the land close to Funchal (particularly in São Martinho) and in Câmara de Lobos, where the best vineyards of the island are to be found, became more valuable for building development, and many of those who had enfranchised their holdings decided to cash in on their investment. The result has been a sad and virtually irreversible loss of vineyards, either to bananas or to building. Although there was a government-assisted scheme for the reconversion of banana plantations back to vineyards (and other forms of exploitation), very few farmers were tempted by it.

All this has exacerbated the already deleterious effects of inheritance laws based on the Napoleonic model which have operated for almost two centuries, whereby all children have an equal right to inherit property. This has resulted either in the multiple ownership of land or in its division into ever-smaller lots; hence the mosaic configuration of extremely small vineyards in Madeira. In the 1990s some traditional, though relatively small, quintas remained—particularly at Estreito de Câmara de Lobos. The Quinta do Jardim da Serra, built by the indefatigable Consul Veitch and latterly owned by the Araújo family, used to provide the island's best Sercial. In 2003 the property was developed into a hotel which is currently closed. The Quinta do Estreito, then owned by the Veiga França family, has also become a hotel, its vineyard destroyed to make way for the construction of extra buildings and gardens. A small plot of vines in the gardens provides 'atmosphere' for the guests. Another traditional property, the Quinta de São João, with its chapel dating from 1693, now offers rural tourist accommodation and caters for wedding parties. This property extends to 6 hectares, of which half is planted with bananas and half with vines (mainly Tinta Negra, which is sold to Barbeito). It is owned by João César, whose father and grandfather were once the largest wine producers in Estreito de Câmara de Lobos, with a total of 30 hectares yielding some 500 hL of must. These vineyards remain in the family, having been divided between three brothers and their children. In general, however, the vineyards at Câmara de Lobos and Estreito de Câmara de Lobos have become much more divided than on the north of the island, and it is in São Vicente that one now finds the largest producers. In the absence of a *cadastro* it is almost impossible to establish precisely the disposition of larger vineyards. It is possible to get some idea from production figures, but it has to be remembered that large producers will have many parcels of land and these figures do not represent the production of a single vineyard. Thus, for example, in 2012 the largest amount of grapes bought by Justino's from a single grower was 30,000 kilograms. The average for a farmer is about 400 kilograms. To demonstrate how dramatically the volume of production can vary, the smallest amount Justino's received in 2012 was 120 kilograms. About six or seven of the largest producers live in Venezuela, and return to the island only for the vintage. For the majority of producers, big and small, growing grapes is secondary to their main livelihood. One of the two largest producers in the north makes his living by running a taxi firm. The largest producer on the south of the island—who was once pointed out to me walking up the Estreito de Câmara de Lobos road with a load of grass on his back to feed cattle—sells about 30,000 kilograms a year.

Porto Santo

Grapes from Porto Santo, the little island to the north east of the archipelago where vines were first planted before those in Madeira, can legitimately be used to make madeira. The island is climatically quite different from Madeira. It suffers from a chronic shortage of water and over the years this has had an adverse effect on all its crops, to which the deserted terraces covering the island bear eloquent testimony. Quite recent photographs show small vineyards along the shore in front of Vila Baleira, the capital, and stretching towards the south-west point of the island. A few of these now tiny plots still survive. The centre of the island, north of Vila Baleira, was at one time also covered with vineyards, but the airport was driven through them in 1960, and was further extended in 1973. Consequently the production of grapes has decreased enormously. Most of what is now produced is Caracol and Listrão destined for the table. A small number of recently established vineyards have espalier training. Apart from these, one sees grapes being grown in some front gardens in Camacha, and in the remnants of former vineyards to the north and south of the airport runway. They are small, bounded by low freestone walls (called *muros de croché*), which are also found in the Azores, and the vines are trained over the ground without supports (*vinhas da pé*).

The vines in Porto Santo grow in sand, which made them immune to phylloxera. Consequently only a few direct producers were planted. How many, if any, survive I do not know. Porto Santo musts were once popular with madeira wine-makers because of their high alcoholic potential of 13° or more. Listrão ages well and quickly, and is said to mature in one year as much as Tinta Negra will in three. Henriques & Henriques used to buy Listrão in the 1950s and 1960s until the high cost of transport in casks made it prohibitive. As late as 1991 Barbeito was buying up to 3,000 litres of Listrão a year. Being fermented completely dry before shipment to Madeira, it was particularly suitable for addition to their 10 year old blends of Sercial and Verdelho. The high cost of transport again brought this to an end. Until quite recently, Barros e Sousa also used to produce a Listrão madeira. In 2012 the areas of Porto Santo producing grapes for madeira were Verdelho, 0.30 ha; Boal 0.02 ha; and non-noble white varieties—of which Triunfo forms a large part—12.11 ha. Despite all that has been said above, with this area of production Porto Santo has a larger area of vineyards than five of the *concelhos* of Madeira.

The shippers' vineyards

Vizetelly makes it clear that at the end of last century it was common for shippers also to own vineyards, rather as port shippers do today. Thus we learn of vineyards belonging to Krohn, Leacock (the São João vineyard), Donaldson and Davies. The São João vineyard, mentioned by Cossart as late as 1984, is now a thing of the past, and the Quinta do Furão, which he mentions as a new acquisition of the MWC, was relinquished by them in 1993. Pereira D'Oliveira, who up until the end of last century had family vineyards at São Martinho, disposed of them during the 1990s. By the end of the century only Henriques & Henriques (always the owners of family vineyards) were growing grapes. When they decided to build a new vinification centre at Quinta Grande in 1990, they took the opportunity to create a new 10 hectare vineyard on the 17 hectare site. This, with another in the north of the island, was the first vineyard with bulldozed *patamars* in Madeira.[16] It was planned and constructed under the supervision of Miguel Corte Real of Cockburn's, the port shippers. The Douro technicians who built it had to adapt their techniques both to the lie of the land and to the changes in the soil types, which are visible evidence of the diversity of soils encountered in a single vineyard.

Within the vineyard there are four (possibly five) different microclimates, either because of undulations of the contours or because of differences of altitude—600 m to 750 m, which is rather high for Madeira. Originally planted with 54 per cent Verdelho, 28 per cent Sercial, 8 per cent Boal, 6 per cent Malvasia, and 4 per cent Terrantez, these *patamars* have since been remade and replanted. A certain amount of soil erosion has made it necessary to build retaining walls at the foot of the slopes. The Terrantez, Malvasia and Boal have been removed, and in 2011 50 per cent was replanted with Verdelho. The remaining 50 per cent is to be planted with Sercial later. The company also has a smaller 1.3 hectare vineyard at Preços (Câmara de Lobos) planted half and half with Malvasia Cândida and Terrantez.

At the same time that Henriques & Henriques were making their Quinta Grande *patamars*, Sr. Ricardo França created a 5 hectare vineyard west of Ponta Delgada with *patamars* planted with Verdelho and varieties for table wine. Since then nobody has followed their example.

In 2012, the MWC became concerned, in the face of social construction and the increasing needs of other shippers, about whether it would be able in future to obtain all the white varieties it requires—in particular Sercial, Verdelho and Malvasia—and decided to reverse its policy of not farming its own grapes. It has, therefore, rented two properties under long-term agreements. The first is, ironically, at the Quinta do Furão, the very property it sold off in 1993. The 2 hectares of vineyards surround a country hotel and restaurant close to Santana, which continues to be run independently. The vineyards are biologically managed and have been replanted with espalier-trained Sercial (50 per cent) and Verdelho (50 per cent). The development will be completed by 2014.

The second vineyard is at the Quinta do Bispo, a property belonging to the Church at São Jorge, not far from Santana. Here new vineyards are being created on 4.5 hectares of flat land which have been leased for twenty years. Planting was in progress as this text was being written: 50 per cent Malvasia de São Jorge, 25 per cent Sercial and 25 per cent Verdelho. It has been decided to train all the vines on (wooden) *latadas* 2.20 m high in order to obtain the best quality (and to reduce humidity-related illnesses). The MWC is looking for further new properties.

Barbeito maintains a small experimental vineyard at its winery at Câmara de Lobos, but has no plans to grow grapes for commercial production.

Vineyards round the island

Most maps of the vine growing areas of the island are, if not plain inaccurate, at the very least misleading. They usually purport to show where the varieties of *Vitis vinifera* are grown, but make no reference to the hybrid direct producers, which occupy a very considerable area. Moreover, most areas in the north have only minuscule scattered plantings of either recommended or authorized varieties, and shaded areas on maps suggest a density of planting that is simply unreal. Nevertheless, although potentially misleading, I have retained the convention of shaded areas on the vineyard map on page 140 because, however approximate, they do give some sense of where the vineyards can mostly be found. To remedy this vagueness I indicate the proportions of varieties to be found in each *concelho*, based on figures for 2012. However, the reader must understand that, with replanting and restructuring, the situation alters a little from year to year, and a map based on one year alone can be at best only indicative of current vineyard dispositions. To supplement the map, therefore, I shall provide the reader with a wine tour of the island, similar to that of Fructuoso at the end of the sixteenth century. We start from Funchal and work our way clockwise around the island.

Funchal, despite being a city, still produces some grapes, even though the vineyards of São Martinho, which used to be so notable, have almost completely succumbed to urban development. Having been, at the time this book was first written, the fifth largest grape-producing area on the island, it is now, with Santa Cruz, only a little larger in grape production terms than the smallest, Ponta do Sol, although all the classical varieties, with Bastardo and Terrantez, are grown. Câmara de Lobos and Estreito de Câmara de Lobos, though also depleted, remain the best and largest of the grape-growing areas. Production here is mainly of Tinta Negra (averaging 86 per cent of the total crop), but all the classical varieties are grown here. Further west we come to Campanário, of which Quinta Grande forms a part. Still famous for its Boal, Campanário is not, however, as important as it used to be. Almost half of the crop at Ribeira Brava is also Tinta Negra, with some Boal, and tiny amounts of Verdelho, Malvasia and Sercial. Shortly we come to Ponta do Sol, the smallest producing *concelho* on the island with less than a hectare of *Vitis vinifera* vines. There is very little grape cultivation westwards until we get to Arco de Calheta, where Boal is the main crop (45 per cent). Ponta do Pargo, further west still, was once famous for its Sercial (now vanished) but is no longer a significant wine area, the predominant crop being vegetables.

On, now, north to Porto Moniz, on the north-western tip of the island, where we enter the kingdom of direct producers (over 70 per cent). Here, as we descend to the village, the eye is met by a multitude of little plots, each protected against the prevailing wind by *bardos*, the little fences made from shrubs. In winter everything is green, meaning that there is no Tinta Negra in sight. The predominant variety is Jacquet. Verdelho (31 per cent) is the main classical variety, followed by Sercial (19 per cent). Eastwards towards Ribeira da Janela we see small plots of vines precipitately placed on the cliffs and wonder how anyone can ever reach them.

Ribeira da Janela stands at a river mouth, and looking up the river valley one can see terraced vineyards, protected by their *bardos*, stacked on either side. Here it is mainly Verdelho that is grown. Passing through a long tunnel on the way to Seixal, we reach an area known as Contreiros, with a few vineyards, mainly of Sercial, perched on the hillside. The next notable vineyard site is at Seixal, where there is about three times as much Jacquet as Sercial. More extensive vineyards are found to the east of Seixal, again mainly Jacquet, with some Sercial and a tiny bit of Verdelho. Here one can see some of the steepest vineyards on the island, with slopes of up to 65 per cent. Vintagers require the agility of mountain goats.

At the centre of the north coast we come to São Vicente. From here there is a very wide valley running south and inland as far as the pass of Encumeada, along which runs the old road to Ribeira Brava. This is now the second largest vineyard area on the island and getting bigger, with the smallest proportion (around a fifth) of direct producers. With only a tiny amount of classical grapes, over 77 per cent is Tinta Negra. There are plenty of vineyards to the west of the Ribeira Brava road in Feiteiras and Ginjas. Here there is also a little Verdelho, with a single 5 hectare Verdelho vineyard at Feiteiras. However, the majority of São Vicente vineyards are hidden from the view of the traveller on the road south towards Encumeada, and to see them one must turn east off the road near Rosario towards Achada do Til. This takes one back on the other side of the valley via Lameiros to São Vicente. Here most of the vineyards are around one hectare in size. Although we also encounter a great deal of Jacquet, the production of *Vitis vinifera* from São Vicente has been steadily increasing. This is largely due to the restructuring of direct producer vineyards under various government schemes.

Going eastwards again along the north coast, we find some vineyards which are mostly Jacquet, with a little Sercial. There are sporadic terraces along the coast, and at Ponta Delgada a large number of terraces close to the sea on the north of the road as well as inland. Here there are some extensive and impressive vineyards—again mainly of Jacquet, but with a certain amount of Verdelho and Sercial. Ricardo França's 5 hectare vineyard, with 3 hectares of bulldozed terraces, is south of the road. Several of the other vineyards here have espalier-trained vines—evidence of restructuring—but some rows are so close together that it appears to be impossible to work them with a tractor.

From Ponta Delgada one rattles along the old stone-block road towards Boaventura and sees quite a number of vineyards as one approaches the town, this time mainly of Herbemont. Boaventura is built on a little shoulder of land and there are re-entrants to east and west, both covered with vines. Further along one reaches the junction with the road to Fajã Grande and Lombo do Urzal. To the south, looking up the re-entrant, there are more vineyards, as also at Fajã do Caneiro. A tunnel then leads to the area of Arco de São Jorge, part of the *concelho* of Santana, the third largest wine area on the island and notable for the quantity of Complexa (27 per cent) it produces. In the town, if you park by the church and walk about a hundred yards, you have a good view of the MWC's new vineyard at the Quinta do Bispo. For a more comprehensive view of the area's vineyards, pass through the town and climb the road to a vantage point on the east, beyond Arco de São Jorge. Looking down, one realizes that the vineyard area is effectively a small plateau set in a cupped recession of the sea cliffs. Unlike the other main wine areas of the north, there is no river, no valley and no slope. This is another area mainly of direct producers, but several espalier vineyards indicate restructuring. Some Tinta Negra (8.5 per cent) and Sercial (1 per cent) are grown.

The road continues round an outcrop of cliffs, then descends to the mouth of the Ribeira de São Jorge. Vineyards abound on both river banks, and in the upper part of the valley there are several *Vitis vinifera* plantings, including a restructured 2 hectare vineyard of Verdelho. This, as the name indicates, is the home of Malvasia de São Jorge (46 per cent for the *concelho*). From here we proceed to Santana, also a source of Malvasia de São Jorge. Undoubtedly the most eye-catching vineyard here (visible from the road) is the one adjacent to the Quinta do Furão, now a country hotel and restaurant. Newly planted by the MWC, its 2 hectares occupy an almost level site on a headland commanding a magnificent view along the coast to the most easterly point of the island.

Further along the road at Ribeira do Faial the vines are mainly Herbemont, while at Porto da Cruz they are mainly Isabela. This is part of the *concelho* of Machico, a small area for vineyards, of which the majority are direct producers. There are a little Malvasia and some new plantations of Verdelho. The road winds down to Machico on the south coast, and here we turn east. Driving towards the island's most easterly point we arrive (through another old tunnel) at Caniçal. Although never considered much of a grape-growing area, there are several new vineyards north of the town, now a favoured area for growing grapes for making table wines. A little Jacquet is grown at Machico for *vinho seco*, but at Ribeira de Machico and Santo António da Serra the most favoured drink is local cider, which can be found in bars. This has never been an important vine-growing area. Even Fructuoso considered the local wine the worst on the island, and over the centuries the island's wine producers seem to have shared his view. Santa Cruz, where the airport is, shares with Funchal the status of being beaten only by Ponta do Sol as the smallest wine area, being almost 100 per cent direct producers with only minute quantities of the four classical varieties. Between Santa Cruz and Funchal the vines one sees in gardens produce table grapes which are not commercialized. This effectively ends the wine tour, for the area along the south coast from the airport to Funchal has never been important for wine growing, but has traditionally produced other crops such as onions and tropical fruit. The observant visitor will see evidence of abandoned terraces to the west of this area, but these were on the whole never used for vines. Indeed, abandoned terraces are not hard to find in many parts of the island, and some of them undoubtedly date from the era of phylloxera. They give the lie to the guidebook cliché that cultivable land is so scarce in Madeira that not a square metre of it is wasted. Nevertheless, these terraces are often in the most inaccessible places, and not much easily cultivable land lies fallow.

The vintage and the vineyards in 2012

The 2012 Vintage

Production totals for the 2012 Vintage:

Varieties	Production in hL.	Percentage of total harvest
Sercial	508.01	1.12%
Verdelho	996.23	2.19%
Boal	1,372.42	2.80%
Malvasia	943.38	2.07%
Other European Varieties	39.04	85.86%
European Varieties sub-total	42,756.09	94.04%
Direct Producers	2,710.97	5.96%
Total Production	45,467.06	100.00%

Data kindly supplied by IVBAM, IP–RAM.

Vineyard Areas in 2012

In the information alongside Map 3, Vineyard Map of Madeira in 2012, overleaf, areas for each *Vitis vinifera* variety in each *concelho* are given in hectares and as a percentage of the total archipelago vineyard area, which is 476.06 hectares, including 44 hectares of table wine varieties included under 'Other white varieties' and 'Other red varieties'.

Total archipelago vineyard area of each variety

(a) hectares: (b) percentage of the total archipelago vineyard area.

		(a)	(b)
Bastardo	(Ba)	1.73	0.363%
Boal	(Bo)	15.59	3.275%
Complexa	(C)	34.49	7.245%
Malvasia	(M)	36.84	7.738%
Sercial	(S)	16.01	3.363%
Terrantez	(T)	1.52	0.319%
Tinta Negra	(TN)	260.46	54.712%
Verdelho	(V)	50.72	10.654%
Other white varieties	(OW)	28.64	6.016%
Other red varieties	(OR)	30.06	6.315%
		476.06	100.000%

Data kindly supplied by IVBAM, IP–RAM.

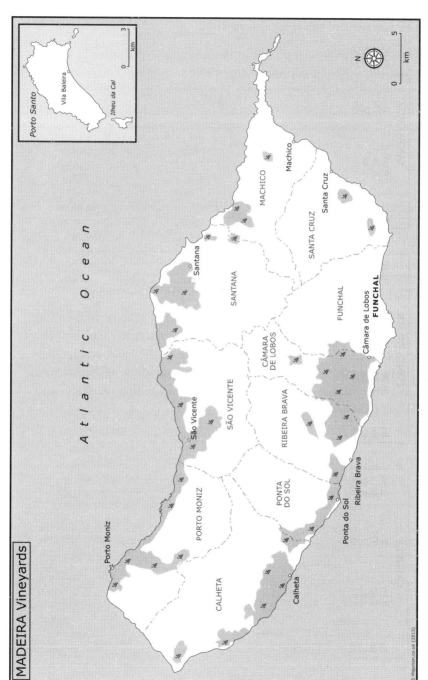

Map 3: Vineyard map of Madeira in 2012.

CALHETA

Ba	0.10	T	0.36
Bo	8.60	TN	0.19
C	2.73	V	5.55
M	0.21	OW	0.08
S	0.08	OR	1.05

Total: 18.95 ha. (3.98%)

CÂMARA DE LOBOS

Ba	0.12	T	.83
Bo	3.20	TN	151.32
C	2.32	V	10.79
M	0.56	OW	0.12
S	4.82	OR	0.17

Total: 174.25 ha. (36.60%)

FUNCHAL

Ba	0.14	T	0.12
Bo	0.23	TN	0.13
C	1.30	V	0.40
M	0.32	OW	0.00
S	0.27	OR	0.15

Total: 3.06 ha. (0.64%)

MACHICO

Ba	0.00	T	0.00
Bo	0.05	TN	0.00
C	0.87	V	0.95
M	0.14	OW	0.16
S	0.00	OR	7.46

Total: 9.63 ha. (2.02%)

PONTA DO SOL

Ba	0.00	T	0.10
Bo	0.20	TN	0.26
C	0.04	V	0.15
M	0.00	OW	0.00
S	0.00	OR	0.05

Total: 0.80 ha. (0.17%)

PORTO MONIZ

Ba	0.00	T	0.00
Bo	0.00	TN	0.04
C	1.62	V	11.10
M	0.06	OW	1.23
S	7.03	OR	14.94

Total: 35.58 ha. (7.47%)

PORTO SANTO

Ba	0.00	T	0.00
Bo	0.02	TN	0.00
C	0.00	V	0.30
M	0.00	OW	14.94
S	0.00	OR	0.00

Total: 15.26 ha. (3.21%)

RIBEIRA BRAVA

Ba	0.00	T	0.03
Bo	2.78	TN	4.55
C	0.47	V	0.32
M	0.55	OW	0.00
S	0.27	OR	0.28

Total: 9.25 ha. (1.94%)

SANTA CRUZ

Ba	0.00	T	0.00
Bo	0.28	TN	0.16
C	1.49	V	0.18
M	0.03	OW	0.00
S	0.17	OR	0.72

Total: 3.03 ha. (0.64%)

SANTANA

Ba	1.37	T	0.08
Bo	0.00	TN	0.13
C	20.31	V	6.41
M	34.17	OW	6.27
S	1.27	OR	3.11

Total: 73.12 ha. (15.36%)

SÃO VICENTE

Ba	0.00	T	0.00
Bo	0.23	TN	103.68
C	3.34	V	14.57
M	0.80	OW	5.84
S	2.10	OR	2.57

Total: 133.13 ha. (27.96%)

9

VITICULTURE AND THE VINTAGE

Old vineyards

In viticultural terms, it is only comparatively recently that very much has changed from the way in which things were done for hundreds of years. To an observer used to the standards of viticulture in France, or even in mainland Portugal, Madeira is only just emerging from a sort of viticultural Middle Ages.

Many of the old vineyards on the steepest slopes are on stone-walled terraces, or *poios* or *socalcos*, laboriously constructed centuries ago. Inclines of 45 per cent are by no means unusual in Madeiran vineyards, and on the north of the island they can be as steep as 65 per cent. In places where the slope is less severe, the terraces are broader and may hold more than one row of vines. The visual effect of these terraces, however, is vastly different from the orderly, stepped-up terracing which is such a familiar sight in the Douro. Here the terraces are adapted to outcrops of rock and other irregularities of the terrain, and being covered with *latadas*, or trellises, which themselves bear the continuous canopy of the vines, they are generally not clearly visible while the vines are in leaf.

Apart from a score or so of more recently planted vineyards which have adopted the espalier (*espaldeira*), or post and wire, system of training, the description of a *latada* vineyard of the eighteenth century[1] might have been written yesterday, except that metal frames have occasionally replaced wood and bamboo for supports. The height of *latadas* is variable. Over paths and around houses they are high enough to walk under without trouble. Elsewhere, they tend to be remarkably close to the ground (1–1.5 m), making it really very difficult to get underneath to weed, carry out treatments and finally to pick the grapes. The theory is that the reflected heat from the ground assists in ripening the grapes.

The growing of crops under trellises is officially discouraged[2] but, for the poorest producers, making the fullest use of the available ground to grow vegetables for the family is still an economic necessity. Many vineyards, especially in the north, are chaotic. In Seixal I once saw a small one which, apart from vines, had tomatoes, cabbages, oranges, avocados, papaya, custard apples, bananas, sugar cane, a peach tree and tangerines within its boundaries. Such diversity is admittedly rare, and potatoes, cabbages, onions and beans are the more usual crops. When potatoes are grown in the winter, while the vine is dormant, they do little harm. Summer crops are the worst, especially as watering them cannot be effected without also watering the vines (which is technically illegal, but practically speaking uncontrollable). Another disadvantage is that fertilizers for crops strengthen the vines and the quality of the grapes diminishes. Where there are no vegetables, it is a common enough sight to see weeds. Vineyard tidiness is not one of Madeira's strong points.

Farmers can obtain both root stock and bench grafts either from licensed commercial suppliers or through IVBAM, which has a licensed nursery. The two root stocks most used are R99 and 1103–P. 5BB and SO4, which were still in use until recently, are no longer recommended, although the latter is occasionally used. Some small farmers in the north continued to use Jacquet and Herbemont until the end of last century, but their use is now forbidden.

For planned *latadas* the approved density of vines is 3,300 per hectare, planted with 2 m between rows and 1.5 m between vines. The training of the vine over the *latada* is effected by means of the following pruning regime. In the first year a cut is made above the first bud, which sends the cane to the level of the *latada*. In the second year, cuts are made at the level of the *latada* to leave three canes, which are trained in different directions over it. The canopy is thereafter developed by choosing a number of canes for training each year, the number depending on the strength of the vine and on the pruner's judgement. The aim is to have as uniform a canopy as possible. In old plantations, weak vines tend not to be replaced and their stronger neighbours are allowed to roam.

The productivity of vines trained on *latadas* varies with the variety. By law the maximum production of a hectare of vines must not exceed 80 hL of must (which must have at least 9° of natural alcohol). Tinta Negra will produce an average of 12 tonnes per hectare; Sercial and Boal 10 tonnes per hectare; Verdelho 9 tonnes per hectare; and Malvazia Cândida 8 tonnes per hectare.[3] These official figures make one blink when one reads in Cossart that 'one hectare of well-cultivated land with the best soil should, in an average year, produce from 15 to 20 tons of grapes, whereas in well-cultivated medium-quality soil only 10 to 15 tons may be expected'.[4] Cossart is talking of almost double the quantities now regarded as normal. Unless he is entirely wide of the mark, we can only conclude that the general quality of grapes must have improved with the reduction in quantity.

The advantage of *latadas* is that closeness to the ground helps in ripening the grapes, especially in the north, where the sweeter varieties can be grown quite well but not always satisfactorily ripened: the difference in sugar between the same varieties from the north and the south can be as much as 1.5°. The disadvantages are that it is difficult to gain access to the vines to carry out treatments and harvest the grapes, and dense foliage has to be lightened to allow sunshine through to the grapes underneath.

Some varieties, including Sercial, Malvasia Cândida and Tinta Negra, seem to do consistently better when trained on *latadas*. In the case of Malvazia Cândida, however, this method of training is particularly advantageous because the flowering is always at the end, rather than in the middle, of the cane. Consequently, yields of Malvasia Cândida on *latadas* tend to be greater.

Farmers use both organic material and chemical products for fertilization, and advice on the most suitable commercial fertilizers, based on the analysis of soils, is available from the Serviços de

Viticultura department of IVBAM. The general consideration is to balance the level of fertilization against the quality of the wine.

Short of the ban on the irrigation of vineyards—and even this is officially relaxed in very dry years—there is virtually no official control over the way in which a farmer chooses to grow his grapes unless, as in the case of restructuring, the farmer is to receive a subsidy towards the cost of replanting or of making a new vineyard. The role of the Serviços de Viticultura, where established vineyards are concerned, is purely advisory.

New vineyards

Vineyards are licensed, and a license is legally necessary before a grower can sell his grapes to be made into wine. Under EU regulations the planting of new (additional) vineyards is not allowed in the demarcated region of Madeira. However, certain other operations are permitted in cases like the following: (a) vineyard reconversion or restructuring whereby, for example, existing *Vitis vinifera* vines are regrafted with different varieties, or direct producers are replaced; (b) when replanting rights are granted from the Reserva Regional Direitos (a regional reserve of replanting rights administered by the government); or (c) when rights pertaining to an existing vineyard are transferred to a new vineyard in a different location, in which case the old vineyard's license becomes valid for the new vineyard.

EU grants for reconversion and restructuring have been available for a number of years and still exist. Under current arrangements such grant-funded schemes apply to minimum areas of 0.05 hectares. The aim is to extend the production of recommended and authorized varieties, although special terms apply to Tinta Negra (of which there is, for the moment, an adequate supply). In general the subsidy is 50 per cent of the approved investment up to a maximum of €56,575.79 per hectare, to which is added (except in the case of Tinta Negra) compensation of €3,046.50 per hectare for loss of income resulting from the process of transformation. In the case of Tinta Negra, the compensation is €0.90 per kg, calculated on the average production of the area for the three years prior to the start of the scheme, up to a limit of 50 per cent of the maximum legally permitted limit for the first three years of new production. The total cost of each scheme must be paid by 30 June following the date on which the scheme is undertaken unless there has been an advance payment (which, as a guarantee, has to be 120 per cent of the value of the subsidy).

The present policy is to recommend the use of espalier training wherever the nature of the site permits. This is an important limitation, because espalier training requires relatively flat terrain and, in Madeira, this is something of a rarity. The advantage of espalier training is that it allows a greater density of planting: 4,500 vines per hectare. Production levels are generally the same as with *latadas* (which have a lower density of up to 4,000 vines per hectare), but benefits include greater exposure of the grapes to sunlight, ease of spraying and applying treatments, and better plant hygiene. However, growers are free to choose a *latada* training system if they wish, even when advised otherwise. Cordon and Guyot (single or double) pruning is general. Given the fruiting habits of Malvasia and Sercial, long pruning is the best option. Malvasia also, for the same reason, does better with *latada* rather than espalier training.

The health of the vines in Madeira is greatly influenced by the generally high temperature and humidity. *Oïdium* and downy mildew therefore remain major problems: 1995 was a particularly bad year for *oïdium*. *Botrytis* (mould) is now less prevalent than mildew, but remains a problem. Apart from leaf removal and other cultural operations that improve the aeration of the vines, spraying with approved preventative and curative products continues to be the best treatment for these problems.

IVBAM—Divisão de Viticultura

Right up until the start of the new century there was a division (often criticised by the shippers) between the the supervision of wine-making and commercialization, which was the responsibility of the IVM, and supervision of vineyards and all other matters viticultural, which was carried out by the Serviços de Produção Agrícola, which was a sub-department of the Divisão de Viticultura, itself part of the Direcção Regional da Agricultura.

In 2003 the competencies of the Serviços de Produção Agrícola were ceded to the IVM and, with them, its staff, experimental vineyards, research installations and all associated equipment and property. At this point the IVM assumed global responsibility for all aspects of madeira production from grape to consumer.

During the transition from the IVM to IVBAM in 2006, a branch of the new organization called the Direcção de Serviços de Viticultura (DSVV) was set up. This new department was itself split into two sub-departments. The first, the Divisão de Viticultura (Div. VITI), largely took over the responsibilities which had belonged to the former Serviços de Produção Agrícola, while the second, called the Divisão de Vinicultura (DV) took charge of IVBAM's wineries, the main one being the Adega de São Vicente, which provides winemaking facilities for producers of table wines.[5]

The DSVV is run by a director (who is an agricultural engineer) with appropriate technical, operational and administrative assistance. The Div.VITI is headed by a biology and agronomy graduate, who has on his staff two technicians, two technical assistants and eighteen operational assistants. The DV will be more fully explained in Appendix 2.

Currently there are experimental stations at Arco de São Jorge, Câmara de Lobos, São Vicente and Caheta (the station previously at Ponta do Pargo no longer exists, nor does the laboratory formerly at Bom Sucesso). Collections of all the recommended and authorized *Vitis vinifera* varieties for fortified and regional table wines have been established, and these are maintained as 'keepers' of the integrity of their genetic heritage. Currently the main focus of the research stations is to have stock nursery plots to supply standard category material for producing bench grafts or *in situ* grafting. Ready-grafted stock, of course, has the advantage of reducing by a year the time taken by growers to establish their vineyards, and of minimizing losses from grafts which fail to take. Bench grafting is carried out at the IVBAM nursery at Caniçal.

The vintage

Sadly, the colourfulness of the traditional vintage has all but disappeared. The only grapes trodden in *lagars* nowadays are to make *vinho seco*, though the procedures remain almost identical to the vintage as it was in the eighteenth century—and indeed, as it was well within living memory. The vintage is the end of a cycle of very hard work. It is a time for co-operation between neighbours, for there are no *rogas*, or roving bands of pickers, as in the Douro. The younger people do the most strenuous jobs, picking the grapes on vertiginous slopes and carrying vintage baskets which can weigh up to 60 kilograms. In the evenings it is time to relax, and there is some serious eating and drinking. Music often accompanies the work in the *lagars*. Processions of *borracheiros* carrying the wine to Funchal were a common sight until the early 1980s. After that, sometimes *borrachos* were still used to carry *vinho seco*, and the odd *borracheiro* could occasionally be seen in the north, especially at Porto da Cruz. That, however, is now history.

For the fortified wine, sadly, the vintage is now a somewhat charmless industrial process, with a street party organized to please the visitors in front of the Turismo office in the Avenida Arriaga in Funchal. The larger shippers employ agents—Justino's has twelve— who will provide technical advice throughout the year, and will negotiate purchases of grapes well before the vintage begins. Until 1992, the IVM, in conjunction with growers and shippers, would fix minimum prices. Currently, IVBAM merely acts for the regional government to buy in grapes which are deemed unsaleable.[6]

The prices for the vintage are determined between shippers and growers independently. Most shippers will pay a higher price for each half degree of sugar (potential alcohol) above 9.00 (the lowest degree permissible) up to, generally speaking, 12.00 degrees. This may be a fixed price for all white varieties and for all red varieties, or may vary for each variety of red and white grapes. The prices will also vary from vintage to vintage. The following are representative prices for the 2012 vintage.

	White varieties				Red varieties	
	Sercial	Verdelho	Boal	Malvasia	TintaNegra	Complexa
Shipper I	€1.50–€1.80	€1.08–€1.48	€1.06–€1.45	€1.08–€1.48	€0.99–€1.14	€0.90–€1.07
Shipper II	€1.20–€1.35	€1.20–€1.35	€1.05–€1.22	€1.20–€1.35	€0.95–€1.03	€0.90–€1.01
Shipper III		€1.04–€1.36			€0.90–€1.19	

These prices will reflect the particular needs of shippers, scarcity of supply, and so on. Equally, some shippers may require certain conditions to be met—for example, quick delivery after picking—and may even offer additional premiums when these conditions are met.

Some growers have been selling to the same firms for three or more generations. Two or three months before the harvest the wine-makers will go round the island to visit their farmers. They will inspect the vineyards and give advice, after which the larger firms will control the maturation of the vines. This is done by the oenologist or wine-maker and his assistant (if he is lucky enough to have one). The agent(s) will continue to deal with the growers and give advice. If a particularly difficult problem arises, they will refer it to the wine-maker. In place of the capacious vintaging baskets which were once used, each shipper issues his agent with distinctively coloured plastic containers holding about 15 kg to pass on to the farmers from whom he is buying. The rate at which these containers are issued can be used to control the rate at which the grapes arrive for vinification. When filled, they are delivered by lorry to the shipper's winery. With the passage of time the authorities, first the IVM and now IVBAM, have tightened the controls under which the vintage takes place. The rather antiquated system which was in place in the 1990s has now given way to an immensely detailed computerized system which was introduced by IVBAM in 2008 after an intensive campaign to update information about each grower's vineyards. This information is recorded by IVBAM in an individual Wine Grower's Record (*Ficha de Viticultor*): it contains the grower's personal and business details (his grower's identification number, VAT number, etc.) and identification details of his vineyard plots (their identification numbers, plantation dates, areas, varieties, unused planting rights, etc.). The details on the Wine Grower's Record are then used to issue a Grower's Card (*Cartão de Viticultor*), which every grape-farmer has to have. The Grower's Card has to be produced when each and every transaction involved in the harvest takes place.

After consultation with representative bodies of shippers and growers IVBAM fixes the official start of the vintage, taking into account weather conditions, the ripeness of the grapes, and other relevant considerations. However, if in individual cases the ripeness of the grapes justifies it, exceptional permission to start picking before the official starting date may be granted. The official harvest period is from 15 September until 15 November, but picking has been known to start as early as 5 August. There are varying dates of maturation around the island, usually depending on altitude and exposure to the sun, and there are various micro-climates. Normally the vintage starts with grapes grown at sea level and on the lower altitudes (Verdelho and Tinta Negra) and ends with late-maturing or high-growing varieties (Malvasia and Sercial). The grapes in the south are ready before those in the north. The harvest is generally over by mid-October, but can last until early November. Traditionally, some grapes are left on the vines in São Martinho until 11 November, because he is the patron saint of wine growers and this is his name day. A street fair is held just below the church.

All growers who are registered with IVBAM and have a Grower's Card are issued with a Vintage Record (*Caderno de Vindimia*). This contains details (taken from the Wine Grower's Record) of each grape-farmer's productive potential, and must be produced when grapes are delivered to purchasers. Into it are entered details of the delivery—the quantity, variety, vineyard parcel source(s), and the recipient's (normally the shipper's) name.

At the same time IVBAM sends out inspection teams consisting of two representatives to carry out a complete audit of all the grapes acquired by the various purchasers, noting the varieties, quantities, health status and potential alcohol of the grapes that have been bought. These details are recorded on a form called a Vintage Supervision Bulletin (*Boletin de Fiscalização da Vindima*). During and after the vintage IVBAM makes a digital record of each grower's harvest manifesto, the details of which have to be confirmed by the production of the Grower's Card, Vintage Record and purchaser's delivery notes. Subsequently, after 15 November, the shippers (purchasers) make two declarations to IVBAM. The first, the Grape Purchasing Declaration (*Declaração de Compras*) states the quantity, variety and vineyard source, etc., of all the grapes acquired from each grower. The second declaration, the Wine Production Declaration (*Declaração de Produção*), details the wine made from these purchases, indicating for each type of wine its variety, its amount, how much wine alcohol and rectified concentrated must have been added to it, etc.

After IVBAM has collated the various declarations and found them to be accurate, the shippers must request recognition by IVBAM of their new wine by supplying documentation identifying each type of wine according to variety, the location of its storage, the containers it is in (type, number and capacity) and the quantity actually in each container. The details are monitored by a team from IVBAM's Departamento de Fiscalização, who visit the shipper's premises to verify the details that have been supplied. The team also collects samples of all the wines that have been declared, and these will later be analyzed by IVBAM's laboratory staff.

All shippers have to report monthly to IVBAM on all operations on, and movements of, wine under their control. After all the above formalities have been carried out, and after the shipper has recorded the new wines as additions to his stocks in his next monthly report, a computerized current account (*conta corrente*) is opened for each of the new wines.[7] The wine is now officially recognized and its commercial life, whether it is sold quickly as a modified wine for use by the catering industry or is kept in cask for decades to become a venerable *garrafeira* madeira, can be charted and controlled by IVBAM. Only when the wine has been fully accounted for and no longer forms part of the shipper's stocks can the current account be finally closed.

10

MAKING AND MATURING THE WINE

Vinification

Only in the 1980s did it become standard practice for the shippers to make their own wine from the grapes they purchased.[1] Before that the wine was made where the grapes had been grown and was then transported, as previously explained, to Funchal by processions of *borracheiros*. At this time the wine was fermented right out and therefore dry. It was then up to the shipper to sweeten the wine to suit his commercial requirements, and this he did in a variety of ways. For the best quality wines he would add *vinho surdo*, which was unfermented grape juice to which 20 per cent spirit had been added to stop it fermenting, or *vinho abafado*, which is similar to *vinho surdo* except that a small amount of fermentation is allowed to take place before it is smothered by the addition of alcohol (thereby preserving some of its natural sugar). Lesser quality wines were sweetened with *arrobo*, which was grape juice to which sugar and tartaric acid had been added. This mixture was then boiled down to a syrup one third of its original volume, the tartaric acid converting the sugar into equal amounts of glucose and fructose. The lowest qualities were produced by doctoring the dry wine with *calda*, which was simply boiled-down sugar, or caramel.[2] Under EU regulations none of these is now legal, and sweetening is effected, when necessary, by adding rectified concentrated must. It is interesting to note, however, that as late as 1984, when the now current method of making the sweeter wines was beginning to replace the traditional ways just described, Cossart speculates about whether, with ageing, wine made by the new method would 'lose vinosity and richness sooner than that sweetened with surdo'.[3] I fear I shall not live long enough to find out.

'Does anyone know how to make madeira?' was the name of an article written in 1991,[4] but the shippers had had to ask themselves the same question in the 1980s when a delegation had gone to Brussels to negotiate the status of madeira after Portugal's entry into the EU. 'We must defend our traditional way of making madeira' was the cry, but when it came to defining what the negotiators had to defend, the diversity of practices gave rise to problems. Thanks partly to pressure from the OIV (Office International de la Vigne et du Vin)—effectively the guardians of the EU's wine-making standards—and partly to the arrival on the island of modern wine-making equipment, there is now a measure of uniformity in vinification practice. The method now universally used is a large-scale application of the principle of *vinho abafado*, and it is employed in making both the generic madeira from Tinta Negra and in making the traditional single variety wines. Needless to say, there are small variations between shippers, but none of radical importance.

In the account which follows I shall deal first with the making of the generic wine, almost exclusively from Tinta Negra and Complexa, and then with the traditional varieties. I shall indicate where appropriate the practice of individual shippers in relation to what generally happens. Note that almost all generic wines are given *estufagem*, while the remaining generic wines and wines made from traditional varieties, which do not have *estufagem*, are aged as *canteiro* wines—that is in casks kept in moderately warm stores.

Generic madeira

Grapes are received at the winery and are weighed and tested for sugar (the indicator of potential alcohol). The normal potential alcohol for white varieties is 10.5–11° Baumé, and for Tinta Negra 9–10°. The legal minimum, as explained in the last chapter, is 9°.

The grapes are then poured into hoppers. The next part of the operation is the destalking of the grapes, which is total. At this point the wine-maker has a choice between pumping the crushed grapes and skins direct to the fermentation tanks or into a wine press. Henriques & Henriques have an automatic facility to enable them to do either; in other cases, it is a matter of connecting up the requisite pumps and piping. There are various types of press in use, and some producers use more than one kind. A continuous press (as used by Borges) will allow skins and even occasional bits of stalk to remain part of the must (the pressed grape juice). Pneumatic presses, on the other hand, provide skin-free liquid and can be adjusted to different pressures. A high pressure can extract more juice but may also extract elements from the skins that impart unwanted bitterness to the wine. Pneumatic presses are becoming standard.

When the must is pumped into the fermentation tanks it is normal to add 50 milligrams per litre of sulphur dioxide to control the bacteria. Sometimes grapes from the north which have spent three or four hours in their containers become a little oxidized, and sulphur dioxide acts as an anti-oxidant. The sulphur is added in the form of a sulphite solution (around 50 milligrams per litre). Some shippers (Barbeito, Justino's, D'Oliveira) also add pectolitic enzymes—about 1.5 grams per hectolitre—before fermentation in order to realize the full potential of aromas and flavours of the grapes, and to clarify the wine a little before *estufagem*. It is also permissible by law to add some concentrated must, which boosts sugar levels, either during or after fermentation. The permitted amount is limited to the equivalent of 2° Baumé, and only 8 per cent of the harvest may be so treated.[5] If the must is deficient in acidity—normally never a problem in Madeira—gypsum, in conjunction with tartaric acid, can be added. This helps to balance the wine. Not more than 1.5 grams per litre are used (the legal limit being 2 grams per litre).

In practice, for generic wine some fermentation on the skins (maceration) is now general. Some shippers give all red grapes full maceration (Barbeito, Henriques & Henriques). Others confine maceration to the must which will be used to produce sweet and medium-sweet madeira (MWC, Justino's and Borges). The object of maceration is mainly to extract as much colour as possible from the skins because the polyphenol concentration is normally largest in the wines with most colour. Thus, if a 3 year old wine has good colour, this reduces the amount of caramel which needs to be added.

Vinification takes place in stainless steel tanks. The most sophisticated have built-in temperature control, which can be of two types. The first has internal coils through which cold water is pumped; the second, which is becoming more common and is certainly better, consists of jackets round the outside of the tanks through which a coolant is pumped. The control of temperature is often computerized. Most shippers have vinification tanks in which, to aid extraction of colour, the must is pumped over the cap of skins which forms on top of the must. Barbeito, on the other hand, has a stainless steel robotic *lagar* with mechanical feet (the only one in Madeira), which simulates ten men crushing the grapes for ten minutes every two hours for seven days. This apparently provides extra maceration and oxidation within the *lagar* resulting in darker-coloured, fuller-bodied musts. Normally the natural yeasts are sufficient to get the fermentation under way, and no commercial yeasts have to be used.

The temperatures which shippers consider optimum for the fermentation of red grapes vary only a little. For example, Borges and Justino's prefer to ferment between 28°–30°; Barbeito between 27°–28°; but the MWC is somewhat lower at 24°–26°. Many shippers now publish technical details of individual wines on their websites, so the reader may often be able to find out precise information about a particular wine, including the fermentation temperature, in this way. In the past, temperatures were not controlled at all and this could result in wines with very high volatile acidity—high enough, indeed, to constitute vinegar. Most winemakers believe that the oxidizing effects on the alcohol in the wine are reduced at low temperatures, and that when the volatile acidity is kept low the wines in general mature better. This can be of particular importance for wines destined to be sold at three years old. High acidity reduces the potential of oxidation, and during two or three years of maturation you do not get much characterization of the wine.

Where shippers have computer-controlled equipment (MWC, Justino's, Henriques & Henriques), the maintenance of a steady temperature does not require separate continuous monitoring. Without such equipment vigilance is essential—even to the extent of checking temperature, degree of sugar content, density and alcohol level every hour. What is most crucial, however, is the sugar level. During vinification the amount of sugar decreases as it is turned into alcohol, at the rate of 18 grams per litre of reducing sugars to produce one degree of alcohol. The wine-maker has to stop the fermentation completely by adding more alcohol (in the form of spirit) when the sugar level gets down to the degree of natural sweetness appropriate to the type of wine he is producing.[6] Fermentation times vary for each type. For a sweet wine, fermentation can take anything from eight to twenty-four hours, depending on temperature, etc.; for a medium-sweet wine, it can take up to three days; for a medium-dry wine, fermentation can take from three to four days; and for a dry wine which is fermented right out, five or even six days.

After fermentation is completed, the *bagaço* (lees) left in the fermentation tanks is pressed, the quality of subsequent pressings decreasing each time. The lowest grade of pressings is generally used for modified wine. Better quality pressings can be added to blends to increase colour, body, etc. Pressings can account for as much as 8 per cent of the total volume of wine.

Cane-sugar spirit (*aguardente*) was used for fortification until its use was banned in favour of wine alcohol in 1967. In 1973 it was made compulsory for producers to purchase alcohol from the Junta delegation. This monopoly was inherited by the IVM and lasted until 1992. Now 96 per cent rectified spirit (mainly from France and Spain) is used, and shippers can purchase it for themselves, though its quality has to be checked by IVBAM. The process of fortification is simplicity itself. The wine-maker will have a set of tables which show how much alcohol needs to be added to the partially fermented must, based on density and temperature measurements, to arrive at the desired degree of sweetness. Older wine-makers will have this in a booklet entitled *O Adegueiro* ('The Cellarman'), which was published by the IVM. Generally speaking, by adding about 21 per cent spirit for sweet wine, between 13 and 16 per cent for medium-sweet wine, 12 to 13 per cent for medium-dry wine, and 9 per cent for dry wine, the wine-maker ends up with wine with the sweetness he wants at 17° alcohol, which is the level at which madeira is generally kept within the lodges.[7] The simplest way to fortify is to pump the wine into tanks containing the requisite amount of spirit (or vice-versa).

This wine, called *vinho claro*, is now allowed to rest briefly for a period called the first *estágio*. This provides an opportunity to assess the wines and prepare them for the next stage of the process, *estufagem*, which is the heating of the wines in *estufas*. Most firms (MWC, Henriques & Henriques, Borges, Barbeito and Justino's) clarify and filter the wine before *estufagem*. Gelatine is the most usual clarifying agent, though bentonite, which helps to stabilize the proteins in the wine, is also used. Clarification of a tank takes about thirteen days. Filtering techniques are more varied, and include diatomaceous earth filters ('Spanish earth') and filtering pads. Centrifuges were in use by some shippers during the 1980s, but they were expensive and have fallen out of favour. The shippers who fine the wine before *estufagem* believe that this removes undesirable components from the *vinho claro*, such as thermo-resistant yeasts which can develop after *estufagem*; it can also lessen the risk of faults such as mercaptan developing, and help the wines to retain their primary characteristics—particularly their aromas—and a low volatile acidity.

At this point some shippers will select a small amount of the Tinta Negra for ageing in cask like the traditional varieties,[8] but the main part will go for *estufagem*, which generally starts in January or February. It is in their handling of this process, which has aroused controversy since it was invented, that we begin to see more noteworthy differences between the shippers. Formerly (until the early 1990s), when wine was fermented completely dry, it was not uncommon for wine destined for the cheaper blends—and in the case of some shippers, all their blends—to be put into the *estufas* before the alcohol level had been corrected to 17°.[9] This possibly had an advantage insofar as there was a marginal saving in alcohol, some of which is lost during *estufagem*. The disadvantage was that, with a relatively low alcohol level, the lactic and malic acids in the wine (there being no malolactic fermentation in madeira) meant it was more apt to develop excess acidity and disagreeable smells and tastes. At the moment, however, fortification before *estufagem* is general.

All *estufa* tanks, whether made of stainless steel, or expoxy-lined concrete, are essentially the same, and all have a facility for heating the wine either by means of internal hot water piping or by means of external jackets. Again, as with the most modern fermentation tanks, automatic temperature may be included. Often, when the legal limit to which the wine may be heated is reached—that is 50°C—the heating is automatically switched off. *Estufa* tanks must, by law, be equipped with a maximum-minimum type of thermometer gauge to record the upper limit of heating. There is no lower limit. The tanks can have a small tap for draining off a sample of the contents. The shipper has to give a minimum of five days' notice of the implementation of *estufagem* to IVBAM. A representative will oversee the filling, seal the containers with tape and wax, and may take samples for analysis in the Institute's laboratory. The wine now has to remain in the *estufa* for a minimum of ninety days, and at the end of this period the representative from IVBAM will return to check that the seals are intact and that the maximum temperature has not been exceeded. Some shippers may extend the period of *estufagem* if they consider it would benefit the wine—for example, if it has not lost enough of its red colour, or the levels of total acidity and sulphur dioxide are too high. The degree of sweetness of the wine makes no difference to the amount of *estufagem* it receives.

The simplest form of heating is to raise the wine gradually to a preset temperature, keep it there for the three months, and then let it cool down. Although the chosen temperatures vary a good deal, this is what most shippers do. All are constrained to accept the minimum period of ninety days. Barbeito uses jacketed tanks and raises the temperature to 50°C, after which the wine is allowed to cool down to 42°C, at which point the heating restarts, and this process is continued for the rest of the period. Henriques & Henriques use tanks with heated jackets and hold the wine temperature at 45°C. Their tanks also have internal paddles to circulate the wine and ensure that it is evenly heated. Justino's heat slowly to 45°C over a week, then to 50°C over a further two weeks, which temperature is then maintained for the rest of the period. The wine is pumped over, again to distribute the heat evenly. Borges maintain the wine at between 40°C and 45°C, while D'Oliveira keeps the wine at between 42°C and 43°C. The MWC uses epoxy-lined concrete tanks and keeps the wine at 45°C for four months. After the *estufagem* has been stopped a representative of IVBAM again visits the establishment to remove the seals and to take further samples for analysis. The wines are slowly allowed to cool down to ambient or near-ambient temperature over a period of up to four weeks. If this is not done the wines can become excessively oxidized. Wines which were not filtered or clarified before *estufagem* are subjected to this treatment now, and wines that have had pre-*estufagem* filtration may, if required, receive further treatment. *Estufagem*, as has always been known, has a considerable effect on the wine. The aim is to give it a more mature character simulating wood aging—it being reckoned that three months of *estufagem* is equivalent to about two years of *canteiro* ageing. The wine develops the characteristic slightly toasted rancio aromas of madeira. Handled badly, *estufagem* can 'rip the guts out of the wine', as one shipper expressed it, and cause it to develop disagreeable stewed tastes and baked smells. In general there is some evaporation during the process—but not, I am told, in the most up-to-date stainless steel vessels—and the wine gains in sweetness as the sugars are caramelized, loses colour and increases in volatility. If any bad tastes and smells are present after *estufagem*, they can generally be remedied by the use of charcoal (*carvão*), but this tends to destroy the desirable characteristics of the wine (by reducing colour, flavour and smell) as much as it corrects the faults.

Modern stainless steel tanks, with their superior insulation, lose heat very slowly and trap the smell of the cooking wine. When concrete tanks are used, the area in which they are kept becomes something like a sauna, and a rich smell, somewhere between that of a gingerbread bakery and a blackcurrant jam factory, pervades the atmosphere. Pipes of *canteiro* wine which are showing difficulties after a year may be 'assisted' by being kept here for a short while. There used to be *armazems de calor*, stores which were heated to about 35°C by means of hot water pipes round their walls, in which casks would be kept for six months. This method is not used any more.

After *estufagem* has been completed, the wine-maker then has to re-examine the wine, deal with any faults, and decide on its quality. The wines are assessed and divided into lots (*lotes*). Some wine will be earmarked for the lowest quality (modified wine); the rest will be destined to provide various types of aged wines. It now has a second *estágio* and remains undisturbed for about three months or longer. It will generally be put into large wooden vats to continue to mature.

Varietal madeiras

The making of Sercial, Verdelho, Boal and Malvazia is not greatly different from that of Tinta Negra, except that *estufagem*, which is against the law for vintage wines, is never used.[10] This is principally because, if you use *estufagem* or artificial heat, you get a dry extract (what would be left if the water and alcohol were taken away) of about 20 grams per litre, which is too low for a vintage. All vintage wines are consequently *canteiro* wines. This description of the vinification of traditional varieties will therefore concentrate mainly on the significant differences from that of generic wines and on other matters of note.

Shippers vary in the degree to which they make special arrangements for the traditional varieties. As the quantity of grapes is so small, they either set aside special days for their reception, or receive them only 'by appointment'. Until some time in the 1980s it was usual to ferment these in lodge casks (*bica aberta*). Some firms (the MWC, Borges and Barros e Sousa) occasionally continue to do this (though usually in stainless steel rather than in casks).

The MWC has dedicated facilities for the reception of red and white varieties. The size and type of stainless steel container used for vinifying white varieties will be related to the often relatively small quantity of grapes being vinified. Traditional varieties are generally vinified without any maceration, but the MWC allows chilled skin contact for a limited period varying from twenty-four hours to 36 hours prior to fermentation. This is to increase the extraction from the grapes. Justino's also chill the must because this helps to precipitate unwanted solids. The chilled wine has to be heated a little to allow fermentation to start. Vinification temperatures are much lower than for the red varieties and vary not just from variety to variety but for each individual wine, so it is impossible to generalize. The MWC usually ferments within the range 18°C–22°C. Justino's favours 16°C. Fermentation times also vary widely, ranging from about four days (for Malvasia) to ten days (for Sercial). As with generic madeiras, some companies publish technical production details of specific wines on their websites.

The traditional varieties are fortified on the same lines as the generic wines, and then rested for a while. They are then racked and fined, put into cask and allocated to a warm but not artificially heated store. This is also when they are analysed and classified according to their organoleptic qualities. For example, the best Verdelho, with vintage wine potential, may be designated 'Verdelho A', while 'Verdelho B' will appear more suitable for an eventual 5 or 10 year old wine. As he does with all his stocks, the wine-maker or oenologist will monitor the progress of these wines year by year. It will become increasingly clear which wines have the potential to age to become a vintage, and which are falling short. The latter are progressively designated as suitable for aged blends. Most wine-makers, however, develop a feel for wines of vintage quality, and say that after ten years they have a good idea which they are.

Maturing the wine

Madeira is essentially a wood-aged wine. In this respect it is like tawny port; but whereas tawny port has a bottled-aged brother known as vintage port, madeira has nothing corresponding. All madeira is wood-aged. Whether it is stored in casks or in large wooden vats, the aim is the same: to allow it a slow, controlled reaction with oxygen while its volume reduces and its components become increasingly concentrated. During the ageing process, therefore, the proportions by volume of sugar, acidity, alcohol and dry extract increase, and the wine develops in complexity and flavour. That is why, generally speaking, old wood-matured madeira has more character than young wine, and why it is worth storing, even at the cost of evaporation and diminishing quantities. It is most important that the wine can breathe through the wood. Without this—when, for example, it is stored in stainless steel tanks or glass demijohns—the wine will stay virtually (although not completely) inert.

The process of ageing in wood constitutes the maderization of the wine. When we talk of a maderized table wine, we mean that it has a nasty taste and smell because the air has got to it too rapidly (generally because of a faulty or dried-out cork) and the oxygen has reacted with the wine adversely. It has become oxidized. But when the oxygen gets to the wine very slowly through the wood, which acts in a way as a filter, and there is a lot of alcohol present, far from reacting adversely, the wine is stabilized by it. The chemical analysis of this process is extremely complicated, and not entirely understood.[11] Briefly, the high levels of acidity and alcohol in fortified madeira and the relatively small amount of oxygen to which it is subjected inhibit the formation of acetic acid, while the oxygen reacts with amino acids and proteins in the wine to change them slowly into other chemicals such as aldehydes, which give the wine the smells and flavours associated with wood ageing, sometimes referred to as tertiary characteristics. As it ages, therefore, madeira is gradually stabilized by oxygen, which removes by chemical reaction those elements of the wine which tend to destabilize it. In time (after about ten years) the wine reaches a stage at which it becomes relatively immune to damage from exposure to the air. That is why, after a bottle of old madeira has been opened, it does not 'go off', but remains drinkable for at least several months.

According to Noël Cossart, the most suitable wood for ageing madeira, after seasoning, is American white oak, which is mild and does not impart a taste to the wine, though it is an important component in the development of certain flavours.[12] Most tuns and vats are made from American oak, but Baltic oak and Brazilian satinwood are also much used for large vats. Henriques & Henriques prefer to use reconditioned whisky and sherry casks. Because wooden casks are practically no longer used for shipping wine, many firms have a large supply of them and at present have no need to purchase new ones. With careful cooperage casks can be used almost indefinitely. When they are new they have to be seasoned carefully—formerly achieved by using them to ferment the wine—to avoid imparting strong wood tastes to the madeira.

As the wine matures in cask it changes, and how it does so depends largely upon the conditions in which it is kept. Evaporation, for example, is less from large vats than from casks because the surface area of the wood exposed to the air is smaller in relation to the volume of wine. In lodge pipes, for example, evaporation averages almost 4 per cent a year, or 18.5 per cent every five years, in ordinary atmospheric conditions. There is less evaporation of water and more of alcohol in conditions of high humidity, and this is inimical to the evolution of the wine. Dry, warm conditions are most conducive to a good evolution. For this reason, the MWC finds its São Francisco lodge in the centre of town better for maturing and concentrating the wines than its Mercês lodge, which being at a higher altitude is cooler. Justino's believe that their maturing cellar is on the cold side and are about to install solar heating panels to help remedy the situation. Conversely, evaporation can be excessive in very hot, dry conditions, such as occur when, each August, Madeira is subjected to arid winds (the *leste*) from the Sahara. Putting unusual conditions to one side and taking the 4 per cent average annual figure, this means that over seventeen years the shipper will lose half of his wine in lodge pipes through evaporation. It is consequently very easy to understand why old vintages which have been kept in wood, their rarity apart, become so very expensive. In fact, after a certain point (around ten years), when the wine's evolution is considerable, the shipper may decide to store the wine in larger wooden containers to reduce the evaporation.

Policies vary with regard to the topping up of casks. Some shippers will leave the wine undisturbed for a few years, but others check every cask during the course of the year (to test for faults) and take this opportunity to top up. Invariably this is now done with wine of the same variety and of the same vintage,[13] but a small 'breathing' space is always left in each cask. In the case of *garrafeira* wines of considerable age and generally well beyond twenty years, when the quantity is so diminished that topping up the cask becomes impossible and evaporation losses too expensive to bear, the wine will be transferred to glass demijohns, usually with a capacity of 20 or more litres. Once this happens the evolution of the wine is halted.

There is another tricky problem, however, which shippers are reluctant to talk about. Wine, as it ages in cask and reduces in volume, increases in viscosity. If one were simply to leave the wine to reduce in this way, in about sixty years or thereabouts it would have become as black as treacle and of much the same consistency. Leave it longer and it starts to solidify. In Rutherglen, Australia, I was offered a taste of a 100 year old muscat, looking like meat extract, on a teaspoon. Not only this, but the concentration of flavour becomes so overpowering that tasting the wine ceases to be pleasurable, while the concentration of alcohol burns the throat. It follows, therefore, that in order to keep the wine in condition it has to be refreshed from time to time. This does not need to be much or often, but it does have to happen. One port producer in the Douro, who let me taste wines which had been in cask for from sixty to over a hundred years, told me that they had been minimally refreshed by 5 per cent every thirty years. This had stopped them from getting like the Rutherglen muscat, but they were still treacly and very unpleasant to drink. It follows, therefore, that to be fit for marketing, old vintage wines which have been in cask for over sixty years will have had to be refreshed at some stage. Cossart cites vintages which have been in cask for over 140 years.[14] Indeed, when vintage wines lack the concentration which should be expected of such old wines, they may have been over-refreshed.

Why then is there such secrecy and evasion over this issue? One reason is that the refreshing of vintage wines is strictly speaking illegal—although I once managed to get a spokesman for the IVM to agree that it has to be done. Another reason may be that, if the wines are refreshed with different wine, this compromises their genuineness as a single vintage. The public likes to think it is getting a product which has not been 'tampered with'. Some shippers may escape this problem by removing the wines from cask before they start to reach the unpleasurable drinking stage, but I suspect that judicious refreshing is the normal response. It is nothing to be ashamed of, and anyone who understands the way in which forti-fied wine ages in cask will expect it to happen. There is in fact a way to solve the problem and maintain the integrity of the vintage, which is to store a little of the wine in demijohns once it is twenty years old. As it will not develop viscosity while stored in glass, this wine is ideal for refreshing the wine in cask at a later stage. This is what one shipper in Oporto does with his older cask wines, but it does not happen, so far as I am aware, in Madeira.

The characteristic development of the components of the wine is that at first they drop and then, as the wine concentrates, they increase. Thus, when you start with a cask of wine at 17 per cent alcohol by volume, after one year it comes down to 16.8 per cent; after three years it will have increased to about 17.1 or 17.2 per cent; and after five years it will have increased to 17.5 per cent. The alcohol level will then increase steadily, so that wines which have been in cask for thirty or forty years sometimes reach 22 or 23 per cent—by which time they are a liquorous wine. It is the same with acidity. Normally you start with a wine which has 9 or 10 grams per litre of total acidity.[15] After fortification this comes down to 8 grams per litre, and after *estufagem* or three years in cask it comes down further to 6 grams per litre. After that, acidity is like alcohol and increases with age, and after thirty or forty years can rise to 14 grams per litre total acidity. Volatile acidity, which after twenty years will be about one gram per litre, can rise to as much as 2.2 grams per litre in old wines—though without imparting the flavour of vinegar, because most of this volatile acidity comes with concen-tration in the cask and thus is in balance with the other flavours that develop. When you taste such wines, however, they are so round that nobody guesses that the total acidity is so high. A Verdelho which had been in cask for seventy-five years was recently found to have 24° alcohol and 17 grams per litre of total acidity. The sugar also concentrates, but this may not be so noticeable because it tends to be masked by the acidity and the two maintain a sort of balance. However, in very old wines—particularly ones made before there were strict guidelines on sweetness—this can blur the borderline between the different styles of wine, making it for example quite possible to mistake a Verdelho for a Boal. Finally, cask ageing affects the colour of the wine. Those which are dark to start with tend to lose colour during the first two years and then steadily gain in intensity. Light wines gain colour right from the start.

How a wine develops depends ultimately not just on how it is kept but on what it was like to start with. Only the very best wines, probably no more than about 5 per cent of the traditional varieties, will show themselves capable of the development necessary to become a *garrafeira* wine. The others fall in between the lowest grades and that summit, and are therefore suited possibly as *colheitas*, but more probably for blending. It is therefore the work of the blender that we must next consider.

11

FROM CASK TO CUSTOMER

Official classification of wines

Madeira is a fortified wine with a Protected Designation of Origin (Denominación de Origen Protegida—DOP) produced in the demarcated Region of Madeira. There are legal restrictions on what madeiras, and what sorts of blends of madeiras, can be put on the market. When this book first appeared in 1998 the range of styles then available had basically been established in 1982,[1] when legislation defined a series of descriptive terms for use on labels. In the late 1980s the IVM issued a proposal to alter certain of these provisions and add others.[2] It was not immediately acted upon, but was nevertheless adopted by the trade although it did not have the force of law. A further legal decree to amend and supplement the 1982 law[3] came into force just after publication of the first edition, and this defines the present legal structure of the trade. Amongst other things it recognizes and defines certain styles of madeira.

In these definitions the following terms correspond with the degree Baumé indicated. Extra dry—below 0.5°; Dry—below 1.5°; Medium Dry—between 1.0° and 2.5°; Medium sweet—2.5° and 3.5°; Sweet—over 3.5°. Traditionally, amongst wines made from recommended varieties, Sercial is dry or extra dry; Verdelho is medium dry; Boal is medium sweet; and Malvazia is sweet.

Rainwater. A wine with a colour between 'golden' and 'half-golden', which is between 1° and 2.5° Baumé, and is of good quality.

Seleccionado (Selected, Choice, Finest). A wine of requisite quality which has been aged for a minimum of three years, is invariably made from authorized varieties (mainly Tinta Negra) and can be dry, medium-dry, medium-sweet or sweet.

Reserva (Reserve, Old). A wine of the standard required of a 5 year old wine. When made from recommended varieties its sweetness will correspond to the sweetness value of that particular variety. When made from other recommended (Tinta Negra) or authorized varieties, it may be dry, medium dry, medium sweet/rich, or sweet/rich.

Reserva Velha (Old Reserve, Very Old). A wine of the standard required of a 10 year old wine. When made from recommended varieties its sweetness will correspond to the sweetness value of that particular variety. When made from other recommended (Tinta Negra) or authorized varieties, it may be dry, medium dry, medium sweet/rich, or sweet/rich.

Reserva Especial. A wine of the standard of a 10 year old wine of outstanding quality.

Superior. A term used in conjunction with a wine of outstanding quality obtained from traditional recommended varieties for which a specific current account (*conta corrente*) exists. Thus: 'Boal Superior', Superior Verdelho', etc.

Garrafeira (or *Frasqueira*).[4] When this designation is associated with a vintage year, the wine must have been made from a traditional recommended variety and have been aged in wood for a minimum of twenty years before being bottled. In addition it must have entries in a current account before and after being bottled. There is no approved English translation of *garrafeira* or *frasqueira* as they apply to madeira. In practice, the shippers speak of these as vintage wines, wine merchants in English-speaking countries list and offer them as such, and I doubt if anyone who has written in English about madeira during the last half century has not done so too. However, for reasons which will shortly appear, the standard English usage of 'vintage wine' to indicate wine made from the harvest of a specific year does not fit easily (and perhaps not at all) into the legally recognized categories of madeira, and in this case does not take account of the twenty years of cask ageing which is an essential part of the concept of a *garrafeira*—or its equivalent, *frasqueira*—madeira. This matter will be discussed further below.

Colheita. This is the Portuguese word for 'harvest', and in this context indicates a wine obtained from a single harvest, of outstanding quality, which has been aged in wood for a minimum of five years, with an indication of the year of the harvest. The term may be applied both to wines made from traditional varieties and to wines from other varieties provided that no more than 10 per cent of the total volume of the harvest is marketed as *colheita* with no indication of vine variety. The latter may only be designated as dry, medium dry, medium sweet/rich, or sweet/rich, followed by the year of the harvest. It will be apparent now that, because the year of the harvest is indicated, *colheitas* (like *garrafeiras*) also qualify in normal English usage for the epithet 'vintage', but this takes no account of the requirement that they have been aged for a minimum of five years—and, by implication, for less than twenty. To make the distinction clearer by using the epithet 'vintage', we might say that *garrafeira* madeiras are vintage wines (that is, from a single harvest) that have been aged in wood for a minimum of twenty years, whereas *colheita* madeiras are vintage wines that have been aged in wood for more than five but less than twenty years. However, to avoid confusion I shall continue to use the official Portuguese terms as above defined, although I shall limit the use of the term *garrafeira / frasqueira* to wines with harvest dates later than twenty-two years before the term was invented and introduced in the 1982 legislation—that is to say, with harvest dates from 1960 onwards. Earlier dated wines I shall continue to call 'vintage' wines. In parenthesis, it is worth pointing out that the English term 'vintage', although it does not appear in any legislation regarding madeira, does appear in legislation regarding port. The Instituto do Vinho do Porto and the port shippers generally are totally opposed to the extension of the English term to refer to madeira—which is part of the explanation of why the wretched Madeirans cannot use the term for their product and find themselves in this linguistically unsatisfactory situation. Why the port trade should have a monopoly of an English term I simply do not know.

Canteiro. A wine which, having been fortified immediately after fermentation and not having undergone any *estufagem*, has been aged in wood for a minimum of two years, has a specific current account, and has not been bottled less than three years after 1 January of the year following the harvest. The beginning and end of the *canteiro* process must be notified to IVBAM, which can take samples for analysis and seal the container.

Solera. The definition currently in use applies to new soleras, and not to those established in the nineteenth or early twentieth centuries. A wine from a specific harvest year from which an amount not exceeding 10 per cent is removed from cask for bottling each year, being replaced by an equal quantity of another wine of the same quality, which operation may be repeated a further nine times, after which all the wine in the *solera* must be bottled at one time.

Madeira without an indication of age. The humblest bottles of madeira do not have any of the above qualifiers on their labels. They are plain madeira of the lowest bottle quality, sold with less than 3 years of ageing. I call this 'cooking' madeira. This is madeira which can be sold six months after *estufagem* has been completed and after 31 October of the second year following the harvest.

Madeira with an indication of age. Madeira may be marketed with an indication of age 'whenever the organoleptical characteristics of the wine conform to the quality standards typical of a wine of that age'. The following designations may be used: 5, 10, 15, 20, 30 and over-40 years of age. It is important to realize that these indications rely entirely on, and are justified only in terms of their possession of organoleptical characteristics considered by IVBAM to be representative of a wine of the age in question. The wine does not need to be exactly of the age specified. Normally it will be a blend of different proportions of a number of wines, some of which will be younger and some of which will be older—perhaps considerably older—than the age indicated. The matter is determined by the experienced tasting panel of IVBAM in line with what it considers to be characteristic of good quality wine of the age in question.

Modified wine. On 8 May 2001 the export of wine in bulk (that is, unbottled) became illegal,[5] and on 5 June 2001[6] the legal framework for the (exceptional) export of madeira wine modified for food use was established. Modified wine is specially designed for use by European food and catering industries, the modification consisting of the addition of 10 grams per litre of salt and 40 milligrams per hectolitre of pepper, which is in the form of an essence and may be omitted at the purchaser's request, and occasionally malt dextrose. Modified wine may be exported in large containers. Unmodified wine (that is, without additives)—known as disqualified wine—may also be sold direct to the confectionary industry, the pharmaceutical industry, and to manufacturers of prestige products. Importers of disqualified wine have to certify that it will be used solely for products that require the wine not to be modified, and that it will not be otherwise bottled or sold.

Blending

The role of the blender is one of the most important in any shipping company. He starts with the stocks of wine that have accumulated in store after every vintage, and has to produce blends of these to suit the shipper's commercial requirements and to comply with the legally recognized types of blends. Not all companies work in exactly the same way, but the following account, modelled on practice at the MWC, is typical. Most shippers, unless they are starting up, have already-established brands. The blender's job is therefore twofold: to continue to produce these brands with as much consistency of style as possible and, when required, to create new ones. The procedures are the same in each case. Most shippers maintain minimum stocks of each brand. As these are sold it becomes necessary to replace them and, on the basis of actual sales and forecast sales, the blender will work out a production timetable. He will also have to bear in mind large volume sales periods such as Christmas, and the necessity of emptying as many tanks as possible immediately prior to the next vintage. Let us, for the sake of argument, suppose that he needs to produce another batch of 3 year old Dry. This is how he will set about it.

He will have a computer record of all the company's stocks of wines. For each commercial brand he will have details of the amount previously blended, how much was bottled, stock movements to indicate the present position, and how much (if any) is still in store waiting to be bottled. For each of the stock lots—the blending materials—in store, the computer file will record the lot number, the identification number of the storage vat, the number of litres, its age and maturity, and the history of problems (if any) the wine has suffered.

The blender knows his stock lots like he knows his children, and he will therefore have a good idea about which of them are likely to be suitable components for continuing a blend. In the case of the 3 year old Dry, he will instruct the cellarman to draw small quantities from those lots he is going to work with and send them to the laboratory. Here he will make up one or two trial blends, usually of about two litres and incorporating six or seven different wines, which will be submitted to a small company jury (who of course will have a sample of the existing version of the brand with which to compare them). If they approve one of the trial blends, the blender will then ask the cellarman to make up a large quantity to the same recipe, using up the existing stocks of the component wines as far as is possible. This becomes what is known as the 'base wine' for the blend. A sample of this is also sent to the laboratory for analysis—a process described in the next section of this chapter—and the blender will adjust and refine the sample, tweaking it until it is just right. He may decide that he has to add another wine to impart a certain characteristic of the brand which is missing, or he may subtract something. He may have to adjust its colour, for example, either by adding caramel or (only in dire necessity) by using a charcoal filter to reduce it. He may have to adjust the sweetness so that it falls within the legal limits; this is done by adding rectified concentrated must or, less commonly, by blending with drier wine. He may have to adjust the level of alcohol. When he is satisfied, this new sample is then submitted to the jury and, if it is approved, the cellarman is instructed to make up a commercial quantity, using the base lot as the foundation, but incorporating the changes made to the second laboratory sample. Finally, to help maintain the style of the brand, the remaining stocks of the last batch (say about 5 per cent) will be added to the new batch, which will be rested for a few months.

There may be enough of the base wine to make more than one commercial batch, in which case what remains is stored for future use. During a year a large firm may have to make up on average two or more replacement blends for its brands. The procedure outlined above applies to the whole range of brands. It should be noted that when wine is sold under a varietal name shippers are permitted to blend in up to 15 per cent of wine made from other varieties (e.g. Tinta Negra); all shippers, as far as I am aware, take considerable advantage of this concession. All wines (including *garrafeiras*) may be bottled in smallish batches (leaving some to age further in cask) or, depending on quantity, all at one time.

Legal controls

Madeira can only be marketed after it has reached a minimum age. As we have seen, a *garrafeira* madeira must have been aged for a minimum of twenty years, a *colheita* for a minimum of five years, and a *canteiro* wine cannot be sold less than three years after 1 January of the year following the year in which it was made. Wines that have been subject to *estufagem* can only be bottled and sold six months after *estufagem* has been completed, but never before 31 October of the second year following the harvest. In the case of modified and disqualified wine, sales are not permitted until at least six months after fortification and three months after *estufagem*, but not in any case before 31 October of the year after it was made.

When the shipper's blender has selected and made a trial blend of the wine his company wishes to sell he needs to ensure that it conforms to all the technical norms laid down by law (largely in compliance with the standards set by the OIV). He may also have to take other values into consideration. Certain importing countries (such as Germany, the United States, Canada and Switzerland) impose standards of their own—e.g. an absence of lead or calcium—and the blender has to ensure that the wine conforms to the requirements of all recipient countries. Some countries, such as Canada and Switzerland, restrict the upper alcohol limit of wine. The most important current standards are the following:

Alcoholic strength:	17–22 per cent at 20°C†
Total alcoholic strength:	≥ 17.5% vol at 20°C
Degree of sugar:	Extra Dry: ≤ 0.5° Baumé
	Dry/Sercial: < 1.5° Baumé
	Medium-Dry/Verdelho: 1–2.5° Baumé
	Medium-Sweet/Boal: 2.5–3.5° Baumé
	Sweet/Malvazia: > 3.5° Baumé.
Volatile acidity:[7]	Wines less than or equal to 10 years: 20 meq/l
	Wines over 10 and under 20 years: 25 meq/l
	Wines of 20 years or more: 30 meq/l
Sorbic acid:	≤ 200 mg/l
Total sulphur dioxide:	For wines with < 5 g/l total sugar: ≤ 150 mg/l
	For wines with ≥ 5 g/l total sugar: ≤ 200 mg/l
Malvidin (3.5 malvidin diglucoside)	≤ 15 mg/l

† Exceptionally, after IVBAM authorization, madeira can be exported at as low as 15.5 per cent to countries with climates that do not compromise its conservation.

There are no longer any legal limits or stipulations regarding fixed acidity, tartaric acid, pH, or non-reducing extract.

After having rested and prior to bottling, commercial blends will be cold stabilized by being held at between −5° and −7°C for about six days so that tartrates are precipitated, and they may also, using a plate filter, receive a light sterilization filtration. Most firms use cold stabilization for their 3 and 5 year old madeiras, whilst some, like the MWC, use it for all aged wines up to 15 years old. When the wine is ready for bottling the company submits it to IVBAM for approval. The procedure is as follows. The shipper delivers four bottles of 75 cl capacity (or the equivalent thereof) to IVBAM. One bottle is immediately returned with a security seal to prevent any tampering with its contents. A wax seal is placed on the cork, and from this seal a cotton ribbon is led to the label, over which another seal is placed in such a way that any attempt to open the bottle or tamper with its label would be immediately obvious. This bottle is held by the shipper in case his wine is rejected by IVBAM and he subsequently wishes to appeal against the rejection. Of the other three bottles being held by IVBAM, two are used for testing the wine and one is kept in reserve against the possibility of an appeal. If the wine passes the physico-chemical analysis it is then subjected to organoleptical examination by IVBAM's tasting panel (*Núcleo da Câmara de Provadores*—Chamber of Tasters' Nucleus— NCP). This consists of a team of a variable number of tasters consisting of oenologists, winemakers from shippers' companies, and other qualified experts 'of renowned and undisputed competence'. The only information about the wine available to the panel is the designation for which approval is being sought and its degree of sweetness. The wine is assessed under eight headings covering the wine's appearance, bouquet and taste.

If the wine fails to pass either the physico-chemical analysis or the NCP rejects the wine because it is not of the requisite character and quality of the designation under which it was submitted, the shipper has ten business days in which to appeal the finding, and the reserve bottles are used in its reassessment. If the wine fails examination a second time the shipper will have to reblend his wine and submit a new application (or he might decide to use the component wines for other blends). If, on the other hand, the shipper's wine is approved, IVBAM will certify it and issue appropriate documentation. Within the EU madeira is shipped under an e-AD (Electronic Aministrative Document). Before that can be issued IVBAM has to certify the wine on the website of the Tax and Customs Authority (Autoridade Tributária e Aduaneira—AT) after conducting a wide range of further administrative and physical controls to ensure that the wine in question is genuine and as previously certified. IVBAM will also, on request, issue the shipper with a Certificate of Origin and a Certificate of Analysis of the wine. If the wine is being exported out of the EU the Certificate of Origin is mandatory, as is an e-AD to cover transit to the port of exit from the EU.

After certification by IVBAM the wine has to be bottled within six months. Guarantee seals (*selos de garantia*) are issued for all bottles of the approved batch with capacities ranging from 0.375 l to 1.5 l, and these have to be affixed at the time the wine is bottled. The seals are made of white paper and are glued to the neck of the bottle, on top of the cork, and to the base of the capsule. The shipper has a current account for the supply of these seals which are charged at €0.0115 each for bottles with a capacity of less than 0.6 l and €0.0173 each for bottles with a capacity above 0.6 l. The seals are numbered and these are recorded for each batch of approved wine. Their deployment is subject to various legal compliance controls.

In the case of miniature bottles (with a capacity no greater than 200 millilitres) the use of paper seals is replaced by specially manufactured capsules with an imprint of the armorial shield of the Autonomous Region of Madeira and the inscription of the icon of IVBAM. In this case the shipper's current account will be charged €0.0115 for each capsule-guarantee seal supplied. A commercialization fee of €0.0860/litre is charged for shipping modified or disqualified wine.

The guarantee seal is IVBAM's assurance to the eventual purchaser that the wine in the bottle conforms to the standards required by law and fits the description on the label, which is itself subject to a multiplicity of other legal requirements. These include the legal requirements common to all wine regions within the EU, as well as the individual requirements of importing countries outside the EU.

Finally, in addition to adhering to the procedures outlined above, the shipper has to fulfil other legal obligations (first introduced in 1957). One of the most important of these is the maintenance of minimum stocks. The system is similar to that in Oporto, and has the aim of stabilizing commerce and keeping fly-by-night operators out of the market. The minimum stock level is sufficient volume to cover the export of wine for 18 months, based on the average actual exports during the previous three years, or 600 hL, whichever is the higher. A stock declaration (as at 31 July each year) has to be submitted to IVBAM by 15 September each year. No shipper may export more than is compatible with the maintenance of his minimum stock unless he has given notice to IVBAM that he is winding up his business. In addition, each shipper has an obligation to buy grapes at the next vintage. His obligation is based on 75 per cent of his exports during the year up to 31 July immediately before the vintage, except that (in broad terms) he may have to buy more or less, depending on whether his stock level is below or above the minimum required.

12

THE MADEIRAS OF TODAY AND YESTERDAY

The characteristics of madeira

In this chapter I shall try to describe the qualities of madeira and how it should be assessed. Like any wine, madeira has to have the balance of components appropriate to its character, and in assessing it the professional will find this out by looking at it, smelling it, and finally by tasting it. The analysis of its attributes is a factual matter. In some cases (like colour, acidity and sweetness) it is a question of what is appropriate, but mostly the taster is looking for a large number and high degree of the positive characteristics, and a low number and low degree of negative characteristics. In the case of madeira, these can be illustrated diagrammatically by the table of opposites shown on page 180.

By considering these factors the taster will acquire an overall impression of quality. The best sort of glass to use for tasting and drinking madeira is a plain, medium-sized, tulip-shaped glass. Small, traditional port glasses are hopeless: they do not give one the opportunity to swirl the wine and release its bouquet. The wine should always be at room temperature and, except for the cheapest extra-dry and dry qualities, never chilled. As with any wine of quality, decanting helps the wine to breathe and prevents any sediment from getting into the glass.

Madeira, of course, has very distinctive characteristics which make it fairly recognizable even to unpractised tasters. These are the aromas which arise from wood ageing and the distinctive tastes mostly associated with caramelized sugar. When the wine is very old, however, these characteristics become very similar to those of other wood-aged wines—such as port and sherry—of a like age, and it is not at all impossible to mistake one wine for the other.

COLOUR

Pale	Dark
(–) Dull (turbid)	Bright (+)

BOUQUET

(–) Acetic	Clean acidity (+)
(–) Simple	Complex (+)

PALATE

(–) Light	Weighty (+)
Dry	Sweet
(–) Fruitless	Fruity (+)
(–) Flavourless	Flavoursome (+)
(+/–) High acidity	Low acidity (-/+)
(–) Coarseness	Finesse (+)
(–) Simple	Complex (+)
(–) Unbalanced	Balanced (+)

FINISH

(–) Short	Long (+)
(–) Simple	Complex (+)

Indeed, although it is often said that madeira is unique, this is not entirely true. The people who say so are usually referring to the uniqueness of the *estufagem* process, but technically there is nothing to choose between a *canteiro* madeira and a *colheita* port: both are fortified to much the same level, and both are slowly matured in quite similarly sized casks at ambient temperatures. What differentiates them is that the grape varieties used in making them are, except in the rare cases of Bastardo and Moscatel, completely different.

The flavours and aromas associated with oxidation can be divided into several types: those associated with wood, such as pinewoods and eucalyptus; phenolic flavours, such as vanilla and turpentine; caramel flavours, such as black treacle, toffee, barley sugar, honey, coffee and chocolate; spicy flavours, such as cloves, cinnamon and saffron; nutty flavours, particularly almonds and walnuts; dried fruit flavours, such as apricots, plums and raisins; citrus flavours, in particular orange; and others less easy to classify, such as yeastiness and smokiness.

Excessive acidity and volatility with evident overtones of vinegar were common enough features of cheaper madeiras until the 1980s but, thanks to technical improvements in *estufagem*, I have to say that nowadays this is no longer so. Indeed, acid balance is generally good. Some people have a higher tolerance of acidity in wines than others. Mine is relatively low, so faults in the acid balance of madeiras are particularly evident to me. Nor do you often meet with the stewed flavours which were once an equally common manifestation of poor *estufagem*. It is clear to me that the general standard of making the commercial wines has greatly improved within the last twenty years.

In what follows I shall first consider the madeiras that are currently being produced and I shall then have a brief look at the older madeiras that are of interest to madeira enthusiasts and collectors.

The four classical grape varieties

The wines made from the classical varieties have individual characteristics which may be briefly summarized here.

Sercial. The palest of madeiras, its colour is similar to that of a very mature Sauternes or of a Tokaji: a kind of orange-gold tawny. Rather pungent when young, the smell is characterized by aromas of oranges and dried fruits. The oranges carry through to the taste, which develops a certain nuttiness with maturity, while the smell mellows and suggests overtones of turpentine. Very old Sercials seem to fade more readily than other varieties, but develop wonderful balsamic qualities with a patina of age which really defy description. Sercial is generally (and rightly) regarded as an aperitif wine, but it can be drunk with hors d'oeuvres. Old Sercial makes a good palate-cleansing end to a meal for those who do not like to finish on a sweet note.

Verdelho. In colour there is little to choose between this and Sercial, but Verdelho may be a degree darker. Less brusque than Sercial when young, the nose tends to be honeyed and slightly chocolaty, and the taste is reminiscent of candied citrus fruits, but more gently rounded than Sercial. With age Verdelho develops considerably in intensity and is the favourite variety of many shippers. It can be drunk (as indeed can all the other varieties) at any time of day. It is pleasant as a pick-me-up in mid-morning, as an aperitif, and used to be the traditional accompaniment to turtle soup in the days before killing turtles for soup became impossibly politically incorrect.

Boal. The darkest of all varieties, Boal has a tawny colour approaching the darker hues to be found in tortoiseshell. Its smell is akin to barley sugar, and a rich mixture of caramel and dried fruit flavours, such as apricot, predominates on the palate. With age the sweetness which is so obvious in young Boal tends to be modified and it can taste similar to old Verdelho. Strictly a dessert wine, it makes a pleasant accompaniment to nuts and fruit, but I prefer to drink it by itself, without the distraction of food.

Malvazia. In former days the cheaper Malvazia look-alikes were sold, as the cheaper sweet blends are today, with the darkest colour (because of market demand, the shippers say). However, genuine Malvazia, until it has considerably matured, is perceptibly a shade lighter than Boal, although of the same general tone. The open and expressive bouquet, even when young, is unmistakably like vanilla cream toffee, sometimes with a hint of meatiness. The taste is also idiosyncratic, combining hints of caramel and barley sugar with marmalade, and, as with Boal, its pronounced sweetness is attenuated with age. Good Malvazia is never cloying, and deserves to be enjoyed by itself at the end of a meal.

Madeiras with an indication of age

In the original edition of this book this section started with a tirade against 'the most disgusting madeira I know'. This was the free welcoming glass served on presentation of the menu in Funchal's tourist restaurants. Its quality was dire, and I speculated that it was often bootleg madeira made from direct producers. Far from tempting tourists to find out more about madeira, it seemed almost calculated to steer them away from it. Happily, I can report that the quality of this gesture of hospitality—now much less frequent than it used to be—has improved: although basic, it is not usually undrinkable, although I would still maintain that it is not much of an advertisement for the delights of drinking madeira.

Before starting the discussion of these generic madeiras, which are the commercial bread and butter of the trade, it is worth repeating that madeiras with an indication of age are not precisely of the age indicated (although, legally, they could be), but are blends of older and younger wines purporting to have the characteristics considered typical of the age in question. The recognised indications of age are 3, 5, 10, 15, 20, 30 and over-40 years. If you think of the spectrum of development of wood-aged madeiras then, exactly as you would expect, the older the indicated age of a wine the more development it will have—more depth and complexity of flavour, more development of aromas, especially those associated with wood ageing, and the more it will approach the character of a *garrafeira* wine. The indications of age are like steps along a line of seamless development—arbitrary points between childhood and adulthood.

3 year old and 5 year old madeiras

The port enthusiast does not, on the whole, find much to interest him among young ruby ports, and the same is true of the younger madeiras; the real madeira aficionado is unlikely to get worked up about 3 or 5 year old blends of Tinta Negra. They are mostly well enough made, but there is a limit to what can be done in such a short time. Part of the trouble is that Tinta Negra, whatever its versatility, is a grape with a certain asperity, and this is difficult to disguise in wine so young (even after *estufagem*). The 3 year old wines, therefore, almost always have a rather harsh edge to them, and this is perhaps why they seem to be generally more acceptable in their sweeter than in their drier versions. They are also more fragrant in their sweeter forms—the drier ones tend to have a smell reminiscent of wet cardboard. Moreover, they lack anything more than a whisper of an approximation to the varietal characters of the grapes after which they were until recently named, and which they are still presumably intended to resemble. That said, they are popular with the public: one shipper told me that he sells a hundred bottles of his 3 year old blends for every bottle of a 5 year old blend. At best, they are an honest drink, but without sophistication; at their (now happily infrequent) worst, they are unlikely to give pleasure to even a relatively unsophisticated palate. What is truly grotesque is the use of the English word 'Finest' to describe this category of wine. The wine is the lowest of the aged qualities on the market, but it is described by a word implying that it is the best, under legislation originally introduced 'to protect consumers against the confusions to which labelling so often gives rise'.

When we turn to 5 year old wine we naturally find some advance in quality, though hardly a marked one. Two years is not an immense period of time in the world of wine. The situation is complicated by the fact that, except for its Miles label, the MWC uses traditional varieties, whilst Borges, Henriques & Henriques, Justino's and D'Oliveira use Tinta Negra. Barbeito uses both. I have to say of the wines made from Tinta Negra that many of the remarks made about 3 year old wines equally apply. The asperity is only marginally less apparent, and there is still not much by way of convincing simulation of the traditional varieties (if that is still the aim—though there is no reason why it should be).

As far as the 5 year old traditional varieties are concerned, Verdelho is perhaps the most successful, being the variety which tends to mature quickest. Rainwater is therefore usually an agreeable, if light and undemanding, drink. The sweeter varieties can also be attractive, and they have much more individuality than their Tinta Negra equivalents. I have not, however, found a Sercial in this category which I have liked. It has always been recognized as the most awkward variety when young, and used to have to be a minimum of 7 years old before sale. I wonder if it is worth the effort of trying to produce it. There is, after all, no fundamental reason—apart from tidiness—why a shipper should produce all four traditional varieties in a particular age range.

10 and 15 year old madeiras

All the shippers except D'Oliveira, Faria and Barros e Sousa use traditional varieties for their 10 year old blends; Justino's have 10 year old ranges of both varietal and non-varietal wines. I cannot be enthusiastic about the non-varietals. On the other hand, it is only at this point, with the varietals, that commercial madeiras start to become of interest to the serious madeira drinker, for here we are dealing with individual varieties which have had enough ageing to show their true characters. The wines generally have more fragrance, more weight and style, and begin to hint at the glories which older wines can achieve. It is salutary, perhaps, to reflect on the fact that these wines are not only twice the age of the next range down, but are older than most of the madeiras sold in the eighteenth and nineteenth centuries.[1]

Although they are not cheap, these are the wines for everyday drinking. One hopes, therefore, that the trade will find a way of opening the public's eyes to their delights. Because of evaporation during maturation, the cost of a 10 year old wine is always going to be considerably more than that of a 5 year old wine. However, if in the course of time the proportion of traditional varieties in comparison with Tinta Negra can be increased, the differential in the cost of grapes will probably diminish.

15 year old madeiras are produced from varietals by Borges, Henriques & Henriques and the MWC. D'Oliveira has a range of non-varietal 15 year olds. I can be unreservedly generous in my praise and enthusiasm for 15 year old varietal madeiras. They are, in a sense, junior vintage wines, and act as a bridge between 10 year old wines and the *garrafeiras*. Five more years in cask produce an enormous difference in maturity and an almost exponential leap in quality. For the drinker who jibs at the price of vintage wines, but who requires something of their quality, they are one possible answer. Indeed, being blended for immediate drinking, they lack the rawness of some young *garrafeira* wines, and may even be preferable.

20, 30 and over-40 year old madeiras

These categories of aged madeiras have only been recognized since 1998.[2] Previously the oldest recognized indication of age was 15 years. They were introduced because there was concern that some shippers had old wines without the documentation necessary to sell them as *garrafeiras* and some route had to be found for their commercialization. They could, of course, have found a use as components of blends, but it was recognized that this would not solve the problem when stocks of such wines had considerable depth, and also it failed to recognize that such wines could be of superlative quality in their own right.

As one would expect, wines of 20, 30 and over-40 years of age will in general show considerably more evolution than the 15 year old madeiras—more depth and complexity on the nose and palate and, indeed, more of the development characteristic of a *garrafeira*.

In fact, the introduction of these categories, which are similar to categories of aged wine in Oporto, has not resulted in a flood of new releases on the market, but the ones that have appeared have had a warm reception. Borges, specifically to mark a special occasion, produced a 40 year old madeira to celebrate the quincentenary of Funchal's recognition as a city in 1508; Blandy's has produced a 20 year old Terrantez for an individual customer; while Henriques & Henriques also offer a 20 year old Malvazia and a 20 year old Terrantez. Barbeito currently lists a 'Special Lot' 30 year old Malvazia, as well as a 'Lot 7199' 20 year old Malvazia, and Borges offer a 20 year old Verdelho.

It remains to be seen whether these older categories of aged madeiras will prove useful to the trade and attractive to the public. Luís D'Oliveira believes that his firm's customers would be more likely to prefer a *garrafeira* to a wine with an indication of age if the cost to the customer is much the same. In the end, perhaps only the skill of a blender in producing aged wines of such superlative quality that they can compete with *garrafeiras* will sway the customer towards these categories. As yet the outcome remains to be seen.

Modern soleras

So far as I am aware no shipper has thought it worthwhile to start a new solera under the current rules. The sad fact is that the status of madeira soleras was overlooked during negotiations with the EU, and this led to much subsequent confusion and beating of breasts. Many shippers share the view that it is wrong, and even bordering on fraudulent, to sell bottles with a date from two centuries ago on them when there is nothing like wine from two centuries ago in them. It is hard to disagree with that but, on the other hand, it is equally hard to see the point of establishing a solera for just ten years and, on the face of it, unlikely that the solera will result in a wine of sufficient interest to justify the trouble of setting it up. Consequently, soleras as newly defined are not yet an important part of the spectrum of madeira products and may never become so.

Garrafeira madeiras

The definition of a *garrafeira / frasqueira* wine is precise: it has to be made from a recommended variety, to be of a certain quality, and it has to have been aged in wood for a minimum of twenty years. Previously it also had to have been in bottle for a minimum of two years before being sold, but this stipulation was dropped. The category was first introduced in 1982.[3] Before that there were just dated wines. The twenty years stipulation was not arbitrary—it was chosen as the age at which traditionally wood-aged madeiras generally begin to display the degrees of depth and subtlety characteristic of full maturity. There was no suggestion that shippers were at this time cutting corners and selling dated wines with less ageing than the new legal minimum. Indeed, if anything, ageing periods were then considerably longer. However, it laid down a marker, a benchmark, and thereby defined the top category of madeira. There was no break or change in the way such wines were produced: nevertheless, because the term was invented in 1982, there is a sense in which only 20 year old dated wines produced after that date should count as *garrafeira* madeiras.

In 1973 the Delegation of the JNV established current accounts for existing stocks of dated wines held at that date by shippers. The accounts were based purely on their owners' declarations, and no supporting documentation was required to authenticate the wines or their age. They were, so to speak, taken on trust. Since then only those dated wines that were declared then, and the wines that have been made since 1982—which, of course, may date back to twenty years earlier—and which meet the requirements of *garrafeira* wines, can legally be sold as such by the shippers.

These wines are the glory of madeira and, with the best examples of dated wines from the past, the yardstick by which it is judged to be a world class wine. I have already quoted from George Saintsbury, in whose opinion good madeira is comparable only to burgundy. His enthusiasm is not unique, however, and it is shared by many contemporary wine writers such as Michael Broadbent and Jancis Robinson. The fascination of vintage madeira arises not only from its apparent capacity to survive over centuries as a wine which can be drunk with pleasure, but because at its best it is capable of making such a strong statement about the wine potential of the grape.

Over the last thirty years the *garrafeiras* and other registered dated wines have been diminishing in quantity and getting scarcer and scarcer, although visitors to Madeira are regularly astonished by the number of comparatively old vintages still being sold by the shippers. Many tourists are mesmerized by the dates on the bottles, and a surprising number of expensive *garrafeiras* are bought as suitable presents for Uncle Henry and Aunt May on their birthdays. One-day visitors from cruise liners which regularly stop at Madeira descend like gannets and make huge inroads into the available vintages. Even the odd Russian billionaire, arriving on his personal jet and buying old wines, untasted, solely on their high prices, makes an appearance from time to time. This is forcing some companies to make defensive price increases to conserve their irreplaceable stocks and, inevitably, this pressure has been showing itself in the appearance on the market over the past fifteen years of *garrafeira* wines which are just on the twenty-year limit of being legally marketable. When I first began going to the island in the 1970s, about the youngest vintage available was 1940 and most were fifty or more years old. Shippers would nurse their dated wines until they felt they had reached their optimum development—different in each case—before bottling them and putting them on sale. Some still do, but others, reluctant perhaps to keep their capital tied up for longer than is necessary and finding their older *garrafeiras* running out, yield to the temptation to put their wines on the market as soon as the law permits.

It will be sad if this becomes the general rule, because in very few cases has a *garrafeira* reached its full development at twenty years; or rather, if it has, then it was never of the potential which used to be thought absolutely indispensable for a wine to be considered of 'vintage' quality. One hopes, therefore, that in their efforts to maintain and improve quality, shippers will continue to mature their *garrafeiras* for much longer than the minimum period required by law—even if such wines when they eventually appear on the market will inevitably have to carry a very large price tag.

Nevertheless, despite these worries and reservations, I believe that the best of the *garrafeiras* presently on offer are every bit as good as the best of the past, and that the enthusiast does not yet need to be apprehensive that the kind of madeira which so impressed George Saintsbury has now become only a memory.

Colheitas

Since 1982 it has also been possible to bottle and sell dated wines which, not having been aged in wood for twenty years, cannot be considered as *garrafeira* wines. The original legal formulation of this rule read as follows: 'An indication of age or of a vintage year is reserved for wines of noble varieties and can only be used when the product has a minimum age of 7 years for wines made from the Sercial variety, and of 5 years for wines of the remaining varieties'.[4] This provision was replaced by Portaria No. 125/98 of 29 July, which gave the category the name *colheita* and reduced the ageing required by Sercial to 5 years, in line with the other varieties. Although non-*garrafeira* dated wines were permitted before 1998 very few shippers bothered to produce them. As far as I am aware, the MWC—in the form of special editions for promotional purposes and not for general release—and Barros e Sousa were the only two.

Colheitas certainly add to the diversity of the market. Many are made from Tinta Negra. This is possible because, with better vinification and *estufagem*, these wines now have a low level of volatility, so the character of the wine is not masked. Apart from that, the introduction of *colheitas* made from traditional varieties offers the public the opportunity to drink young varietal wines with a certain individuality of character—unlike young wines with an indication of age, which tend to be blended to a uniform style. After five years these wines are just beginning to show their varietal character in an attractive, if not fully developed, direct form. Moreover, the *colheitas* in the lower part of the age spectrum—those, say, which have been aged for up to ten or twelve years—generally lack the weight of a potential *garrafeira*, and this comparative lightness combined with often considerable residual fruitiness makes for a delightfully winning, elegant mouthful. Add to this the fact that they are generally sold in 50 centilitre bottles and, apart from offering a new range of tasting experiences to the madeira drinker, you have something of an affordable bargain. The older *colheitas* (which have been aged for from around twelve to nineteen years) may be expected to become progressively very close in style and character to a *garrafeira* and some will in fact be wines which were being groomed as future *garrafeiras* but did not quite make the grade. One might think of them as unofficial junior *garrafeiras*. These are the other possible solution for the drinker who wants a quality of wine close to that of a *garrafeira* at a more reasonable price.

If there is a problem with *colheitas*, then it is perhaps the one I have already alluded to—the difficulty for the public to distinguish between two types of dated wine. Both, to the rest of the world, are vintage wines. Why should the customer know the definition of *colheita*—or of *garrafeira* come to that? There is room for further confusion insofar as in the world of port a *colheita* is a tawny port that has had at least seven years wood ageing. Add to this the fact that, although 'Harvest Wine' is accepted as an appropriate English labelling equivalent of *colheita*, the MWC (uniquely) confines the description 'Harvest Wine' to *colheitas* of up to six years of ageing, and uses '*colheita*' to refer to dated wines with more than six (and, of course, less than twenty) years of ageing. None of which makes it easy for the customer to understand what he is buying.

Old madeiras for enthusiasts

Over the last thirty years there has been a steady increase in the number of people seeking out old bottles of madeira, not only in Europe and the United States, but latterly in Japan, China, Russia and other countries (like, for example, Latvia) not previously noted for much if any interest in the wine. At the same time the prices of prestigious old quality wine of practically all sorts has skyrocketed as worldwide demand has increased, and madeira has been no exception to this trend. Enthusiasts acquire their old bottles at sales of madeira at auction,[5] from specialist brokers and from private cellars both on the island and elsewhere. Surprising amounts of old madeira have surfaced. There have, of course, been many noted collectors in the past, amongst them Braheem Kassab, Sir Stephen Gaselee and Walter Grabham—individual bottles which belonged to them still appear from time to time—and more recently Harry Johnson, Mills B. Lane, Lenoir Josey and Graham Lyons, whose collections have been auctioned over the past four decades. Other notable auctions have disposed not only of large family collections (such as madeiras from the Torre Bella estate in 1988, the Quinta do Serrado and the Acciaioly madeiras in 1989, the Goelet collection in 1999, and the Leacock collection in 2008) but of individual bottles of special interest. There are still collectors with notable cellars; there are still investors with stocks eventually to be disposed of; there are still families on the island with treasured old wines. One shipper told me in 1997 that he could take me to a private cellar with over sixty old vintage wines in cask, 'each one better than the last'. I believe they are still there. Undoubtedly, as more and more bottles are consumed by madeira enthusiasts the legacy from the past is diminishing, but I do not think the well is soon about to run dry.

Old bottles can be labelled, but many are just hand-stencilled (sometimes rather crudely) with what is frequently rather chalky and easily rubbed-off white distemper or paint. The stencilling simply gives brief details of the type of wine the bottle contains, a date, and a shipper's name (although some do not even have that). Buying old bottles, therefore, involves taking much on trust. The risks of making costly mistakes can be lessened, however, by appraising the appearance of bottles in an intelligent and informed way. Some of the following information may help you as you do this.

The study of old bottles is complex and detailed and beyond the scope of this book. The oldest madeira bottles from the eighteenth century are of a handblown global shape. They are very rare. One encounters mallet-shaped bottles from the late eighteenth and early nineteenth century, and dump bottles have been used right up until the mid-twentieth century. More common are nineteenth-century two- and three-part moulded bottles, usually made from slightly opaque glass and similar in shape to current madeira bottles, and with quite a deep punt on the base. They tend to be heavier than their modern equivalents of the same size, and are often very slightly tapered. Quite common are very heavy burgundy- and champagne-shaped bottles dating from the second half of the nineteenth century. They often purport to contain wine dating from the first half of the nineteenth century (or even earlier). Clear glass bottles are relatively unusual for madeira, but they do exist. More alarming is to find madeira in old whisky bottles. Their use arose from a shortage of suitable new bottles after World War Two. Despite their appearance they are probably genuine, but they are not very collectable.

Most of the corks encountered in older bottles of madeira are astonishingly short, in comparison not just with long vintage port corks but also with those used for table wine. Many are barely two centimetres in length, suggesting either perpetual cork shortages or more-than-Scottish meanness, but they do their job adequately if they are periodically changed. Just occasionally stopper corks (with a crimped plastic or metal top) are encountered in post World War Two bottles of dated wine, but old bottles will generally have a thick wax seal or a lead foil capsule. It is not unusual to find a foil capsule under a wax seal. Needless to say quality wines have never been sold in wicker- or raffia-covered bottles, but wicker coverings over capsules were used quite extensively by some twentieth century shippers.

A useful indication of probable genuineness is the occurrence of the JNV seal. Before 1980 quality control was in the hands of the Delegation of the JNV, which in the late 1950s and early 1960s carried out a check on substantial stocks of old bottled wine on the island. Random samples were examined, and if the wine was judged consistent with the variety and date attributed to it, then the remaining bottles were branded with a small seal in brown wax superimposed on the existing wax seal or, occasionally, on the neck of the bottle. This seal is rectangular and measures 1.75 x 3 cm. Inside a border it displays at the top the letters 'JNV' slanting downwards from left to right, and at the bottom, separated by a squiggle, the letters 'REF'. I have also come across a round black wax seal, the diameter of a cork, with 'Junta Nacional do Vinho Madeira' encircling a crown with 'Delegação' underneath it. The presence of the JNV wax seal must give the purchaser of old bottles some confidence that the wine has a chance of being genuine.

Returning now to the stencilling on old bottles, instead of indicating a grape variety and a vintage, the contents may simply be described as *Vinho Velho* (Old Wine), *Vinho Vehlissimo* (Very Old Wine) or simply as *Madeira*. These are indications of a very basic wine and are unlikely to prove interesting. In some cases *velho* or *velhissimo* is tagged on to the grape variety in addition to a vintage date: thus, *Boal Velhissimo* (Very Old Boal). The age indication may just be stylistic and should not be taken too seriously. More frequently the grape variety may simply be indicated by a single letter: 'S' for Sercial, 'V', 'B', and 'M'. 'T' for Terrantez is also found. Older bottles occasionally display in addition two or three initials which indicate the person who originally owned the wine or from whom it was inherited. *RAV*, for example, might signify Rui Abreu Vasconcelos, and a bottle bearing such initials would typically be passed down through the Vasconcelos family or its relatives, identifiable as having belonged once to their ancestor Rui Abreu. It is encouraging to know that the wine has a pedigree, and this may be indicated by the words '*Herdeiros de RAV*' (the heirs of *RAV*). Occasionally a place name is used instead of, or in addition to, a grape variety. *Cama de Lobos* is certainly the most famous and most frequent of these, but others met with include *Campanário, Ponta do Pargo* and *São Martinho*. In the United States it is not uncommon to find madeiras named after the ships which brought them from Madeira during the nineteenth century.[6]

Labels have also quite often been used for vintage wines since the end of the nineteenth century, sometimes by themselves, sometimes in conjunction with stencilling. Water staining or a slightly singed or burnt look to indicate age may be fraudulent. A more convincing indication of age is the fragility of the paper. Clearly, the most reassuring labels will have helpful information on them. Some bottles purporting to be old Terrantez have labels printed with a traditional Portuguese ditty: *As uvas de Terrantez, não as comas nem as dês, para vinho Deus as fez* (Terrantez grapes are not for eating or giving away: God made them for wine). I would tend to avoid such bottles. On the other hand, small narrow horizontal strip labels indicating a date of bottling or recorking are likely to be completely genuine. Hand-written labels may be unappealing, but they may well be authentic and are usually an indication that the bottle came originally from a private cellar.

What can I say about dates? Generally, when the bottle bears a shipper's name, the date is the date of the vintage of the wine inside. If the wine is from a private family cellar it is possible that it is from a particular vintage just by repute or family tradition. Or perhaps the date indicates something else, like the birth year of a child the wine was bottled to celebrate. There is even the possibility that it is the date of a family solera, or simply the date of bottling. It may just be the presumed date of the wine's vintage, for few old wines in family cellars have any supporting documentation. It is probably only the oldest-established shippers who have proper records that can verify with reasonable certainty the *bona fides* of their old dated wines. Such shippers may have made the wines themselves, although in the case of wines which predate the establishment of the firm they will have been obtained from elsewhere (such as from other shippers, shippers going out of business, the stocks of the original makers, or from the cellars of private families). All of which leads me to urge the reader to resist, to some extent, the lure of dates. What is important, at the end of the day, is what is inside the bottle.[7]

There is a great deal that we do not know about the contents of many old dated wines, so we just have to treat them as presumed vintage wines (in the English idiom). We do not know how much wood ageing the wines had before being bottled; we do not know if they had any *estufagem*; we do not know if they contain an admixture of wine made from direct producers, which wines made after *phylloxera* wrought its havoc may well have; and, for very old wines, we do not know at what stage they were fortified. We do not usually know anything about these matters when we buy a bottle with nothing more than a grape variety and a date stencilled on it. But, of course, with chemical analysis it may be possible, after we open the bottle, to find out.

I once had in my cellar a bottle purporting to be Moscatel, 1715, the oldest madeira vintage known to me. I asked myself could it be genuine? The fact that 1715 is some thirty years before the fortification of madeira became common must put in doubt the ability of wine of this vintage to have survived late into the twentieth century. It is of course just possible that it was fortified thirty or more years after it was made. Fortification as part of the process of vinification did not become common until well into the nineteenth century, and before that fortification was carried out just prior to shipping. A shipper suggested another possibility—that the wine might have been made on Porto Santo, where the climate produces grapes with very high degrees of potential alcohol.[8] I was curious to see if I could establish the probability of its authenticity and, when I opened the bottle, I sent off a sample for gas chromatography analysis by a chemist who had previously examined around a dozen early nineteenth- and late eighteenth-century madeiras. The result showed two interesting things. Firstly, the level of alcohol was 17.35 per cent by volume, indicating that the wine must certainly have been fortified. Secondly, the levels of the numerous volatile esters and aldehydes were unusual for a madeira of such a great age and suggested a much younger (nineteenth-century) wine. The disappointing conclusion was therefore that, although clearly very old, this was not likely to be an authentic 1715 wine. That said, it also has to be pointed out that analysts on the island are usually very reluctant to put too specific a date on old wines submitted for analysis, and that 'over sixty years old' is about the limit to which most of them will commit themselves.

One lesson to be learned from this is that a healthy measure of scepticism with regard to bottles with extremely old dates on them is useful in order to counteract the uncritical excitement and awe they engender in some enthusiasts. Sadly, perhaps, we live in an age of vintage-year worship; dates fascinate us and we are apt to pay too much attention to them. The ageing aspect of madeira can be exaggerated. It is certainly true that, like Tokaji, madeira appears to be capable of indefinite life, and André Simon was right to say that 'no other wine will be not merely acceptable, but superlative a hundred years after it was made'.[9] However, it is certainly not true that greater age necessarily means better to drink. In the notes on various vintage wines in the next chapter, the reader will note how many disappointments there were amongst the really old vintages and, conversely, how many splendid wines are to be found amongst less venerable vintages still obtainable on the island. Age is not in itself a guide to quality. Madeira can dry out like any other wine, and eventually does; and like vintage port, after more than about a hundred years in bottle there is a risk of madeira becoming spirity. It is always happier in cask than it is in bottle. Although, when properly looked after, madeira may well be able to live indefinitely in cask, in bottle it is subject to many of the same hazards as other wines, though it may take much longer for madeira to react to them.

Another reason for not letting oneself be hypnotized by vintage years is that, in order to be bottled as a vintage at all, the quality of a madeira already has to be extremely high. This makes the question of whether it is from this or that vintage much less important than it is for a table wine. Yet another important factor which influences the quality of the wine is how long it has spent in cask before being bottled. As was explained in the section on the maturation of madeira, the wine ages while it is in wood, but this development is arrested when it is put in a container through which it cannot breathe. A madeira from a remote vintage year which was bottled after thirty years in wood, and has spent twice that time in bottle, will not be as 'old' a wine, in terms of cask ageing, as a madeira from a more recent vintage which has just been bottled after spending sixty years in wood. This illustrates how important it can be to know the bottling date of a vintage madeira: information which sadly is only infrequently available.

Because madeira in a bottle can breathe a little through the cork, it is not quite true to say that its development is totally arrested: it is, however, all but arrested.[10] This has the consequence that when the bottle is opened madeira requires a long time to re-oxygenate itself (breathe) before it relaxes and starts to give off the aromas and to show all the flavours it had in cask. These become dormant in the bottle and it takes time for the wine to come to life again. The longer the wine has been in bottle, the more time it takes to recapture these qualities; a madeira which has been in bottle for upwards of sixty years may require two, three or even four days to regain its composure. I can only echo the words of Noël Cossart on this subject: 'The period of allowing old wine to breathe cannot be overdone in the case of madeira'.[11] Sadly, the contents of many old bottles are consumed before the wine has had an opportunity to get back into condition. Sometimes, when a wine has been in bottle for more than about fifteen years, it gives off a turpentine-like bottle stink when opened. Normally this will clear after a short time, particularly if the wine is oxygenated a little by decanting it once or twice. But when a madeira has been in bottle for more than half a century and has, as it were, gone into hibernation, it can develop a rather papery smell which is difficult to describe but instantly recognizable, and all its qualities seem muted. In this case the wine is 'bottle sick'. Normally, if you are lucky, this will disappear as the wine recovers its health (which may, as mentioned above, take several days), but this does not always happen.

Bottle sickness must be carefully distinguished from bottle age. Unlike the shippers themselves, some madeira drinkers actually prefer their vintage madeira to have spent some time in bottle. This taste is parallel to the fashion which used to exist for bottle-aged sherry. When I first started to drink madeira I belonged to this band, but more recently, having had opportunities to compare wine from cask with the same wine out of bottle, I am less sure. The main characteristic of bottle age is a certain austerity and dryness which the madeira, particularly if it is a sweet one, develops on its finish. The wine is somehow more elegant, with a better defined, leaner profile. It is not necessarily better, however, for that is ultimately a matter of personal taste.

The custom on the island is to keep bottles standing upright instead of binning them horizontally. The main reason for this is because madeira attacks corks rather rapidly, and the wine is able to breathe a little better when the air inside the bottle is next to the cork. The general humidity of the island appears to help prevent the corks from drying out, but in well-kept cellars it is common to recork bottles every thirty years or so. In some cellars a back label gives the recorking history of old bottles—Henriques & Henriques do this for their oldest wines. Less often, old vintage wines are rebottled. In this case it is normal to give the wine a light filtering through muslin to oxygenate it slightly. The advantage of recorking is that it reduces ullage and ensures that the wine is in good condition. Failure to recork will eventually result in the cork drying out and excess evaporation taking place. I have seen really old bottles with corks so shrivelled that they had ceased to adhere to the sides of the bottle and were kept in place only by the wax seal.

It is a pity that this policy of recorking is insufficiently understood by collectors of old madeiras, who are sometimes suspicious of it on the grounds that it might mean that the contents of the bottle have been tampered with. That is an argument only for ensuring that the bottle has a good provenance and that the recorking has been reputably carried out. The quest for authenticity can be carried too far where corks are concerned, and a wine that has been regularly recorked is much more likely to be in good condition than one that has not.

After many years madeira—like all wines which have not been filtered to death—casts a crust which tends to adhere to the bottle. With time a little sediment, which may remain loose, may also be deposited at the bottom of the bottle. Sometimes this is a fine powder, but mostly it has the consistency of coffee grounds. It is therefore worth taking care while decanting the bottle, which is something I would always recommend.

Despite island custom, some merchants in England do bin bottles of madeira on their sides. Whether this is true of other countries I cannot say. My advice to purchasers of old bottles of madeira is to maintain the regime to which the bottle has been subjected. It is often easy to establish this by holding the bottle up to the light and looking at the pattern of crusting inside the bottle. Just as madeiras mature more rapidly in warmer climates, so the process of crusting occurs more quickly in Madeira than, for example, in England. If the bottle has been stored upright the crusting will start at the level of the wine in the neck of the bottle. If the bottle has been stored on its side the staining on the bottle will tend to be greater on the lower side of the neck, and will continue up to the bottom of the cork. Otherwise, madeira is fairly tolerant of storage conditions, and can (and prefers to) be stored at a higher temperature than is recommended for other wines, provided the atmosphere is not too dry. A warm and humid ambience is fine; a dry and very cold one is not so good.

About the old bottled wines themselves it is really not possible to say much that is sensible by way of generalization. Each bottle is different and, one hopes, a pleasant surprise on opening rather than an expensive disappointment. But about one category, old soleras, I do have something more to say. While agreeing with critics of the traditional system of topping up soleras over long periods of time that indicating the date of the vintage of the original foundation wine is potentially misleading, the fact remains that the traditional solera system did seem to produce often wonderful results from the point of view of quality. Some old soleras are amongst the most delicious madeiras you can hope to taste. I remember with fondness three of Blandy's old wines—Verdelho Solera 1822, Bual Solera 1826 and Sercial Solera 1835—which, when I was warden of a university hall of residence in the 1970s, were regularly sold in the Junior Common Room bar at under £2 a bottle. I recently tasted a Cossart Gordon 1860 Solera Sercial which was of superb quality, and the famous Cossart Gordon Solera 1808 Malmsey is favourably assessed in Chapter 13.

What is their secret? Part of it, I suspect, lies in their approachableness. Unlike very old vintage wines, which can arrive at formidable levels of concentration in cask, old soleras sometimes appear to have a better balance, more freshness and more elegance. This may be due to their being frequently refreshed with younger wine and, for the drinker who is overwhelmed by the weight of some vintage wines, soleras can be the answer. Whereas a small glass of an old vintage can sate the drinker, soleras offer more drinkability. And, unlike even the 15 year old wines, which are blended as nearly to a standard as possible, soleras have considerable individuality. Bottles of older soleras appearing at auction now command prices akin to those of dated wines. *Pace* the late Richard Blandy, who was so opposed to traditional soleras, the discriminating public knows a good thing when it tastes it.

In the next chapter I shall survey many dated wines ranging from old to young, amongst them some very famous madeiras and a few that are still available for purchase. This is not in any way a consumer guide, but is intended to illustrate by example some of the contentions made in this chapter.

13

NOTES ON SOME VINTAGE MADEIRAS

All the madeiras noted in this chapter, with only four exceptions, were tasted between November 1996 and May 1997. I hope that this may have given some consistency to my notes. Some madeiras were from my own collection and tasted with friends; others I was able to taste through the generosity of friends in Madeira and in England, and through the generosity of shippers who allowed me access to their *garrafeira* wines. I decided to include four wines which I had tasted previously because of their rarity, and because they were in differing ways so remarkable. I also decided, after much agonizing, to include three wines which are not strictly speaking dated wines, but which from their superb quality might well have been. The madeiras have all been assessed on a scale of one to five stars. As almost all vintage madeiras are of a high standard—otherwise they would not have been kept for so long—this marking system is comparative within what is itself a high-quality bracket. Thus a ★★ mark indicates a wine of a high standard, while ★★★★★ indicates an awesome achievement, at the very pinnacle of vinous excellence. The marking is on the basis of how the wines are now. Some of the younger wines will no doubt improve if kept longer in cask, but it is sheer speculation to predict how they will appear in thirty, forty or more years' time. In bottle they will not develop quickly, and so they have been assessed for what they are now and are likely to remain within my lifetime. I have allowed myself the indulgence of awarding a rosette (✿) to wines which struck me as exceptional, or for which I have a special affection.

One of the dangers of trying to describe madeiras is repetitiveness. Superlatives can too easily be overworked, and descriptions can run to excess. I have tried to err on the side of prosaic description rather than flamboyance (though some readers may find this hard to believe). The privilege of tasting so many remarkable wines in such a relatively short period offered a unique opportunity to make comparisons which are normally impossible, and this alone made it seem worthwhile to try to record the experience here. My notes will also, I hope, enable the reader to infer much about the development of madeiras in bottle, and will put flesh on some of the bones of assertions in the previous chapter.

I have unashamedly purloined one of Michael Broadbent's descriptive terms: 'tangy'. It so aptly indicates citrous acidity that it would be impossible to think of a better word. I also use the terms 'fudge' and 'fudgy', in an idiosyncratic way, to try to pin down the characteristic of butter toffee which characterizes madeiras of all sorts. My use of these terms does not necessarily denote sweetness. I often detect in dry wines, however paradoxical it may seem, the taste of butter and caramel allied to a certain texture, without any sweetness.

Descriptions of the colour of wines are naturally dependent on the lighting conditions in which the wine is tasted. In some situations when tasting these wines there was insufficient light, and even reflecting the light off a white surface can, in such circumstances, give misleading results. In general I have used the word 'tawny' as the generic colour term in preference to others. It should be understood as the colour of a wood port which has lost its ruddiness.

The arrangement of the notes is self-explanatory. Where I have had information about the provenance of the wines—much of which has been derived from Christie's wine sale catalogues and is printed here by kind permission—and when it has seemed sensible to record details about the bottles and other circumstantial aspects of the wines, I have done so. The reader should note that, when it comes to buying old bottles, with or without a shipper's name, it is impossible to over-emphasize the importance of a sound provenance. The notes are printed in vintage date order. An explanation of references to the JNV seal of authenticity can be found in the previous chapter.[1]

Vintage and *Garrafeira* madeiras

1715 Terrantez   João Carlos d'Aguiar & Cia

Tasted in Gloucestershire in January 1986. In a thick glass burgundy-shaped bottle with a deep punt. Crumbly wax seal. Crudely stencilled 'TERRANTEZ/1715/J C A & C'. Ullaged to mid-shoulder. Dense crust entirely coating the inside of the bottle. Purchased in Funchal in September 1973. I have at last been able to identify the shipper. I have seen eight identical bottles from the celebrated Kassab collection. Braheem Kassab was a Syrian embroidery merchant who put his personal seal, embossed 'BAK', on the bottles he collected earlier this century, which are therefore easy to identify; what remained of his cellar was sold at a Christie's London auction in June 1986. The wine initially suffered from bottle sickness, but improved over two or three days.

Dark tawny, with ruby and green glints, and very green rim; subdued, but balanced and attractive bouquet, with a little healthy volatility, but not spirity; faded and gentle, with vestigial sweetness, rounded, slightly toasted, with bitter accents; moderately intense finish, bitterness more apparent, but no great length. Is the date remotely genuine? Patently a very old wine, with all the hallmarks of Terrantez, but it seemed, though faded, too well preserved to be true. It drank, basically, like a madeira of the post-fortification era; just possibly it was fortified after having been aged. If so, the spirit was still remarkably well married to the wine. This wine will always remain a puzzle. It would be absurd to award it stars after eleven years, but it certainly deserved several.

1715 Moscatel

Purchased in Madeira in December 1983. In a dark green glass, two-part moulded bottle. Stencilled 'Moscatel/1715'. Healthy moist cork under thick wax seal. Dense crust entirely coating the inside of the bottle. No sediment on decanting. The wine took four days to shake off most of its bottle sickness. Alcohol: 17.35 per cent by volume. This wine is discussed further on p. 195.

Dark tawny with green-yellow substratum; a firm if unassertive bouquet, fudge and black treacle, with the merest whiff of paperiness which disappeared in the glass; fairly concentrated and sweet, rich barley sugar, with considerable but balanced acidity, and a slightly herbal, medicinal character; not as weighty in the mouth as some, but with a clean, long and uncloying finish. Fascinating and very drinkable. ★★★★

1789 Sercial

From a private island source. Three-part moulded bottle, with stencilled date and original owner's initials 'RT'. Hard wax seal and sound cork. Ullaged to mid-shoulder. Light crusting.

Pale, amber-gold tawny; after two days it developed a subdued, attractive nutty bouquet with the patina of age, hints of eucalyptus, vanilla, discreetly perfumed soap—too subtle to describe adequately; similar on the palate to the 1795 Sercial, but with less depth and slightly drier; gentle finish of no great length, with an aftertaste of melted snow. Wonderfully preserved. ★★★★

1789 Verdelho

In elegant, tapered, mid-nineteenth-century punted green bottle. Labelled. JNV wax authenticity seal. Very heavy crusting. Purchased in Funchal in September 1973 for £14.50.

Orange, verging on green, on the dark side for Verdelho; intense, rounded, fudgy nose, no excess volatility, but a hint of mould; delicate, a little faded on the palate, with the patina of age, but the mouldiness becoming increasingly disturbing; quite long but dirty finish. Probably a faulty bottle, but still a major disappointment. ★

1789 Cama de Lobos   Avery's of Bristol

Last tasted in Gloucestershire in May 1985. This wine, from the Torre Bella vineyards, belonged to Russell Manners Gordon, the first Conde de Torre Bella. Known in the Cossart family as 'Old Gordon's Madeira', some was sold by Cossart Gordon to Ronald Avery. It was matured in cask until put into 20–litre demijohns in 1900, and was bottled in 1950.[2]

Lively tawny, with russet and green toning; quite fudgy and volatile bouquet, full and open, with a suggestion of toasted almonds; still quite sweet on entry, with a symphony of dried fruit flavours, refined richness, controlled acidity, then a sudden gear-change to relatively austere dryness in the throat; massive length, acidity apparent, but finishing with a heavenly fudginess. No hint of decay. Stupendous wine—but, as will be apparent from the Preface to the first edition, perhaps I cannot be wholly impartial about it.   ✿ ★ ★ ★ ★ ★

1790 Malvazia

Thick green glass, punted, two-part moulded, burgundy-shaped bottle. Thick wax seal with JNV wax authentication seal on top. Heavily crusted. Crumbling cork, consistent with being 60–80 years old. Purchased privately in Funchal in 1973 and reputed to have come from the cellar of the Conde de Carvalhal—though this I doubt.

Dark, dense but bright, bronze and amber, with ruddy overtones and very green rim; very alive, fudgy, cigar box, chocolaty bouquet, with well-controlled undertow of acidity; coated the glass; very beguiling, intensely sweet, richly textured, well balanced, with layers of flavour associated with tobacco, vanilla and caramel; immensely long finish, singing on and on. Fantastic wine, clearly very old, but so amazingly well-preserved it prompts a doubt: can it really be over two hundred years old? A port shipper specializing in old *colheitas* thought it could. Reminiscent of the Henriques & Henriques *Reserva Malvasia* (q.v.).   ★ ★ ★ ★ ★

1790 Moscatel

Extremely elegant, two-part moulded green glass bottle with deep punt. Stencilled. Wax seal, with JNV seal of authenticity super-imposed. Purchased in Funchal in December 1983 from the same source as the preceding bottle.

Mahogany and olive green; bottle sickness dispelled after two days and the wine came to life with a rather spirity, treacly aroma; intensely sweet, Demerara sugar, rather lacking in concentration; moderate length. Very acceptable, particularly in view of age, but not in the top flight. ★★★(★)

1792 Madeira   Blandy's

The so-called 'Napoleon' madeira. Bottled in 1840. Mid-nine-teenth-century moulded green bottle, with meagre but intact wax seal. Old, short cork, which broke. Irregular, quite heavy crusting, but no deposit. Remains of label. See Appendix 6 for further details of this wine. Bought at Christie's in 1977.

Pale orange-green; rather ethereal, spirity bouquet, hints of malt whisky and fudge; reminiscent of armagnac; elements of a sound madeira detectable, even if a touch fiery and starting to dry out; gentle, faded, and not at all disagreeable; dry, rather short finish. Not quite a ghost, but has seen better days. ★★

1795 Sercial

From a private island source. Three-part moulded bottle. Stencilled with date and original owner's initials 'JRT'. Wax seal and sound cork. Ullaged to top shoulder. Consistent light crusting.

Pale, amber-gold tawny; initial papery bottle stink cleared to leave a balsamic, clean bouquet with lifted volatility, hints of fudge, alto-gether surprisingly alive and attractive; full palate, extracted, fla-voursome, with overtones of cream and butterscotch, dry, and with plenty of supporting acidity; finishes quite gently, but with consid-erable length. Complete. Delicious and remarkable. ★★★★★

1795 Terrantez — Barbeito

This wine originally belonged to the Hinton family, from whom it was acquired by Oscar Acciaioly. On his death his stock of wines was divided between his two sons by his first wife (who later sold them at Christie's) and his second wife, who sold them to Mário Barbeito.

Medium-dark, russet tawny, with amber highlights and olive green rim; mellow, delicate bouquet with hints of fudge and surprisingly fruity for age; intense, vinous, quite sharp entry, with bone dry, characteristically bitter, clean acidic finish of considerable length. Beautifully balanced and delicious.   ★ ★ ★ ★ (★)

1795 Messias — F. F. Ferraz

Bottle with 'F. F. Ferraz/Madeira' etched on shoulder. Labelled. Lead capsule covered with waxed raffia, and bearing two JNV wax seals. Messias is Portuguese for 'messiah', presumably indicating a wine of messianic quality! Purchased at Christie's in April 1970. F. F. Ferraz, when asked about the wine, replied that it had not been shipped by them since joining the Madeira Wine Association in 1937, so must have been bottled prior to that date. A former clerk with the company recalled that it was 'as dry as a Terrantez'.

Amazingly, more pale green-yellow with orange than tawny with green; harmonious honey and dried apricots on the nose, with gently lifted, cognac-like intensity; bone-dry entry, intensely flavoursome, with hints of prunes, concentrated vinosity; extremely dry, lingering, rather smoky finish. A shade dried out perhaps, but otherwise wonderfully integrated and well preserved, with the patina of a wine of great age. Fascinating.   ★ ★ ★ ★ ★

1802 Terrantez — Oscar Acciaioly

Special Reserve. Oscar Acciaioly was descended from Simão Acciaioly, who came to Madeira in 1515. This wine was sold by Oscar's sons at Christie's in 1989.

Very dense, reddish mahogany with yellow-green rim; complex, highly perfumed, fruity bouquet with some vanilla and pungent, lifted acidity; heavy and viscous, coating the glass; slightly unctuous, some sweetness, but dominant impression of strong acidity allied to rich, black treacly flavours; sweet and bitter on the finish, with great length, the treacle persisting. Balanced and impressive. ★★★★★

1808 Sercial

From a private island source. Eighteenth-/nineteenth-century blown glass bottle. Wax seal. Stencilled 'SS 1808 MS'. Cork estimated to be 50–60 years old. According to Noël Cossart, the highlight of the collection belonging to Sir Stephen Gaselee—the famous collector of madeiras in the first half of the twentieth century—was an unblended 1808 Sercial from the vineyards of Conde de Carvalhal, bought from Lomelino, who had rebottled it in 1914. He goes on: I was told by Dr Alfredo Leal that it was the best Sercial he knew ... and it is only from this particular bottling that we know that there was a fine Sercial produced in 1808'.[3] There are no means of telling whether this is the same wine. However, a bottle bearing the Kassab seal,[4] but otherwise identical to this one, was sold at Christie's in June 1986.

A darker orange-tawny than is normal for Sercial, with hints of green; a meat extract, yeasty smell took two days to clear, leaving a slightly muted but harmonious, rather generalized madeira bouquet with some volatility; amazingly full palate, quite extracted, faintly herby and very individual, dry and acidic; great length, with refreshing acidity and an aftertaste of Boal. So unlike aged Sercial and akin to Bastardo it astonishes, but it could never become my favourite Sercial. ★★★★

1811 Malvazia Cândida

From a private island source. Old, machine-made green glass bottle. Labelled. 'P W' stencilled on bottle. Hard wax seal with JNV authentication seal superimposed. The most shrivelled (relatively

long) cork I have ever seen, not adhering to the sides of the neck,
but kept in place by the wax seal. Heavy crusting. 13.4 per cent
alcohol (by gas chromatography analysis).

Extremely pale, amber gold, with greenish hues throughout; very
bottle sick; after 24 hours a faded, aged aroma combining vanilla
with singed paper, not wholly agreeable, but with hints of former
richness; after 48 hours the bouquet developed into a harmonious,
quite pungent, sweet vanilla, reminiscent of the smell of a cognac
glass after the last drops have evaporated; dried out and hollow,
with pronounced smoky, tobacco flavour and the merest hint of
acetic acid; slightly dirty, short finish, with lingering acidity on the
tongue. What on earth is this? It seems, apart from the bouquet, so
far removed from even the ghost of a sweet fortified wine that it is
difficult to believe it is really Malvazia. Patently old, but not evidently fortified—though it probably was. Fascinating, if you can
conquer the expectations to which the label gives rise.   [★]

1822 Verdelho   Cossart Gordon

Tasted in January 1994 at a MWC tasting in London. This wine
was originally part of the Grabham collection, also mentioned on
pp. 191 and 295 ff.

Dark, dense tawny, almost opaque; lively, complex bouquet, with
some volatility and bottle-aged roundness; very concentrated, palate-
coating, almost chewy, allied to considerable but not discordant acidity; a long, ravishingly complex finish. Stupendous—a real winner.
 ★ ★ ★ ★ ★

1827 Boal   Quinta do Serrado

Matured in cask until 1935, then put into demijohns; bottled in
1988 prior to sale at Christie's in 1989. From Câmara de Lobos.

Intensely dark mahogany, green highlights; a bouquet of great
depth and richness, with molasses and vanilla; opulent, mouth-
coating, so concentrated it is like a quintessence of madeira, yet

quite sweet and with refreshing acidity; amazing length, a kaleido-scope of flavours remaining in the throat. Revelatory of what madeira can achieve. ✿ ★ ★ ★ ★ ★

1830 Malvazia Quinta do Serrado

Matured in cask until 1935, then put into demijohns; bottled in 1988 prior to sale at Christie's in 1989. From Câmara de Lobos.

Mahogany with a green substratum; pungent, aromatic, slightly volatile, rich, toffeeish; very concentrated and complex, mouth-filling, with quite fiery acidity; explosive finish, very long, leaving tongue-tingling acidity. This wine shows its long wood ageing in its concentration, but although impressive, attracts respect rather than love, and is not in my view a very characteristic Malvazia. ★ ★ ★ ★

1834 Malvazia Barbeito

Medium tawny, and light for the age of the wine; lovely rich, hon-eyed aromas offset by a clean, slightly varnished, lift—intense and attractive; rich and refined, mouth-filling, butter toffee, with sup-porting acidity; finishes cleanly, with decent length. ★ ★ ★ (★)

1839 Malvazia—Fajã dos Padres Blandy's

One of the few bottles to surface at auction in Britain, this was purchased in 1983.

Orange-green; highly aromatic and wonderfully full, vanilla, toffee apple, with hints of raisin and malt, paradigmatic of Malvazia, and with no unwanted volatility; the sweetness modified by a cer-tain dryness which does not affect the overall richness, with layers of flavour ranging through barley sugar, cream toffee and dried fruits, supremely elegant and balanced; clean acidity and dry, lin-gering finish. Seductive nectar. Wonderfully preserved. It is easy to understand why the *Fajã* had its reputation, and how deserved it was. ✿ ★ ★ ★ ★ ★

1846 Terrantez — Blandy's

Tasted in January 1994 at a MWC tasting in London.

Darkish mahogany, but bright, with lively green rim; the bouquet a symphony of aromas, with great depth and complexity; on the palate perhaps the most concentrated wine I have ever tasted (and that just after a Cossart Gordon 1862 Terrantez); intense vinosity, the quintessence of the grape allied to zinging acidity, creating an overpowering impression of richness; a finish of incredible length which went on and on and on. Monumental. ❀ ★ ★ ★ ★ ★

1846 Terrantez — Cossart Gordon

Purchased originally from H. M. Borges, and bottled in 1900. Purchased at Christie's in 1974.

Dark tawny, with a yellow-green rim; characteristic dark-toned bouquet of dates, herbs, fudge, agreeable volatility; lean, compact, but with considerable extract, bitter-sweet; dry, long, smoky finish. A sophisticated, mellowed, stylish wine of wonderful quality, but without the memorable qualities of the Blandy's bottling described above. ★ ★ ★ ★

1846 Campanário — Blandy's

This wine, named after the area in which it was produced, once belonged to the collector Sir Stephen Gaselee.[5] Purchased in England in January 1970 for £5.10.0d. In three-part moulded bottle.

Dark tawny, with pronounced green rim—almost green with tawny highlights against strong sunlight; fragrant, Boal-type bouquet, without much volatility; elegant, balanced, flavoursome rather than assertive, with overtones of Malvazia, still some sweetness, although quite dry; moderate finish. By no means a blockbuster, but nonetheless impressively complete. Delicious. ★ ★ ★ ★ (★)

1846 Verdelho   Avery's of Bristol

Reserva Velhissima around 1846. Produced by the Visconde de Val Pariso at Porto Moniz. Bought in cask by Noël Cossart from his son, Dr John Bianchi, when he was Portuguese ambassador in Washington, and bottled in 1936. Noël Cossart's verdict: 'Magnificent'.

Quite dark tawny, with lively highlights; astonishing and intensely resinous bouquet of crushed geranium leaves (indicative of a wine fault, geraniol, which is lactic acid bacteria from sorbic acid), rather unpleasant; amazingly powerful and concentrated on the palate, vinous, a little dried out and spirity, with the resin flavour coming through strongly; assertive but short aftertaste; wholly unattractive and disappointing.   [★★]

1862 Terrantez   Avery's of Bristol

This wine was aged in cask until 1905, when it was put into demijohns. It was bottled in 1936. Made from grapes grown on the properties belonging to João Alexandrino Santos, from whom it was purchased in cask. Purchased from Avery's.

Dark tawny, ruby and orange highlights, orange-green rim; astonishingly full and assertive bouquet, quite volatile, showing candied peel, coconut and kiwi fruit; immensely weighty on the palate, intense, with layer upon layer of rich, smoky, concentrated extract, and then some, but behind the opulence, a steely backbone of acidity which holds it all together; almost medicinally dry, with a bitter finish and a length which goes on and on and on. Sensational. A giant amongst giants. Cossart's view that this is 'the best Terrantez ever vintaged—surpasses all others' is challenged only by Blandy's Terrantez 1846.   ✿ ★★★★★

1863 Boal   Barbeito

Dark tawny, showing olive green on rim; moderately powerful, toasted bouquet with rich, clean volatility; fairly sweet palate with some depth but not much complexity; clean acidic finish of moderate length.   ★★(★)

1864 Sercial

From a private island source. Early twentieth-century machine-made bottle. Label indicates that the wine originated in Câmara de Lobos, and was inherited from Dr Francisco E. Henriques. This may be the same Sercial 1864 that was purchased by Sir Stephen Gaselee from Dona Eugenia Bianchi Henriques, who inherited it from her grandfather, Barone Carlo de Bianchi.[6]

Orange-yellow, shot with lime green; rather ethereal, patinated, soft old Sercial bouquet, similar to the 1875 Sercial but with deeper toning, gentle but satisfying; clean, slightly honeyed, nutty flavour with a little depth; a little acidity but not much length. Very refined, subtle, rather faded but still positive. Delicious. ★★★(★)

1870 Malvazia—Fajã dos Padres

A clear glass, hand-blown, cognac-type bottle. Labelled. Rebottled in 1950. Private island source.

Very light amber, yellow and orange, with green rim; still bottle sick after 48 hours, but much improved by oxygenating the wine in the glass; restrained, rather spirity nose, light and lifted, faintly rubbery, but a harmonious, slightly citrus, 'old malmsey' aroma still detectable; very sweet, not very concentrated, lacking acidity, but very elegant; dry, rather short but clean finish. Pleasant but unremarkable. ★(★)

1870 Terrantez   Blandy's

At least fifty years in bottle. Unfortunately, I have been unable to establish anything about the origins of this wine, which was purchased in England.

Dark tawny, orange highlights, greening rim; complex, rich, fudgy nose, quite acidic; positive, bitterly acidic entry, weighty, lots of extract, mouth-filling; clean, fresh acidic finish with considerable length and a hint of sweetness at the end. A wine of sophistication and character. ★★★★(★)

1870 Bastardo
Blandy's

Originally from the cellars of Padre Henriques, vicar of Estreito de Câmara de Lobos. Some of this wine was sold to Sir Stephen Gaselee and acquired by Avery's of Bristol after his death.

Medium-dark tawny, orange-green highlights; dry, volatile marmalade nose, a bit varnishy; some glycerine on the palate, but high acidity and a dry, citrous zing do not disguise some lack of depth; long, intensely tangy finish. ★★(★)

1875 Sercial

From a private island source. Three-part moulded bottle.

Mature, orange-yellow; extraordinarily fragrant, almost sweet aromas, with hints of linseed oil and almonds, but ultra-refined and with an evident patina of age; gentle and faded on the palate and not bone dry, with a slightly flat flavour of hazelnuts, and some remaining supportive acidity; modest, unassertive, clean finish. Subdued maybe, but gracious, refined, evocative, and in its way delicious. ★★★

1875 Moscatel
Pereira D'Oliveira

Very dense, dark mahogany, with virgin olive oil green rim; on the nose, treacle and chocolate, a little raisiny, powerful but without much lift; weighty, complex and concentrated, quintessence of barley sugar; acidity masked by the intense sweetness; persistent without being throat-filling. The most powerful Moscatel madeira I have encountered, and impressive. Remarkable of its kind, but something of a curiosity. ★★★★(★)

1879 Verdelho
Torre Bella Estate

From Câmara de Lobos. Recorked in April 1987. Sold in the Captain David Fairlie sale at Christie's on 24 November 1988.

Pale, medium orange-gold, greening on the rim; fragrant, balanced nose with no exaggerated acidity; concentrated, citrus orange, slightly smoky, very dry; refined and subtle strength; good length, with acidity to the fore. Delicious. ★★★★

1882 Verdelho Cossart Gordon

Really dark mahogany, with russet tints, but very bright; steely, focused bouquet, concentrated, with overtones of marmalade and fudge; complex, clean fruit offset by intensely tangy acidity, producing delicious balance; medium-sweet finish, clinging, with tanginess predominating. Attractive. ★★★★

1883 Tinta Blandy's

Bottled in 1936 or 1937. Made with grapes from the Porto Moniz vineyard of the Visconde de Val Pariso. Purchased from Avery of Bristol in June 1967 for £3 0s. 7d.

A light golden colour, yellow, gold, orange and green throughout in strong natural light; fruity, slightly sweet and fudgy, rounded Boal-type bouquet, lacking volatility; at first flat, one-dimensional, dried out and somewhat woody on the palate, with a rather astringent, long, dry finish; but after 48 hours settled down a little and developed more of a Boal character, with more apparent residual sweetness and depth; but, sadly, the wine has dried out a little, and a papery taste on the finish was still evident. Not wholly agreeable when first tasted, but more enjoyable later. ★★(★)

1885 Verdelho Barbeito

Medium-dark tawny with yellowish green rim; weighty, deep-toned bouquet without much liveliness; notable lack of intensity on the palate, but finishing with nice, persistent, tangy acidity. ★★

1890 Verdelho Pereira D'Oliveira

Very dark, glowing, russet mahogany—amongst D'Oliveira's densest wines; toasted, brûlé, pungently volatile bouquet; big, concentrated layers of flavour, balanced with strong acidity; long, tangy finish. ★★★★

1890 Boal   Artur de Barros e Sousa

Medium-dark tawny, with green rim; very pungent, rich and concentrated nose, hints of coconut; explosion of concentrated fruit, apricots, layer upon layer of flavour; mouth-filling, with long, long, slightly tangy finish. Astonishingly big and weighty, but structured and balanced. Close to perfection. ★★★★★

1890 Moscat Velho   Artur de Barros e Sousa

Mahogany shot through with green; rather volatile, with some treacle; very sweet, soft, a little hollow and not particularly flavoursome; initially throat-filling, but no great length. Seems to lack any special Moscatel character. ★★★

1892 Sercial   Cossart Gordon

At least thirty years in bottle.

Very mature Sauternes, orange-yellow; pleasant, clean, fragrant and lifted volatility; explosive on the palate, flavoursome, with hints of coconut and dates, bone dry and with searing acidity; a long, cleansing, acidic finish. Bracing but balanced. ★★★★

1897 Boal   T. T. da Camara Lomelino

Mahogany, with red glints and a yellow rim, like very mature claret; pungent bouquet, a little varnishy, showing candied sugar, chocolate and roasted almonds; mouth-filling, very intense, rich but refined and focused, with controlled acidity; long, fairly acidic finish. Fine specimen of a Boal. ★★★★

1899 Terrantez   Cossart Gordon

Bottle stencilled 'AO–SM', indicating the wine belonged (until 1984) to Agostinho D'Oliveira-São Martinho. 5.5° Baumé, 1.5 volatile acidity.

Dark orange with hints of green; could easily be mistaken for Malvazia from the bouquet, which is rich caramel and butter toffee, very forthcoming; explosive entry, mouth-filling, concentrated, complex and for Terrantez surprisingly sweet; long and dry on the finish, but lacks the whiplash intensity of the best Terrantez. Wonderful to drink, but more interesting than typical. ★★★(★)

1900 Boal   Adegas do Torreão

Medium-dark tawny, hints of gold; full, slightly burnt-sugar nose; restrained sweetness, lacking a little in power, but balanced and of decent quality; dry finish of moderate length. Elegant and pleasing. ★★(★)

1901 Malvazia   Barbeito

Tawny with pale orange tones; rather flat and dirty, meat extract smell (a bottle stink, perhaps, which never quite cleared); rich, butter toffee, vanilla, quite concentrated and palate-coating, with refreshing acidity; finishing quite dry with moderate length. A second bottle had no stink and was much more attractive. (★)/★★★(★)

1901 Malvazia   Adegas do Torreão

Heavily crusted bottle.

Dark tawny, yellow glints; full, generous, cream toffee, classic Malvazia bouquet, considerable volatility; mouth-filling, rich and concentrated butterscotch, sweetness cut by acidity; exhilarating intensity in the throat, quite long acidic finish. Still youthful, and a little four-square and lacking in elegance, but its sheer power overcomes such criticism. ★★★(★)

1903 Boal   Pereira D'Oliveira

Very deep tawny; rich, variegated, deep-toned vanilla bouquet; hugely concentrated barley sugar, sweet, but with a wonderful acid balance; big, lingering finish. The weight of this wine does not, however, submerge its Boal character. Excellent; combines power with charm. ★ ★ ★ ★ ★

1907 Malvazia   Pereira D'Oliveira

The birth year of both the parents of the D'Oliveira brothers, and therefore for many years the family celebratory wine.

Almost opaque, dense ruddy mahogany, even darker than the 1912 Verdelho, with brilliant amber glints; pungent, with characteristic butter toffee varietal bouquet; glass-coating; so concentrated on the palate that one has to work at it, almost a wine to chew; sweet but, with high controlled acidity, not in the least cloying; persistent, but without the full finish one expects. A blockbuster wine, commanding respect rather than love, of which a few sips suffice. Tasted a second time six months later: on this occasion noted for the treacly character of the nose and treacly concentration on the palate—neither easily recognizable as Malvazia. ★ ★ ★ ★

1908 Boal   Cossart Gordon

Bottled in 1984 after 76 years in cask.

Dark mahogany with russet tints, not showing much age on the rim; forthcoming aromas of burnt sugar, coffee and chocolate, lively, but focused and refined; powerful, vinous, concentrated, with high but integrated acidity; clean, full palate finishing very long. Very good, satisfying wine. ★ ★ ★ ★

1910 Sercial   Barbeito

Lively medium tawny with amber glints; fairly intense, fresh and harmonious bouquet, characteristic, with attractive acidity; full palate, clean and balanced; moderately long finish. A long-time favourite of mine. ★ ★ ★ ★

1910 Sercial   Cossart Gordon

Bottled in 1984.

Golden-orange; moderately assertive bouquet, rounded and nutty, hints of orange peel and fudge, stylish and well bred; powerful entry, considerable depth, full but delicate; deliciously complex, clean, bone-dry finish of moderate persistence. Very fine. ★★★★

1912 Verdelho   Pereira D'Oliveira

Dense, ruddy mahogany, with olive green rim; intensely perfumed, complex, flowery nose with an exhilarating but refined volatile lift; a full palate—concentrated vinosity, hints of fudge—opening out to a powerful, lingering aftertaste of black treacle devoid of any sort of cloying sweetness. Another winner.   ★★★★★

1920 Malvazia   T. T. da Camara Lomelino

Dark mahogany; pungent volatility, burnt sugar and toffee apple; sweet, concentrated, mouth-filling, raw acidity; tangy, tonsil-tickling finish. Clumsy, crude, lacking balance and any clear Malvazia character. Still too young?   ★(★)

1920 Malmsey   Cossart Gordon

Said by Noël Cossart to be the last vintage made from Malvasia Cândida, and from grapes from the Fajã dos Padres (but see p. 128).

Dark tawny with green toning; very aromatic, with the unmistakable cream toffee bouquet of genuine Malvazia; concentrated, with hints of treacle, sweet and luscious; long finish. A wonderful Malvazia, if still too young-seeming.   ★★★(★)

1922 Boal   Pereira D'Oliveira

Dense, ruddy mahogany, with yellow-green rim, just beginning to coat the glass; the bouquet grew and opened out, a rich symphony of aromas like *crème brulée* and roasted nuts; very concentrated and sweet, but with good balancing acidity; powerful and persistent finish. A reference wine. ★ ★ ★ ★ ★

1927 Bastardo — Adegas do Torreão

Tawny with green, yellow and orange tones; faintly Malvazia on the nose, and rather volatile; intense, austerely dry, and very acidic on entry; long, dry, acidic finish. Contrasts strongly with the sweeter, typically MWC Bastardo style—like a Sercial with lots of body. Not better, but very different. Impresses mainly because of its concentration. ★ ★ ★ (★)

1934 Malmsey — Henriques & Henriques

Bottled over twenty years ago.

Dark mahogany, with striking yellow toning; rich, quite lifted bouquet; rich, layered and concentrated, intensely sweet; but the sweetness is cut by the tangy acidity of the long-lasting finish. A fine wine. ★ ★ ★ (★)

1937 Sercial — Pereira D'Oliveira

Dark tawny with orange-gold highlights; pungent and characteristic bouquet with hints of fudge, varnish and strong acidity; explosive fullness on palate, big but rounded, with an astringent, very long finish; totally dry, with a deliciously lingering fudge flavour. ★ ★ ★

1954 Verdelho — Justino Henriques

Fairly dark tawny with amber-orange and olive green tints; nice restrained caramel aroma, with a bit of lift, balanced; distinctly sweet, but harmonious and concentrated; good length. Attractive, with overtones of Boal. ★ ★

1954 Bastardo — Blandy's

Bottled in 1992.

Tawny with gold and orange glints; quite volatile nose, a little dusty, with hints of barley sugar and dried fruits; apricots and caramel on palate; sweetness cut and balanced by considerable, but unaggressive, acidity; a touch raw, but stylish; medium length with agreeably fruity finish. ★★★

1957 Boal — Barbeito

Medium tawny; modest but delicate bouquet, with harmonious volatility; quite rich, nutty, full palate with adequate acidity; finishes a little disappointingly. Needs further development. ★★

1958 Boal — Cossart Gordon

Dark orange-tawny; high-toned, focused aroma of dried fruits; rich, textured, considerable acidity; long acidic finish with toffee-ish aftertaste. Promising. ★★★(★)

1959 Boal — Blandy's

Medium tawny; lacking power, but otherwise complete and satisfying bouquet; similar palate to the 1958 Boal, but much more delicate; moderate finish. Modest but attractive. ★★

1964 Boal — Justino Henriques

Extremely dark tawny with orange highlights and a glint of gold on the rim; attractive aroma, typical of Boal, sweet, but a little lacking in power and with a hint of varnish; a big mouthful, quite tangy, with an agreeable barley sugar aftertaste. Finishes well. Attractive. ★★★

1966 Verdelho   Pereira D'Oliveira

Dark tawny with russet-orange highlights; focused, well-bred but unassertive bouquet; ripe, concentrated and flowery on the palate with a tangy, dry finish.   ★(★)

1968 Boal   Pereira D'Oliveira

Dark tawny with ruddy tints; forthcoming and harmonious blend of singed aromas, already well developed, with a slight volatile lift; fruity palate, its sweetness cut by considerable acidity, finishing rather dry and quite long.   ★★

1969 Bastardo   Cossart Gordon

Bottled in 1982. 3° Baumé.

Medium-dark orange tawny; harmonious, quite lifted, toasted aroma of dried apricots; slight sweetness, masked with an astringent hint of almonds; toffee-ish, with slightly bitter overtones, reminiscent of Terrantez; longish, quite dry finish, not too astringent. Elegant and powerful, but hardly medium-sweet as described.   ★★★

1971 Sercial   Cossart Gordon

Pale amber tawny; candied peel, rather muted and clumsy with hardly any vibrancy; brittle, nervous, without much depth. Rather ordinary.   ★

1972 Verdelho   Madeira Wine Institute

Pale, medium orange gold; rounded, rather clumsy nose, not particularly pungent but showing some volatility; biting acidity on the palate, even raw; finishes short.   ★

1972 Verdelho   Cossart Gordon

Orange tawny; rather subdued nose; tongue-tingling acidity and some intensity of flavour; modest finish. Still very young and undeveloped.   ★★

1974 Terrantez **Cossart Gordon**

2.5° Baumé.

Pale orange tawny; young, crisp, undeveloped Verdelho-like bouquet; quite sweet, rounded, rather lacking in characteristic bitterness, but finishes long and quite dry. Needs a long time to develop. ★★(?)

Non-dated wines

Malvazia—Solera 1808 **Cossart Gordon**

Made into a solera in 1873 and not topped up after 1953.[7] The best wine, in my opinion, at a Cossart Gordon tasting in 1979, beating in quality all the vintage wines shown on that occasion. Tasted on this occasion against the 1920, 1870, 1839 and 1830 Malvazias discussed above.

Very dark tawny, slightly ruddy, hints of green; bottle stink took three days to clear; rich, harmonious, characteristic Malvazia toffee aroma, with slight volatility; unctuous entry, the sweetness disciplined by quite sharp acidity, luscious, considerable depth of flavour, rather malty, but does not flower in the mouth as it should; slightly burnt finish, moderately persistent but leaving the tongue tingling. This wine grows on one, and its attraction is perhaps the blend of obviously aged characteristics with youthful zest—which is possibly what shows that this is a solera wine. Misses being of the very top quality only by a whisker. ★★★★(★)

Grand Old Boal **Henriques & Henriques**

Old bottled, and recorked in 1927, 1955 and 1975. Bottle absolutely black from interior crusting. Thought to date from the first quarter of the nineteenth century. For further details see p. 238.

Darker than medium tawny, with orange tints, and showing olive green towards the rim; very rich and pungent on the nose, without any excess volatility, and a mature fudgy aroma—Boal at its most typical; rich, concentrated, with vanilla predominant, but balanced; wonderfully focused long finish, persistent black treacle aftertaste, going on and on, but nevertheless dry. A lovely wine. Classic.

★★★★★

Reserva Malvasia   **Henriques & Henriques**

Rebottled in 1964 and similar in age to Grand Old Boal.

Very dark tawny, golden highlights, shot with olive green; complex, nutty and fudgy, ethereal bouquet, redolent of age and maturity, totally captivating; hugely concentrated, many-layered wine with an explosive entry and almost chewy consistency; ravishing, intense, but controlled and uncloying sweetness; an exceedingly long, very intense and lingering finish. The quintessence of Malvazia and, for me, perfection.   ✿ ★ ★ ★ ★ ★

PART III

THE PRODUCERS

14

THE PRODUCERS

Artur de Barros e Sousa, Lda[1]

This small firm—technically a *partidista* and not a shipper, because it has no export license—came into being at the instigation of Dr Pedro José Lomelino (1864–1930)[2] who came from an important if not particularly wealthy Funchal family. Although prominent in public life—he was for a time Funchal's deputy district civil governor and for many years director of the Municipal Superior Primary School—he continued to practise medicine. Being fond of wine, Dr Lomelino bought parcels of good madeira when he could and, according to family tradition, he often got paid with wine for his medical services.[3] He thus amassed a sizeable collection, and when, early in the 1920s, his nephew Artur de Barros e Sousa had to return from Brazil because the climate was unsuitable for his asthma, Dr Lomelino offered him work sorting out the wines. Artur was so successful in this that shortly afterwards Dr Lomelino offered to set him up in the wine business. The resulting company was first registered in 1921 under the name of Lomelino (not to be confused with the other firm of this name which became part of the Madeira Wine Company), but was re-registered the following year in the name Artur de Barros e Sousa, Lda. Artur had a daughter Virginia who married Edmundo Menezes de Olim, and they had three sons, two of which currently run the company. Artur is the wine-maker—somewhat unusually a teetotal one—and Edmundo is principally on the sales side. Rui, who used to be a sleeping partner, left the firm a few years ago.

Barros e Sousa has never had a very high profile as a madeira producer. Many years ago it exported to Trinidad and Venezuela, but for more than quarter of a century its market has been home sales on the island. It will, however, despatch orders abroad to individual customers. So far as I am aware, its existence had never before been acknowledged in any book about madeira in English until the first edition of this volume, whereas in Portuguese wine books and guides it has for a long time been accorded an important place. Even its lodge in the Rua dos Ferreiros (next door to that of Pereira D'Oliveira) is inconspicuous and easily missed, unless you happen to peer into its shadowy doorway and its trade sign catches your eye. Once inside, however, you pass through a time warp into a setting which cannot have changed very significantly since the firm first occupied these premises more than ninety years ago, and whose quaintness is more suggestive of the nineteenth century than of the beginning of the twenty-first. A cobbled passage leads to a wider area which serves both as a workplace and shop, and beyond this is the office. To the right a door leads into a small yard off which there is a modest three-storey wine store. Whereas the old-world atmosphere is maintained in some other establishments largely as a part of their marketing image, in the case of Barros e Sousa it is just how things happen to be. Hardly anything is mechanized—a pump is used to take wine to the upper floors of the store—but otherwise one has entered a world of traditional artisan craftsmanship, totally removed from the frankly industrialized wine production met with elsewhere on the island. Not only does Barros e Sousa carry out all the processes of production, bottling, labelling, etc. by hand, but it is the only firm on the island not to use any *estufagem* in the maturing of any of its wines. Such is its pride in this that on some of its labels there used to be a printed offer of £1,000 to anyone able to prove that the firm's everyday drinking wines are not products of the *canteiro* system. It is partly this avoidance of *estufagem* that has earned Barros e Sousa the reputation it has in Portugal for the quality of its wines. Sadly, some larger firms scoff at this claim and look down their noses at a little firm so rooted in the past. I, on the other hand, find it heartening that a small enterprise of this kind—consisting of the Olim brothers and a cellar hand—with a clear commitment to traditional values has managed to survive in a brutal commercial world.

The Olim family used to own vineyards on Porto Santo and brought must to Madeira from the island. Gradually this diminished until only the must for their Listrão Branco, a speciality of which they had a monopoly, remained. Now that Porto Santo has ceased to be a significant source of grapes for wine making, all the firm's grape requirements are bought from growers in Madeira. The company's wine-making facilities are at the Rua dos Ferreiros, where the must (the result of mechanical pressing) is fermented in wooden pipes. All varieties are fermented off their skins. For standard blends Artur prefers to use Complexa, which he buys from São Jorge in the north. This, he finds, is particularly good for sweet wine, but also satisfactory for medium-sweet and medium-dry. No filtration is ever used, and the health of the wines is maintained by regular racking and washing out of casks. Clarification is carried out only prior to bottling: gelatine for Sercial, egg whites for Verdelho, Boal and Malvazia. Production normally ranges from 25–40 hL, and occasionally much higher.

When Barros e Sousa sells Reserva wines they are a blend of whatever varieties Artur has to hand. 'Tutti frutti' is how Artur describes them. Most of these Reservas (which by law have to be a minimum of five years old) actually have an average age of almost ten years. 'Five year old wine is no good to me,' Artur says. This may be why other firms have voiced suspicions about the 'no *estufagem*' claim, for the wines certainly have a roundness and maturity that could not be achieved in five years without *estufagem*. How is it possible to sell such wines in competition with the larger firms which do use *estufagem*? Part, at least, of the answer must lie in the smallness of the scale of the operation: no advertising, no back-up staff, very little capital investment apart from the wine itself.

The firm used to be one of the few prepared to take the trouble to vinify varieties like Terrantez, Bastardo and Moscatel in quite minuscule amounts. Sadly, Artur has not been able to obtain grapes of these varieties for many years now, so for Barros e Sousa these madeiras, like Listrão, are now past history. 'The vineyard from which I used to get my Terrantez is now under Madeira Shopping', he explains with some exasperation (Madeira Shopping is Madeira's largest shopping centre, at São António, north of São Martinho). Unlike, for example, the MWC, Artur preferred to vinify Terrantez and Bastardo in a bone dry style, which he thinks best displays their characters. Moscatel, unlike other varieties, was allowed to macerate for several months. The first lees were put into a fine-grained bag, then hung up and allowed to drip—a very traditional procedure, and the nearest thing to filtration to be found in this company. The wine was then, like Terrantez, clarified with milk (Bastardo, according to Artur, never requires clarification). Once Artur stops making wine traditional methods like this will, I fear, be lost for ever.

Barros e Sousa sells a full range of the standard qualities up to the 15 year old category, together with some relatively young vintages and a few *colheitas*. The company aims uncompromisingly at quality, and I find the wines well made, honest and attractive. However, Artur and Edmundo are getting older, and their families have no interest in continuing the business, so it has been up for sale for some time. Who will buy it? 'God will decide', Artur says fatalistically. When that happens Madeira will, sadly, have lost probably the last of its remaining practitioners of traditional artisan madeira wine-making.

H. M. Borges, Sucrs., Lda

Henrique Menezes Borges began as a food importer, but he ploughed his profits into the purchase of old wines of which he built up a large stock. In 1877, therefore, in addition to running his importing business, he became a *partidista* and thereby founded the firm which now bears his name. He supplied many firms,[4] but was particularly associated with Krohn Brothers, who specialized in exporting to Russia. Henrique Menezes Borges died in 1916, leaving two sons, João and Henrique, and a daughter, Maria da Conceição. The company, which was situated in the Rua do Seminário, then became styled H. M. Borges, Sucessors, Lda. In 1922, when the firm itself began to export madeira, it moved to its present lodge in the Rua 31 de Janeiro, which had previously been a flour mill. In 1925 Borges acquired a company called the Adega Exportadora de Vinhos da Madeira. Maria subsequently married João Henriques Gonçalves, proprietor of a madeira firm of the same name, which was merged with Borges in 1926. In 1932 Gonçalves bought the Borges firm from Maria and her brothers, but retained the name, and in the same year Borges merged with another firm, Araújo, Henriques & Co. João Araújo (now dead) became a partner in Borges. Finally, in 1935 Borges Madeira, Lda, was created as an associate firm of Araújo Henriques and H. M. Borges.

João and Maria Gonçalves had two sons and a daughter. Their sons, Jorge and Fernando eventually took over the firm, but Jorge died in 2004 and Fernando in 2011, so the company is now owned by the fourth generation of the family. The running of the company is in the hands of one of Jorge's daughters, Isabel Borges Gonçalves, and one of Fernando's daughters, Dr Helena Borges Fontes, both of whom formerly worked with their parents. The wine-maker is Ivo Couto, who took over the job from Jorge in 2003, having been a wine-maker at the MWC and then, until it folded, at Silva Vinhos.

The company's lodge is small and compact. In front, next to the street, is the characterful tasting room to which tourists are welcomed. Next to this is the office, and next to the office (but out of sight) is the laboratory. Behind all three is the *adega* and bottling line (installed in 2005). The company owns no other premises. Almost all the vinification equipment has been renewed within the last decade. It consists of stainless steel cylinders, with non-automatic temperature controls, which have a capacity of over 94,000 litres. Some concrete tanks are still used for *estufagem*. There is a total storage capacity of 10,000 hL in large satinwood vats of around 35,000 litres capacity. Traditional varieties are fermented in cask (*bica aberta*), Bual and Malvazia with some maceration, and are matured in lodge pipes in a store which is fairly warm but not artificially heated. Borges does not produce modified wine and has no interest in making table wines.

The company deals with about one hundred growers. Tinta Negra and Verdelho grapes are sourced from Estreito de Câmara de Lobos; Sercial from Jardim da Serra; Boal from Campanário; and Malvasia from São Jorge and Santana. Normally the firm will buy 200,000 kilograms per year. In 2012, 1,600 hL of wine were made—slightly more than average.

A half of Borges's production at the turn of the century consisted of bulk wine and, although it was by then reducing the amount of production, the eventual prohibition of bulk exports hit hard. Some important markets, like Belgium and Italy, did not accept the change gracefully. Sweden, however, did, and remains the company's best overseas market. Indeed, it is the destination of half of its total exports—the very competitively priced 3 year old madeira dominates in Sweden. Most export wine is sold under the Borges label, but those of the older amalgamated companies are also still used. In 1997 Borges had 80 per cent of the local market, but by 2009 this situation had changed. The airline prohibition on carrying bottles of wine in cabin baggage played a significant part in this, and since 2009 sales have remained flat. Eighty per cent of production is from Tinta Negra (mainly 3 year old wine); the remainder is from traditional varieties. Borges has increased its range of products, which now includes 10 and 15 year old varietal wines, some *colheitas* and a few *garrafeiras*. The company intends to make more *colheitas*. The very old dated wines which have appeared on the market do not come from the firm, but from the private reserve of another branch of the family.

H. M. Borges is a relatively small family company whose better quality wines have been, in my opinion, of a consistently high standard over the years. The company adds considerably to the diversity of the madeira market, and I hope it will continue to do so.

Cooperativa Agrícola do Funchal, CRL (CAF)

This is the most recent shipper to register with IVBAM. It is located in São Martinho. The co-operative was founded in 1951 to produce and sell wholesale animal foodstuffs. However, it has moved into madeira wine production and purchased grapes from the 2012 harvest. Engineer Paul Mendes is in charge. The company will not, of course, be able to trade for some time, and in 2013 it was attempting to buy old wine from other shippers to build up its reserves. At the time of writing its website was still under construction, so there is little else as yet to report about this new player in the field.

J. Faria & Filhos, Lda.

This is a family firm which started in 1949. It originally manufactured and sold alcoholic and fruit-based drinks such as liqueurs, rum punches, and *aguardente*, a brandy made out of sugar cane (supplied by the Compahnia dos Engenhos do Norte). In 1998 the firm became associated with P. E. Gonçalves, Lda., in an arrangement whereby Gonçalves make madeira which is matured and then marketed by Faria. The company only employs four people, including Luís Faria, the managing director, and his father and mother. In 2006 the firm moved into purpose-built new premises close to the Madeira Shopping complex in Funchal and invested in temperature-controlled stainless steel *estufagem* cylinders (100,000 litres) as well as storage for maturing the wines (100,000 litres in wood, and 650,000 litres in stainless steel). The range of madeiras is modest: generic madeiras without any indication of age, and 5 and 10 year old non-varietals. Some varietal wines are in the pipeline. The island accounts for 60 per cent of sales, and mainland Portugal for 25 per cent. The remaining wine is exported to France, Switzerland, England, USA, South Africa and Panama.

P. E. Gonçalves, Lda.

This, apart from Barros e Sousa, is the only other registered *partidista* on the island. The company has been in business since last century, and recently relocated from Funchal to Câmara de Lobos. In the mid-1990s the firm sold rather basic madeiras on the local and Portuguese domestic markets. Until 2002 it specialised in making *granel*, at that time the lowest quality of wine destined for bulk export, and for many years supplied it to a now-defunct company called Veiga França. At the moment its main activity appears to be supplying madeira to J. Faria & Filhos. The company is run by Hugo Gonçalves, and the wine-maker is his son, Paolo.

Henriques & Henriques—Vinhos, SA

In 1850 João Gonçalves Henriques started a wine company. His own vineyards supplied its needs, and in founding his company João Henriques was not so much breaking new ground as formalizing in business terms what had already been a family activity for a considerable time previously. The reason he decided to form a company is not known, but it may have been because changes in the inheritance laws in Portugal—which had adopted the so-called 'Napoleonic Law'—brought about the progressive division of property holdings, and the formation of a company was one way of keeping land holdings intact. However, when the firm found trading conditions tough in 1912 some vineyards were sold, and yet more land was lost when, after the 1974 Revolution, tenants were able to purchase the freehold of their land. As a result, the company was left with only about 3 hectares of vineyards near its lodge at Bélem in Câmara de Lobos. João Henriques had three sons. The eldest was Francisco Eduardo, and the youngest, named after his father was another João Joaquim—later known familiarly as João de Bélem, which conveniently distinguishes him from his father. The middle brother, António Eduardo, lost his inheritance because he made a pact with his younger brother that the first to get married would lose his inheritance to the other: as things turned out, he was the first to do so. It may well be that the threat of property division lay behind this odd agreement, since its effect was to enable the family to keep its possessions intact. According to John Cossart, whose godfather the youngest son was, the joking nature of the contract would have been completely in tune with his sense of humour and his shrewdness. Perhaps the youngest brother guessed that his middle brother was more likely to marry. At any rate, the middle brother founded his own madeira firm, António Eduardo Henriques. Ironically, it is now incorporated in Henriques & Henriques, having been bought by the youngest brother from his widowed sister-in-law.

After their father's death, the firm was inherited by the eldest and youngest brothers and was reconstituted in 1912 as Henriques & Henriques. In due course the youngest brother, João de Bélem, inherited his eldest brother's share in the business. He invited two of his friends to join the firm; Alberto Jardim (known to everyone as Bertie) and Carlos Nunes Pereira. He then took in Peter Cossart, the younger brother of Noël Cossart of Cossart Gordon. The reason why Peter did not join his own family's firm was because in 1938, despite Noël's opposition, his mother advised him not to. She was convinced that war was coming, and believed that if it did the family firm would be badly affected. She advised Peter either to start a company of his own, which he could not afford to do, or to go in with someone else as an interim measure. As João de Bélem had been a great friend of his parents, and had become virtually a surrogate father to Peter Cossart when his own father had died, he said, 'Look no further—come in with me'. The 'interim measure' became permanent.

Before his death in 1968 Joaquim de Bélem made provision for his three friends, whom he also considered as his partners, by dividing the shares in the firm between them. At the same time he put into the firm all the productive land and several buildings that were his personal property. Bertie's children did not come into the company, although his daughter's husband was in the firm until July 1997. Carlos Nunes Pereira's nephew Luís, the only child of his father's generation of the family, was in the company for more than thirty years and was its wine-maker. He has now retired. Peter Cossart was succeeded in 1991 by his son John, who died suddenly in February 2008 and was the last member of the Cossart family to be directly involved in the island wine trade. This effectively left only Humberto Jardim, who had recently joined the company, as the last representative of the families which had originally owned the company.

Humberto started his working life in Brazil in 1994, and having ventured into areas as diverse as travel agencies, ship's chandlery and electronic equipment, came back to Madeira to work in the company with a mandate to try and stabilize it and its finances. The ills that afflicted the company arose from its brave decision in 1992 to take advantage of EU grants and move out of Funchal. This involved a total investment of €5,500,000 in two related projects. The first was to build a new vinification centre at Quinta Grande, where a 10 hectare vineyard with bulldozed terraces was also established on land that had belonged to the Henriques family since the sixteenth century. The second was to develop the site of the company's original lodge in Câmara de Lobos as a new wine store, office and tourist reception centre. These projects were completed in 1995, but a move of this sort was never going to be easy, and the inevitable stress turned to angst when the contractor went bankrupt half-way through the construction of the new premises. This gave rise to very costly problems which were only beginning to be resolved when, in 2009, Humberto chanced to meet the owner of La Martiniquaise, the French wine and spirits conglomerate that had just acquired Justino's. The consequence of this was that in 2010 Henriques & Henriques was bought (apart from some shares which Humberto has retained) by La Martiniquaise. It is occasionally said that Henriques & Henriques and Justino's are now run as one firm. That is not the case. They remain independently run, except that Henriques & Henriques no longer has its own bottling line and this aspect of production is carried out for it by Justino's. Humberto Jardim is both general manager and wine-maker, having been taught by Luís Pereira before he retired. 'I am a very experimental wine-maker', he says. The involvement of La Martiniquaise has brought not only the stability that was needed, but additional investment in the company. The vinification centre at Ribeira do Escrivão, Quinta Grande, is set in its vineyard and built like a Douro *adega* to take advantage of the sloping hillside site. There are six autovinifiers—three large and three small, to make it possible to vinify small quantities of traditional varieties. These were manufactured on the island by a French firm because this proved to be more economical than having the tanks manufactured on the mainland and shipped to Madeira. The centre's total vinification and *estufagem* capacity is 15,000 hL, and the company has a total storage capacity of 30,000 hL, of which a third is wood storage at Bélem. At Ribeira do Escrivão the 50,000 litre storage tanks, all of stainless steel, are situated in an immense hall on the lower level of the building, and at the south end of this hall there is a separate *estufa* room. After its second *estágio* the wine is taken, generally speaking, to the company's stores at Bélem to mature.

The lodge at Bélem stands at the western edge of Câmara de Lobos. It is an extremely attractive five-storey concrete building clad with red tiling, with a wall of glass facing south, through which a large number of stacked-up casks can be seen. One is immediately reminded of an *armazem do sol*. On entering the reception hall, which is on the second floor, the visitor is greeted by an old wooden *lagar*. This level of the building contains offices, laboratories, tasting rooms and the glass-fronted cask store. The casks are reconditioned ones provided by whisky and sherry firms. After having been used for maturing madeira, for which a fee is charged, they are returned to their owners, the company having benefited in two ways—by earning money and avoiding capital outlays on new casks. This is also where many of the company's large vats made from mahogany, or satinwood from Brazil or Angola, are situated.

Elsewhere in the building are a tourist reception area, adjacent to which there is a retail wine shop decorated with wine memorabilia and old photographs, offices, and a cooper's workshop. The production area has an assortment of stainless steel tanks, including four with a 29,000 litre capacity and internal paddles, which are used for blending.

Like most of the older shippers, Henriques & Henriques has associated companies. These are Carmo Vinhos, Lda, established in 1928; Bélem's Madeira Wine, Lda, and Casa dos Vinhos da Madeira, Lda, both established in 1932; and António Eduardo Henriques Sucrs, Lda, established in 1960. Some of these names are still used on labels, though they are not necessarily targeted at specific markets. The company exports to over twenty different countries. Henriques & Henriques produces a full range of wines in a style which it believes has been fairly constant for over a century, and tends to be weighty and concentrated. Tinta Negra is used for the 3 and 5 year old wines; the 10 and 15 year old madeiras are made from traditional varieties. There are three 20 year old wines, *colheitas*, three old soleras, and a range of twentieth-century *gar-*

rafeiras which have had long cask ageing. However, these apart, the special glory of Henriques & Henriques's offering, in my opinion, is a range of old bottled wines which, although they have no specific vintage year, were reckoned to be old wines in 1850! They are very expensive, but it is amazing that they are still available. They are textbook demonstrations of the peaks which old madeira can scale. At the opposite end of the spectrum, the company makes modified wine.

Whether experimental or not, I find Humberto's wines impressive. His philosophy is quite straightforward: 'In all wine I search for the grape and then wrap around it the character of madeira. The acidity, the sugar level and their equilibrium with the alcohol are all necessary to emphasize the character of the grape.' After having limped along for a bit the company is now in very good shape.

Justino's, Madeira Wines, SA

Until the mid-nineties Vinhos Justino Henriques, as the firm was then called, operated from a charmingly old-fashioned office in the Rua do Carmo in Funchal. Now, under a new name and new management, it is situated in Cancela, a modern business park just north of Caniço, to the east of Funchal, where it has a purpose-built winery.

Founded in 1870, Justino Henriques was originally a small family firm. In the 1930s its trade was almost exclusively with Brazil, but the company ran into financial difficulties and in the 1940s and 1950s it developed a market in Canada. By the early 1960s ownership was diffused widely amongst the descendants of the family and, as often happens when there is a large number of owners getting small dividends, they decided to sell the company.

Justino Henriques then belonged for a time to the owners of the Companhia Vinícola da Madeira (which has since gone out of business). In 1981 it was acquired by Sigfredo da Costa Campos, an extrovert Lisboetan of considerable energy and determination with a wide range of sporting interests. A colonel in the Portuguese air force during the troubles in Angola, he commanded a parachute regiment and was being groomed for high command. But he felt his destiny lay in another direction and decided to abandon his military career, later entering the wine trade almost by accident.

Sigfredo da Costa Campos decided that he must expand the company and almost immediately began to cultivate export markets in Europe, the United States and Japan. Having achieved this aim with considerable success, by 1993 he felt that Justino Henriques had arrived at the point where, in order to develop the company, expand its markets and modernize its premises and wine-making technology, an injection of capital was required. To achieve this without undue financial risk, da Costa Campos sought an alliance with the large French import and distribution group La Martiniquaise. At this time La Martiniquaise not only handled about half of his entire export trade—95 per cent of the company's exports were of bulk wine, which constituted some 35 per cent of the island's bulk wine export total—but was the largest importer of madeira into France.

This, in conjunction with EU grants, made it possible for him in 1994 to move the company out of the centre of Funchal, where the difficulties of operating in scattered old buildings with increasingly out-of-date facilities were exacerbated by the city's traffic congestion, into very functional new premises where the whole operation was put under a single roof, thereby substantially reducing production costs. The dominant impression of the winery was, and still is, one of compactness and logical arrangement. At this time the company consisted of just twelve persons, including Colonel da Costa Campos himself, yet Justino Henriques was the second largest producer of madeira on the island, with around a 25 per cent share of the total.

So the company flourished, and with La Martiniquaise behind it, investment and further modernization have been possible on an almost continuous basis since the beginning of the new century, taking advantage, of course, of EU grants when available. This has resulted in the progressive remodelling and upgrading of the original single building, the provision of a second building and, with guidance from La Martinquaise, the acquisition of technically sophisticated vinification and *estufagem* equipment.

The death in 2008 of Sigfredo da Costa Campos almost derailed this tale of prosperous advance. The da Costa Campos family had no interest in continuing with the firm, but La Martiniquaise, which already owned 70 per cent of the shares, stepped in and acquired the family's interest. The company was re-baptized as Justino's, Madeira Wine, SA, and Juan Teixeira, who had joined the company in 2000 and had learned his wine-making skills under Colonel da Costa Campos, was appointed in 2009 as general manager and wine-maker. Originally from Venezuela, he worked in the Ribatejo in the wine sector for four years before marrying a Madeiran and coming to the island. La Martiniquaise give him a pretty free hand, and the company is 100 per cent independent as regards administration and technology.

The company has a staff of twenty, including one cooper. It employs around twelve agents in Câmara de Lobos, Estreito de Câmara de Lobos and São Jorge. There are no contracts with growers, and over the last ten years Justino's has bought from a variable number ranging from a high of 1,130 (2002) and a low of 574 (2012), but which has only once been less than 40 per cent, and has twice been over 50 per cent, of the total number of grape farmers. Tinta Negra (since 2008, much of it organic) comes from Estreito de Câmara de Lobos and Câmara de Lobos; Complexa comes from Câmara de Lobos and Calheta; Sercial from Câmara de Lobos, Seixal and Ribeira de Janela; Verdelho from São Vicente and Câmara de Lobos; Boal from Câmara de Lobos and Calheta; and Malvasia from São Jorge and Arco de São Jorge. In 2012, Justino's also bought grapes from 27 other growers for the production of table wine, being one of only two madeira producers to operate in this sector.

Currently, Justino's has a storage capacity of 5,750,000 litres in stainless steel, and of 1,750,000 litres in wood—pipes of 300, 350 and 650 litres, *tonéis* of between 1,000 and 3,000 litres, and vats of from 10,000 to 40,000 litres. The *estufagem* capacity is 470,000 litres, and Justino's boasts the largest (100,000 litres) *estufa* on the island, heated by three jackets. The ageing cellar, like the whole complex, is at 350 m above sea level, and this is judged to be too cold, so in 2014 solar panels will be installed to boost the temperature of the *adega*.

Until 2001, when they came to an end, bulk exports were 80 per cent of the company's business. It now produces a modest 25,000 litres of modified wine. As with most shippers, wines made from Tinta Negra and other red varieties are Justino's bread-and-butter products, with 10 per cent allocated to its cheapest brand, 75 per cent to its 3 year old, 10 per cent to its 5 year old, and 5 per cent to its 10 year old qualities. Five *colheitas* of consecutive harvests of Tinta Negra are currently on the market—all of them sweet—along with four *colheitas* made from traditional varieties. Many more of both red and white varieties are being matured with the aim of launching them after more than ten years of ageing, while there are further stocks of traditional varieties in wood that are intended as future *colheitas* or 15 year old madeiras, leading Justino's to claim that it has the largest inventory of potential *colheitas* on the island. The *garrafeiras* range in dates from 1933 to 1980. Many of the older years were purchased from the Companhia Vinícola da Madeira. A selection of Justino's madeiras is also available under the Broadbent label (Broadbent Selections Inc.) in the USA.

Justino's is one of the only two madeira companies producing table wines (white, red and rosé). The local market accounts for 98 per cent of production, with a small amount exported to Germany and Poland. Exports of madeira go to twenty-eight countries, the main markets, in order of importance, being France, USA, Germany, Japan, Austria, Belgium and Holland. The company is energetically seeking out new export markets in the belief that this will contribute towards the stabilization of its financial situation in the face of economic problems nearer home. Justino's madeiras used to be available at Wine and Wicker, a shop close to the old Savoy Hotel but, like the hotel building, the shop has now disappeared. Creating its own outlet in the centre of Funchal is a top priority for the company.

Fifteen years ago I would have said that Justino Henriques, concentrating as it then did on the shipment of bulk wine, was the least impressive of all the madeira shippers. I wrote then: 'The wines have a baked and toasted character which seems quite old-fashioned, and contrasts with the fruitier styles coming into vogue elsewhere'. That was a polite way of saying that I did not like them. The situation is now totally the reverse. Justino's is now the largest shipper on the island both in terms of production and of exports.

The basic wines are now technically excellent and, year by year, as can be confirmed on the company's website, collect a considerable number of awards, making Justino's perhaps the most potentially interesting of today's shippers. It will be fascinating to see how the company progresses as its stocks mature and its inventory gains in depth and diversity.

Madeira Wine Company, SA

Some of the history of this firm, originally known as the Madeira Wine Association, has been told already.[5] In 1981 its name was changed to the Madeira Wine Company (MWC), prompted by the fact that the word 'Association' has no legal significance in Portuguese law. The change was therefore purely nominal and did not mark any alteration in the ownership, structure or running of the firm.

Essentially a single company, during most of the second half of the twentieth century the MWA traded under a large number (though not all) of its associated companies' names. This meant that a complete range of each company's blends, with whatever variations of these were demanded by different markets, had to be produced, and that these were marketed throughout the world through a network of different agents. A more cumbersome and, as it finally turned out, unworkable way of selling madeira could hardly be imagined. Even the general manager, who travelled the world to sell the company's madeira, had to maintain the fiction by having a series of trade cards appropriate to each firm he represented. Ferdinando Bianchi, who was general manager in the 1960s and early 1970s, told me about the situation in the 1950s: 'I travelled quite a lot in Germany. We had seventy or eighty agents. When I travelled there it was a most difficult time for me, because I had to produce different cards. I remember once that I went to Frankfurt, and I travelled under the name of Welsh. The following day I was going to Mainz—that is a distance of about forty or fifty kilometres—and I was travelling under the name of Leacock. And it happened that our agent who came from Mainz wanted me to visit his colleague in Frankfurt who dealt with Welsh. I was so embarrassed to explain to him that I couldn't go there, because I had been there the day before.'

I remember going to the MWA during my first visit to the island in 1973. In the centre of the laboratory there was an island of shelving with an immense number of half-empty bottles. These, I was told, were the reference samples of the entire range of the company's blends. Once opened, they were kept for two years! Latterly, in the 1980s, this crazy system was simplified a bit, and the company traded in the names of only nine companies: Blandy's, Cossart Gordon, Ferraz, Freitas Martins, Gomes, Leacock, Lomelino, Miles and Power Drury (although the labels of some of the other companies were still used). The company's oenologist at this time, Ivo Couto, recalls that even with this simplification the task of providing all the required blends, which came from the common stock of the company, was immense.

The MWA was put in a very serious position when all Portuguese banks were nationalized after the 1974 Revolution. The company dealt with only one bank, and the committee of workers which ran it was more interested in using money to promote socially worthwhile projects than to age stocks of madeira. All lines of credit were suddenly cut off and difficult labour problems arose. The older generation of directors, rather bewildered by events, decided to leave the company. At this time the Blandys and Leacocks were the principal (and equal) shareholders, and within a period of two years Richard Blandy, William Leacock and Anthony Miles entered the company to represent their respective families. The three formed an executive committee to deal with the situation, chaired by Anthony Miles.

Rationalization of the company was long overdue. It badly needed further capitalization, but the shareholders had no faith in the future and held back. Blandy's wanted to develop the company and invest in it: Leacock's did not. A stalemate of some four years ensued, resolved only when Blandy's acquired Leacock's shares and thereby a controlling interest. Meanwhile, although the company had found another bank and loans were secured against stocks, this was a difficult time to trade. In the late 1970s and 1980s the escudo was undergoing devaluation at 12 per cent per annum, bank interest rates rose to 29 per cent per annum and there was at one time 36 per cent inflation per annum. Against this, sales were stagnant and interest repayments rose to over 20 per cent of revenue. For a number of years, therefore, the company did not make a profit.

Under Blandy's control some progress was made, and the financial problems were eventually resolved. But it was a turbulent period for the company, and not just because of adverse trading conditions. During this time there were five different managing directors, four financial directors and four production directors—which hardly suggests a continuous forward direction or an established policy—and as a result, the required radical rationalization did not take place.

Blandy's were well aware of these problems, and they saw others looming on the horizon. During this period multinational companies not only began to buy the best-selling brands but also their distributors, who frequently did not wish to carry what they regarded as fringe, low-volume products—amongst which they numbered madeira. Lines of world-wide distribution began to look shaky. Also, in the run-up to Portugal's entry into the EU, it was becoming clear that the methods used to make madeira were not in line with the best wine-making practice, and that the EU would insist on standards more stringent than those then observed on the island. With all these problems in mind, Blandy's decided to look for a business partner to help resolve the situation and take the company forward.

The Symington family, which then owned six port firms, were approached by Blandy's and became shareholders in the MWC in 1988. It seemed a marriage made in heaven because, as Richard Blandy pointed out: 'There is an identity of interests between us: we are both family firms; we have the same outlook on life and the same way of doing business; and we are both in very similar businesses. In addition, the Symingtons were able to provide the MWC with considerable wine expertise and a wider distribution network than we already had.' Following the Symingtons' entry into the company, the other shareholders, taking advantage of an offered premium, disposed of their interests to the Symingtons, who then took a controlling interest in the firm.

The necessary rationalization of the company soon followed, though not without hiccups. Appalled, they said, by the general standards of viticulture and vinification on most of the island—'We did not know how bad things really were until we arrived', one of the directors told me—the Symingtons immediately began to reform the technical processes of the company's wine-making. A new, Oporto-trained oenologist was soon appointed, and with him came a conscious intention to make a wine with a more open, fruity character (partly achieved by reducing the amount of *estufagem*). The results were fairly swift. So was the reaction of the trade, from whom the Symingtons received a generally hostile reception. The company was accused of trying to turn madeira into a kind of port, and for a while the IVM tasting panel consistently rejected the new style. However, an accommodation was soon reached. The present MWC style is still marked by a strong fruit character, but nobody, I think, would ever mistake the wine for port. Its vindication, in the company's view, is its enthusiastic acceptance by the market.

In organizational terms, the company immediately benefited from the Symington distribution network. It was decided to confine the brands under which the company marketed to four—Blandy's, Cossart Gordon, Leacock and Miles—while maintaining some other company names purely as labels in markets where they had become familiar, and which there was no point in upsetting by needless change. Of these four brands, Blandy's has been and is the most important and, in line with the Symingtom trading philosophy of promoting a family image, since the Blandys are not only the sole family from the original Association to survive as actual owners of the company, but also its most successful brand, it was a natural step to build the future of the MWC round them. The renaming of the company's São Francisco Lodge in the centre of town as The Old Blandy's Wine Lodge—now just The Blandy's Wine Lodge—signalled the change of direction. From this point on the emphasis was to be firmly on Blandy's Madeiras Lda, the company founded in 1925 specifically to manage the wine part of the family's commercial empire.

To madeira drinkers Blandy's is pre-eminently a firm of shippers. What is less widely known is that, from the late nineteenth century onwards, Blandy's has been a group of companies with a wide range of interests besides wine. John Blandy established himself in Funchal in 1811 as a general trader, and with his sons Charles Ridpath and John founded John Blandy and Sons. After phylloxera, wine began to lose its dominance in their concerns, whilst shipping (repair, servicing with coal and water, tugs, lighters and coastal vessels, Lloyd's agency) assumed an ever larger place. Offices were opened in London in 1838 and the Canary Islands in 1886. In the twentieth century these interests became astonishingly diverse, including running a bank, a travel agency, a shipping company and agency for visiting cruise liners, flour milling, running the local newspaper (with the largest provincial circulation in Portugal), commercial and residential property development, the export of orchids and an interest in a luxury hotel chain, which owns the Cliff Bay Hotel on the island. Reid's Hotel, which Blandy's had owned since 1936, was sold in 1996.[6]

Marriages made in heaven do not, however, necessarily last for ever. Not far into the new century there began to be rumours that some members of the Symington family had regrets about its involvement in madeira and wanted a divorce. In 2006, the Symington Family Estates purchased the vineyards and wineries belonging to Cockburn's, the port firm, and acquired the right to produce the port on behalf of the brand owners. In December 2012, it bought the brand outright. The purchases made a big addition to the Symingtons' already huge port production empire, managed by Paul Symington and three of his cousins, and added appreciably to the task of running and developing it in a difficult economic climate. Involvement in madeira, sadly, began to be perceived as a distraction, and in 2011 a decision was taken to disengage, at least partially, to concentrate on their port interests. It was not a complete divorce, however, and was brought about in a completely amicable way: the Symingtons maintained a 10 per cent stake in the MWC, but sold their remaining shares to the Blandys who now have, in what appears to be a natural evolution in promoting the MWC as essentially a family firm, a controlling interest. Moreover, most appropriately, this happened during the bicentenary of the founding of the firm by John Blandy. And, with the Symingtons still with a toehold, very fortunately access to the Symington distribution network remains in place. In the same year as the family took control of the MWC, Christopher Blandy (the son of Adam) became CEO on the retirement of Jacques Faro da Silva. Having spent two years gaining marketing experience with the Symingtons in Vila Nova de Gaia and a spell in Washington, D.C., in the hotel trade, Christopher joined the MWC in 2007, and became a member of the board in 2010. From now on the intention is that the company will be led by a member of the family.

'A cathedral of wine' is how a rival shipper has described the Blandy's Wine Lodge, situated on the Avenida Arriaga in the centre of Funchal. This is one of the two sites occupied by the MWC and it is visited by 200,000 people a year. Originally part of the site of the São Francisco monastery,[7] which was on the adjacent São Francisco Gardens, the buildings enclose one of the oldest mediaeval streets in Funchal and incorporate some walls of the original sixteenth-century buildings. The expulsion of religious orders from Portugal in 1834 brought about the destruction of the monastery and the transformation of the site. The original John Blandy purchased a house at 8 Rua de São Francisco[8]—currently being refurbished to provide four self-catering holiday apartments—and acquired the spacious wine stores which already existed there. In 1925, when Blandy's became part of the MWA, the new company was established in these premises and has remained there ever since. In 1996 and 1997 the fabric of the building was comprehensively renovated, with the installation of smoke detectors and emergency lighting, but without disturbing its character. More recent changes have linked the Blandy's Wine Lodge to an adjacent shopping arcade, making the mediaeval street mentioned above into a public throughfare.

The lodge is indeed atmospheric, consisting of a cluster of old buildings round a cobbled central courtyard with, exotically, palm and banana trees. It is geared to receiving tourists and, in addition to a tasting room decorated with a famous mural painting on madeira wine themes by Max Romer, has an indoor museum of documents and wine artefacts; a semi-outdoor area where there is a cooperage display, and an old wooden *lagar* from Quinta Grande bearing the emblem of the Jesuits; a souvenir shop and a wine shop. There is also a special bar where *garrafeira* wines can be sampled (on payment) by the glass. But although welcoming tourists is an important aspect of its function, this is a working wine lodge, and most of its space is devoted to a series of rooms and attics for *canteiro* maturation of the wine in wood (casks and vats), without a steel tank to be seen. Four of the stores, named after the four companies, hold casks and demijohns. At the top of the building is the Sotão de Amêndoas (the Almond Attic), where the natural temperature reaches 28°C and mainly Blandy's madeiras are kept, while at ground level, next to the tasting room, is the store with the oldest wines still in cask (back to 1920 Boal). Above the tasting room on a specially reinforced floor are twenty-five huge satinwood vats holding about 10,000 litres each (weighing 250 tons overall), while elsewhere, at ground level, there are some of the largest vats on the island. The total storage (all in wood) of the São Francisco lodge is 621,000 litres. Guided tours of the lodge and museum are given every working day.

The MWC's second centre, called Mercês after the street which runs behind it, stands on a site which the company acquired when Lomelino and Miles joined it. Mercês is situated at the top of the Rua dos Ferreiros, and is a workaday set of buildings as unglamourous as the São Francisco lodge is charismatic. Before it was started in 1963, everything was done at the São Francisco lodge and at a small *adega* the company used to own at Estreito de Câmara de Lobos. Mercês is very much the MWC's operational centre, and here we find the company's offices, vinification plant, *estufas*, laboratories, stores and more space for ageing wine. In the 1990s it was planned to move to a new EU-subsidized winery on a spectacular site at Cabo Girão. Alas, at an advanced stage of planning it was discovered that the company had unhappily chosen, as one director put it, 'the one spot on Madeira that wasn't solid rock'. The cost of stabilizing the site would have been prohibitively expensive, so this plan had to be abandoned and in 1998 it was decided to invest in revitalizing the Mercês site. Work was finished in 2001. The plan is still to relocate, but the time is still not ripe.

Looking from the street, the open-air grape reception area and vinification plant, which were installed in 1985, are the first thing to greet the eye. There are two vinification lines: eight stainless steel autovinifiers, with a total capacity of 300,000 litres, capable of dealing with up to 100,000 kg of grapes per day, and, for white varieties, a series of tanks of varying capacities from 7,500 to 25,000 litres, the largest being used also for rosé and white wine. In addition there is a cold treatment tank for white wines made without skin contact. Behind the vinification tanks are others (formerly belonging to Silva Vinhos) which are used for the clarification of wines and the fermentation of some Tinta Negra dry wines. To the left of the vinification plant is a warehouse for dry stock and wet stock ready for shipping, while behind are the offices, laboratory and tasting room. Finally, on the right, we find the cooperage (housing four craftsmen), the *estufas* and the *adega*, with storage of 1,600,000 litres in tanks, an equal amount in wood, and 645,000 litres in stainless steel. Most of the storage is in large vats: 80 per cent are made from American oak and 20 per cent from Brazilian satinwood. The rest is in casks, which are stored at ambient temperature. There is an almost fully automated bottling line with three streams.

The MWC's wine-maker is Francisco Albuquerque, who is related to the Borges family. He has achieved the remarkable feat of winning the coveted Fortified Winemaker of the Year award over three successive years (2006–08), and has brought a shower of international wine trophies and awards to the company. Apart from working for the MWC, he is the enthusiastic producer of perhaps the most impressive Madeira table wine, Primeira Paixão.[9] Francisco is assisted by Filipe Azevedo.

In the 1990s the MWC was the largest producer on the island, but today that honour goes to Justino's. A third of its sales are on the island, and the UK is its biggest export customer (20 per cent), followed by Belgium and the United States, Japan, France and Switzerland, the Netherlands and Finland. The MWC was the first to come to the market with the new-style *colheitas*—a 1994 Harvest Wine Malvazia—and this has turned into its most successful category of wine in the last three years. It built on this commercial success by introducing 'Alvada' in 2002. This is a 5 year old 50–50 blend of Boal and Malvazia, and was the first time a blend of two traditional varieties had been offered to the public. It quickly caught on, particularly in Japan, and the idea has been successfully taken up by Barbeito. In the same vein, Blandy's came out with a limited edition Centennial Blend of all four classical varieties in 2011—but combining dry and sweet varieties in this way may seem like little more than a gimmick, despite the fact that it received some critical acclaim. Sadly the MWC's stocks of old dated wines from before World War Two, apart from Boal 1920, have vanished, and we are now on to post-war dated madeiras which, nevertheless, are of a very high standard. Only twenty years ago the company still had some nineteenth-century madeiras on offer, such as an 1863 Boal, an 1882 Verdelho and an 1899 Terrantez. That tells its own tale. It will be interesting to see how the company develops. I detect a certain hesitation about jettisoning the MWC name, but with the company being Blandy's in almost all but name, I think the present situation will have to resolve itself sooner or later. Whatever happens, I am sure that the firm will very fittingly continue the centuries-old tradition of British involvement in the Madeira wine trade.

Pereira D'Oliveira (Vinhos), Lda

This is a small, long-established family firm. It was founded in 1850 by João Pereira D'Oliveira, the owner of property, including vineyards, at São Martinho. The firm is now run by two brothers, Aníbal and Luís, representing the fifth generation of the family. Aníbal joined the firm in 1958. At that time the firm was run by his father, Agostinho—who, apart from having responsibility for the family farm, also had a job at Funchal city hall—and his brother João (their uncle), who died in 1968. In the same year, with their father now in sole control, Luís also came into the firm, and the two brothers inherited his mantle when he died in 1988. Aníbal, having been wine-maker, is now on the sales side, while Luís, who also helps with sales, looks after administration. Aníbal's son, Filipe, who joined the company in 1987, took over wine-making from his father in 1998. A third brother, Miguel, who is in shipping, is a sleeping partner. Twenty-two people work in the company.

Pereira D'Oliveira incorporates four other firms. The first is Julio Augusto Cunha, dating from 1820, which was purchased by the two brothers' grandfather (another João) at the beginning of the century when the Cunha family ran out of heirs. Next comes João Joaquim Camacho, which became part of the firm through the brothers' mother, to whose family it had belonged. The third is Vasco Luís Pereira e Filhos, and the latest addition, by purchase, Adegas de Torreão, Lda. Pereira D'Oliveira, however, only trades under one name in order to prevent confusion.

The company's present headquarters is a very beautiful and atmospheric lodge in Funchal, just around the corner from the Praça do Município in the Rua dos Ferreiros. The date 1619 above the door indicates the age of the building rather than the firm; apparently it was a school in the eighteenth and nineteenth centuries. Pereira D'Oliveira moved here in 1911 having started off in premises (which they still own) in the Rua Santa Maria and the Travessa do Forno. The firm intends to develop a warehouse it owns near the central market in the Rua Visconde de Anadia to provide another central sales outlet and more space for ageing wines, but plans for this have been put on hold for two reasons. The first is the damage that was caused by the big flood in 2010, and the second is that, in 2001, Pereira D'Oliveira purchased Adegas de Torreão, Lda, a *partidista* firm founded in 1949 by Vasco Loja. With this purchase came a warehouse (adjacent to the MWC's Mercês complex), which, now refurbished, and with a new insulated roof, is used mainly for maturing wine in newly-purchased wooden vats—including one with a capacity of 55,000 litres. It also provides a venue for group tastings in large concrete former *estufa* tanks which have been adapted to provide a novel setting.

The original family farm at São Martinho—comprising livestock, sugar cane, bananas, vineyards, and an *adega* that was used for making the Pereira D'Oliveira wines—no longer exists. It required twenty-six workers, and labour shortages finally sealed its fate. The family started to sell off the 15 hectares of vineyards, which used to supply part of the firm's needs, in the 1990s, and where there used to be vines now there are houses. Pereira D'Oliveira prefers in any case to buy its grapes, because that way it can control the quality better, and it deals with between 80 and 110 producers. Grapes—between 150,000 and 280,000 kilograms each year, depending on the company's needs and the quality of the vintage—are sourced mainly from Estreito de Câmara de Lobos, Campanário (Quinta Grande), Calheta, São Vicente, Seixal and Ponta Delgada. Between 70 and 80 per cent of this is Tinta Negra. The firm is actively looking for a site outside Funchal with planning permission for a new winery and has postponed the acquisition of new equipment until this has been found. Meanwhile, the existing equipment has been moved to Torreão, and *estufagem* of Tinta Negra is carried out in a warehouse owned by the company in Camacha.

Pereira D'Oliveira is blessed with an unrivalled stock of old wines, dating back to 1850. Many of the oldest originate from the family companies it has absorbed over time, whilst others, such as a Bastardo 1927, are part of the unbottled stocks of the recently-acquired Adegas de Torreão. But almost certainly the most important factor in enabling the company to build up and conserve its impressive inventory is the reluctance of Aníbal's and Luís's father, Agostinho, to export any of his madeiras. He absolutely set his face against it, preferring to sell them only on the island, and he was happy just to consolidate stocks and see them build up. Thus, for a period of forty-five years between the 1930s and the 1970s, no wine at all was exported. Only in the 1980s did he belatedly yield to the counsels of his sons. We are the beneficiaries of his stubbornness. It is a matter of wonder that we can still purchase centenarian vintages over the counter from Pereira D'Oliveira when, even by the end of last century, there was no other shipper of which this was true. D'Oliveira wines of up to about eighty years old are, in general, still in cask, while older wines are now kept in demijohns. In my opinion, the house style of the Pereira D'Oliveira vintage wines is characterized by the sort of weight and concentration which indicates long cask ageing and minimal refreshing; they say they do none at all.

There is, of course, a range of aged madeiras. Unusually, these are all blends of Tinta Negra up to and including 15 year old wines. They are clearly well-made wines, especially the older blends. It is all a matter of taste whether you find Tinta Negra an appealing variety. Of more interest to me are the *colheitas*, all of them, by contrast, varietal. These in some cases have been aged close to the limit of the category and display qualities akin to the company's *garrafeiras*.

Pereira D'Oliveira's export market has been increasing steadily over the past fifteen years and accounts for between 60 and 70 per cent of annual sales. The United States (where Vieux Vins has been its agent since 1994) comes top of the list; next comes the United Kingdom (where Bovey Wines has been its agent since 1986); after it, in order, are Belgium, Japan, Canada, Norway, Sweden and five other countries. The company's policy has not been altered by any difficulties in the economic outlook. It intends to go on being a small firm and, as Luís makes clear, has no interest in competing in the world of size comparisons. What is important, he says, is to advance slowly and in a safe way, to remain dedicated to quality, and to endeavour to maintain a good, in-depth stock of old vintages. Madeira enthusiasts will say 'Amen' to that.

Vinhos Barbeito (Madeira), Lda

This company was officially founded in 1948 by Mário Barbeito, but it really began in 1946 when Barbeito started to trade in wine privately with his brother. He was very much a self-made man. Born in 1905, he trained himself as an accountant and worked for the Companhia Vinícola da Madeira. Just after World War Two, Barbeito went to Brazil in search of new customers and returned with an order for 5,000 cases, but a difference of opinion with the firm led him to set up in the wine business on his own. In the postwar climate of uncertainty, it was perhaps a courageous decision. He was evidently quite well off by this time, for not only did he acquire substantial stocks of wine in cask, but right from the start he began to make his own wine. He acquired a building close to Reid's Hotel on the Estrada Monumental which had originally been established as a sugar mill by Pedro Pires in 1887,[10] and started off his new business there.

Mário Barbeito died in 1985. Sadly, our knowledge of how the company developed in its earlier years is somewhat sketchy, for few written records were kept. We do know that he quickly built up exports to Denmark and Sweden, and a little to Norway, both in cask and in bottle. Barbeito was a complex and cultivated man; quite apart from his wine interests, he was a considerable scholar and collector of books, of which he amassed a collection of 23,000. They occupied all the available space in his house, which had to be extended to accommodate them. His special interest was Christopher Columbus, about whom he gathered a notable collection of books and memorabilia over a period of sixty years, and these were latterly housed in a small museum to Columbus situated in the basement of the company's retail outlet, Diogo's Shop, in the centre of Funchal. However, the flood of 2010 inundated the basement in which the museum and book collection were housed, leaving mud to a depth of half a metre which had to be dug out over many days. The books disintegrated into a sort of porridge, and 22,000 volumes were lost. Restoration work continues on the 1,500 that were salvaged. The shop has been discontinued.

In 1972 Mário Barbeito's daughter, Dona Manuela de Freitas, began to help her father with running the business. The first two of her five children were at school and she wanted something to do. She went abroad to find new business, building up the export side of the firm. A gifted and charismatic businesswoman, she proved to be immensely successful and quickly became a popular figure in the trade. In 1980, when her father was seventy-five, Dona Manuela more or less took charge of the company, which she continued to run single-handedly after his death in 1985. In 1991 two of her sons, Miguel and Ricardo, entered the firm, and in the same year the family decided to sell 50 per cent of Barbeito to Kinoshita International Company Ltd. This is a large Japanese firm of wine and spirits distributors which also runs an extensive chain of delicatessen stores. It had been handling Barbeito's exports to Japan since 1967. This was more than a purely commercial marriage, because during the more than twenty years of their business relationship the two families behind the companies had got to know each other well—and coincidentally, both companies are now managed by the third generation of their respective families. Their agreement to join forces, Ricardo de Freitas says, was on both sides as much a matter of the heart as of the head. Although the entry of Miguel and Ricardo into the company secured the family succession, Dona Manuela felt that the company needed an injection of new blood; and so, with Portugal's entry into the EU, Kinoshita were happy to establish a stronger link with Europe. Dona Manuela retired from the company in 1992.

At that point the day-to-day management of the company was in the hands of Ricardo, acting as general manager, and Miguel, who was in charge of other family businesses (motor cycles, office renting and banana production). In 2004, however, Miguel left the company and the youngest brother, José, joined. He has charge of promotion, advertising, and the company's website. Emanuel, yet another brother, joined the company in 2007, and he manages the legal side of the business. Ricardo, a history graduate, who worked for a year as a schoolteacher before deciding to enter the family business, remains as general manager and wine-maker. He exudes energy and enthusiasm for his job. 'I am more patient with wine and less so with other things', he confesses. And, indeed, for wine there is no end to the trouble he is prepared to take.

With the involvement of Kinoshita and Ricardo at the helm, a transformation of the firm's management and accountancy methods took place, Barbeito quickly became the most sophisticatedly computerized of all madeira firms. The Japanese partners remain fully involved. They monitor the performance and financial affairs of the company, are kept fully and constantly informed of all relevant developments, and participate in all important decisions regarding marketing strategy and sales. Nevertheless, the ambience of the company has not changed. As Ricardo de Freitas told me when I interviewed him for the original edition of this book, 'Every day I realize that a part of my grandfather is still here.' He made the point by opening the drawer of his grandfather's desk—at which he still works—to show that Mário Barbeito's box of pens and clothes brush were still there. And, even now, if you look around the private tasting room, you can see Mário's glass-fronted office filing cabinet and, more poignantly, a wooden statue and a globe salvaged from the Columbus museum. Ricardo, when he was a boy, always preferred to help his grandfather with his books instead of going out to play with his friends, so the loss of the Columbus collection has been a very bitter blow to him.

The most important development in the company, however, has been its decision to leave the rented lodge in Funchal where Mário Barbeito started in business. It was an awkward if atmospheric building, and I well remember, on visits there, seeing women working at pasting labels on to the wicker-covered bottles (modelled on the flask-shaped bottles used by Mateus Rosé) that were once an important part of Barbeito's image in Japan. Other women would be hand-corking them, and it made a colourful if quaint scene. It soon became clear that this did not project the image of the go-ahead company that Barbeito was fast becoming, and, despite investment in improved fermentation equipment, development was hampered by the fact that the company made its wine at a vinification centre at Estreito de Câmara de Lobos, while *estufagem* and the maturing of the wine were carried out in somewhat cramped conditions in Funchal. A decision was made to take advantage of EU grants and to move to a new location.

Thus it was that, in June 2008, Barbeito began its move out of Funchal to a new, purpose-designed *adega* at Câmara de Lobos. The move was not completed until November, but the company was able to make the 2008 vintage in its new premises. Situated in an industrial park, the *adega* sits quite prominently on the skyline of the ridge that runs inland from the Cabo Girão, and can be seen from the road that climbs up from the town. Apart from a *canteiro* wine-ageing store at the Adega de Bela Vista in Câmara de Lobos, all the company's activities are now centred here. There is a fermentation capacity of 97,000 litres (including the 7,000 litres capacity robotic *lagar*) for Tinta Negra, and of 78,000 litres (30 x 2,600 litres) for white varieties, and a storage capacity of 275,000 litres in wooden *tonéis*, and 666,000 litres (including fermentation tanks) in stainless steel. Together with a further stainless steel storage capacity of 230,000 litres at the Adega de Bel Vista, this gives a global storage capacity of 1,346,000 litres.

Since 1995 Barbeito has had stainless steel *estufas* with digitally-controlled jacket heating—the first firm to introduce them to Madeira. They work very efficiently and have eliminated the need to carry out extra treatments. They have made a huge improvement to the quality of the Tinta Negra wine. Ricardo is also delighted with the results of using the robotic *lagar*, which came into being through discussions with friends in the Douro between 2004 and 2006. It carries out the same programme as for making port—that is ten minutes crushing every two hours over a period of seven days. Organic Tinta Negra is used. The extra maceration and greater oxidation in the *lagar* gives a darker coloured wine than that obtained by pumping over. The wine, according to Ricardo, has a more consistent evolution of aromas and structure, making it more full-bodied. One part of what is produced is matured as *canteiro* wine. The rest is used to improve the quality and colour of the 3 year old madeira.

The high altitude of the *adega*, which is at approximately the same altitude as the Cabo Girão (580 m), has consequences. One is that, because the ambient temperature remains relatively cool, louvred vents make it possible to use currents of cool air from outside to control the inside temperature during the vintage, especially at night time. This also results in a kind of natural cold filtration. There is also a small experimental vineyard, largely to satisfy Ricardo's curiosity. He planted it first with Verdelho, just to see how well or badly it would do at such a high altitude. It did well. Now he is experimenting with Sercial.

Barbeito has a staff of twenty-two. Over the last five years the company has bought from between 90 and 110 growers. Half of the Tinta Negra comes from São Vicente, and half from Estreito de Câmara de Lobos. Sercial is sourced from Câmara de Lobos and Jardim da Serra, while Verdelho and a little Boal come from São Vicente. Most Boal comes, however, from Prazeres and Raposeira (on the south coast, north west of Calheta), and the Malvazia comes from São Jorge. A small amount of Bastardo has been sourced since 2009 from São Jorge (this is made in a dry style with 1° Baumé). Annual production in the same period has been around 230,000 litres, with annual sales of about 160,000 litres. The company produces neither modified wine nor table wine.

In order of decreasing size, Barbeito's markets are Japan (unsurprisingly), the United States, Madeira, the United Kingdom, Belgium (which occasionally overtakes the UK), mainland Portugal, Russia and Germany. Its global share of the export market is 5.5 per cent, representing 9.6 per cent of its value. Barbeito has excelled in diversifying its products. For example, it is the only firm that produces 5 year old wines from both Tinta Negra and the classical varieties. It also makes ranges of wine for special customers like Emanuel Berk's Rare Wine Company in the United States, for which an affordable Historic Series of 'vintage character' wines reflecting the individuality of the classical varieties has been created. Currently there are nine in the series, and each is named after a place, a ship, and even a family with a special historical association with madeira. It is no exaggeration to say that this series has been hugely influential in generating a new interest in madeira in America. In the same way, Barbeito produces madeiras specially for Fortnum and Mason, the well-known London grocers. The diversity is increased by a number of unique, one-off madeiras such as the special cask series (individual casks of wine of superlative quality are bottled without having been blended), special lots (which include blends of different varieties), limited editions, and ranges of *colheitas and garrafeiras*, or *frasqueiras* as Ricardo prefers to say. And, of course, from 2006 Barbeito has been bottling the Malvazia from the Fajã dos Padres. There is a marketing inventiveness at work here which some other companies might emulate to their advantage.

The style of Barbeito's madeiras is characterized by slightly more acidity than those of other houses. Ricardo aims to produce wines which are extremely elegant at all levels, with a pure varietal character, and are aromatic and well-balanced. His view of the market, and of Barbeito's place in it, remains unchanged. 'We don't want to be a big company; we want to be a company from which people wish to buy wine'. He is fortunate, because there are many people who wish to do just that.

PART IV

PRESENT AND FUTURE

15

TODAY AND TOMORROW

Many of the issues left hanging in the air in the final chapter of the first edition of this book have now been addressed, or are being addressed, or have turned out not to have the urgency they then appeared to possess. Work on the *cadastro* is, at last, in progress. Bulk wine exports, to be bottled abroad, no longer exist. The transition to the new regime of modified and disqualified wines was, as Colonel da Costa Campos predicted, a relatively smooth one. Although the vineyard area of direct producers remains stubbornly large, its reduction is not perceived as the urgent problem that it seemed to be to the IVM. There is as much Tinta Negra as the shippers need at the moment—indeed, in 2012, there was an over-supply and, for the time being, IVBAM has put an embargo on converting any more vineyards to Tinta Negra. If there is a problem it is that the shippers would like to see an increase in the supply of the traditional grape varieties. IVBAM does what it can to encourage growers to increase the supply, but there appears to be a rather stubborn reluctance to respond. Younger growers, however, are coming on the scene, and they appear to be more open to change. Figures for reconversion are disappointing.[1] But, one way or another—and, as we have seen, the MWC has taken the matter into its own hands—an increase in supply will without doubt eventually occur.

Part of the solution to the problem of reducing the number of direct producers has been, and still is, to develop the production of table wine to cater for the needs of tourism. This remains problematic. The quality of the wines being produced at the moment—and there are only about two dozen of them—is frankly rather poor. Although one producer has managed to export his wine to Switzerland this has not resulted in a rush of importers to the island. Cost, as much as quality, is likely to be a limiting consideration. One of the better red wines sells on the island for €26.00, but in quality terms it hardly begins to compare with, for example, a Chilean wine selling in continental Europe at around €8.00. In 1998 the IVM optimistically anticipated that a viable table wine industry would have been established on the island within three years. That certainly did not happen, and the majority of madeira shippers still refuse to get involved. What one can say, after fifteen years, is that a foundation has been laid. But with the number of wine producers having remained static for the last three years the future development of this tiny sector, despite the enthusiasm of IVBAM, remains uncertain.

I am happy to say that ACIF now appears to function smoothly. Honest trade rivalry apart, there is nothing like open warfare between any of the shippers. The advent of IVBAM has altered the landscape: it appears to be more active in pursuit of wine excellence than was the IVM. As Engenheira Paula Cabaço, the President of the Institute, put it: 'We do not work here in a traditional way of public service. We are more emotional about it, and identify with the product'. Nevertheless, IVBAM does not altogether escape criticism. One or two shippers think IVBAM should be more pro-active in trying to protect the trade from unwelcome interference from 'Brussels bureaucrats', but others (perhaps more politically savvy) realize that there are limits to what is possible in this regard, and believe that IVBAM fights for the Madeira corner as effectively as it can. What is, to me, rather fascinating is that in an industry in which amongst the shippers, public relations apart, only one company (Borges) has women in positions of senior management, IVBAM redresses this imbalance by having women as President of the Institute and as directors of the departments of Viticulture, Viniculture, Quality Control, the Tasting Panel (and Public Relations)—to name only a selection.

If I were asked to say what I think has been the most significant development over the last fifteen years I should undoubtedly reply that it is the vast improvement in the quality of wines that have been subjected to *estufagem*. With technical improvements such as digitally-controlled jacket heating, the hazards from which the wine used to suffer have virtually disappeared. It is now difficult to pick and choose between the various shippers' younger aged wines on quality grounds. The choice, as it should be, is an individual one that has to be made on grounds of style.

The matter about which I have most concern for the future is the fate of *garrafeira* (or *frasqueira*) wines—the so-called vintage wines. These have to have spent a minimum of twenty years in cask before being bottled. In the earlier edition of my book I pointed out a growing tendency for some shippers, 'reluctant perhaps to keep their capital tied up for longer than is necessary and finding their older vintages running out, to put their wines on the market as soon as the law permits'.[2] Although, happily, a reasonable if dwindling number of old vintages remain available, the situation today is vastly different from half a century ago. Consider this extract from a book published in 1968:[3]

On the whole the members of the Wine section of the Funchal Chamber of Commerce do not usually market any vintage less than fifty years old. They like their wines to age in cask for as long as possible. The longer the wine is in cask before being bottled the better, assuming it is well looked after. That is why the Madeira shippers are still only selling vintage wines of the last century. It is still considered that any wine of the present century is "too young". When considered in the context of any other wine in the world, it is an astonishing fact that the vintage Madeiras of the twentieth century are still being reserved for later use.

Over the last fifty years this situation has changed. Part of the reason for the availability of old vintages was the plain fact that because madeira was not a fashionable drink the demand was small. As demand picked up, particularly amongst affluent wine buyers, the reserve of old vintages diminished and prices rose defensively. The general widening of demand for fine wine from a growing number of increasingly wealthy new wine enthusiasts from many countries across the world towards the end of last century and the start of this one has led to intense pressure on reserve stocks and a rapid escalation of prices. Apart from the astonishing inventory of old vintages held by Pereira D'Oliveira, only Justino's has much in the way of pre-1970 vintages on offer. The general age for bottling *garrafeiras* appears to be after about thirty years. Some are now bottled after only twenty-two or twenty-three years. I anticipate that the average age of *garrafeiras* will continue to decrease as economic pressures increase. The only good news is that the range of *colheitas* is likely to increase. In other words, the nature of the madeira drinking experience for future generations is, in the long run, set to change. But, to be fair, this book documents many such changes that have taken place across the centuries. The history of madeira has always been one of change.

Just after the first edition of this volume several amendments in the law regarding the production of madeira took effect. Ironically, the same thing may well happen again, because as this book goes to press ACIF is in discussion with IVBAM about further changes. It is too early to predict what they may be. However, it is widely rumoured that Tinta Negra will at last be recognized as a variety that can be sold under its varietal name instead of just with a simple indication of style. This is something I argued for in 1998. Commercially, given the predominance of the variety in quantitative terms, at that time it would have been, and still would be, an honest way of labelling the majority of aged wines. I would be happy to see that. However, the fact that there are already *colheitas* made from Tinta Negra, albeit anonymously (until you read the producer's technical specification), seems to imply that Tinta Negra would be joining the elite club of traditional varieties that can become *garrafeiras*. If that should happen the trade will be delighted—especially those shippers who are nursing *canteiro* stocks of Tinta Negra. I am, I confess, less happy at that prospect. It is not just by an oversight that Tinta Negra has been excluded from being made as a *garrafeira* over so many years. It is because many experienced producers initially believed (and their successors have gone on believing) that the madeira made from Tinta Negra does not possess the intrinsic nobility that characterizes madeira made from the traditional varieties, and does not develop it even when matured over a twenty-year-long period. This is not an issue of quality, in the sense that, with modern vinification methods and care, Tinta Negra wine can be made which is up to the highest standards. It is just, as perhaps Noël Cossart might have put it, that Tinta Negra has a rustic character that sets it apart from its noble cousins: it is a peasant amongst aristocrats. Ultimately, this boils down to a matter of taste, and I have more than a sneaking suspicion that future generations of drinkers will over-rule my hesitations and doubts.

Another unresolved concern, aired in the first edition, which may or may not be about to change in pending legislation, is the still-vexed question of bottling dates. The fact that the EU does not require bottling dates to be indicated as part of the information given on wine bottle labels appears to give Madeira a license to go on ignoring the problem. To put the matter in simple terms, if I buy a bottle of madeira with an indication of age I know how long (on average) the wine has spent in wood. If I buy a 5 year old madeira, I know that it has had more ageing than a 3 year old madeira, and for that reason I expect to pay more for it, because the quality reflects that extra ageing. I also know that it has had less ageing than a 10 year old madeira, so I expect to pay less for it than I would for the 10 year old wine because I realize that, not having been aged for so long, it will probably have less quality. If I buy a bottle with just a date on it then I have no idea whether the wine in it has been aged for a short or a long time. A *colheita* may have been in wood for anything from five to just short of twenty years. There is no reason why a shipper should not bottle the wine in several batches, as often happens with *garrafeira* madeiras, and the wine of each bottling may well have a different character. One shipper, currently selling a *colheita* which has had rather a long period of ageing tells me that he will offer it as a *garrafeira* in a few years time when it has had its twentieth birthday. More worryingly for the purchaser of old vintages, bottles of young dated wines that were being sold when this book was first issued, and which only had a date on them, now look—as I then predicted—as if they might be *garrafeiras*. There is no way of knowing from the appearance of the bottle alone. If Madeira wishes to protect the integrity of its *garrafeiras* it might, therefore, with advantage copy the port trade, which is in an analogous position. For some considerable time it has been mandatory for port shippers to indicate a bottling date on the labels of their *colheitas*, Vintage, Late Bottled Vintage and 10–40 year old ports—for exactly the reasons indicated above. To this I have to add a rider. To my knowledge three shippers already put bottling dates on their bottles—one by stamping it on the top of the capsule (which is already a shade of very dark grey), and two by lazer etching it in a miniscule way on the glass at the base of the bottles. This may be an aid to stock control, but because the customer may not see black against dark grey, or be able even to notice, let alone read, the glass engraving, it does not solve the problem that exercises me, which is imparting knowledge to the customer.

All of which brings me neatly to the question of nomenclature. Where madeira is concerned it is a muddle. *Colheitas* may be called 'Harvest Wines'—but the MWC uniquely gives special meanings to each of these supposedly equivalent terms. Dated wines may be *colheitas* or *garrafeiras* or *frasqueiras*, but not vintage wines. *Garrafeira* and *frasqueira* are interchangeable terms; two firms (the MWC and Barbeito) prefer to use only the latter, others prefer to use only the former. To the buyer of madeira, unless he has done some research, these remain arcane matters. What sort of marketing is it that makes things so difficult for the customer? The root trouble is that the term *colheita* has been given a restricted meaning which it does not have in ordinary usage. Normally it means, simply, 'harvest' or 'vintage', and that is the meaning it ought to have—not 'a dated wine aged in wood for more than five and less than twenty years'. Is there a way out? Well, one solution might be to follow in the footsteps of Oporto. On the analogy of the distinction between Late Bottled Vintage and Vintage, Madeira might opt for Early Bottled Vintage (i.e. the present *colheita*) and Vintage (i.e. the present *garrafeira*). And, yes, let the English-speaking world continue to use, as indeed several of the madeira shippers themselves do, the word 'vintage' to mean vintage—and never mind what they think about that in Oporto. I encourage my friends in Madeira to outright rebellion.

Food and wine matching has become a much-written-about theme. It is, in short, fashionable. At least one shipper, Ricardo de

Freitas, is passionate about marrying up madeira and food. It is also espoused by IVBAM, I believe quite genuinely, and not just because getting people to drink madeira at mealtimes is a way of selling more of it—just as encouraging the use of madeira with mixers to make long drinks, which I am told are very popular in the discos of Funchal, also achieves the same goal. It is a free world, and I am happy if more and more people are introduced to madeira in whatever circumstances. I confess that neither way of consuming madeira has much appeal for me. When I have been served madeiras with food, my judgement has seldom been that the madeira overwhelms the food, but that the food dulls the wine. The match that seems to work best is with Asian food, when the acidity of the madeira and the spiciness of the food sometimes appear to find an equilibrium. Although it is widely contended, I do not think Malvazia works well with chocolate. Quite simply, the chocolate alters the taste of the Malvazia, and that to my mind spoils it. I would certainly not risk ruining a really splendid old madeira by pairing it with food. Such madeiras are, in Francisco Albuquerque's words, 'wines of contemplation', to have their complexity explored and to be savoured without distraction. As for matching humbler madeiras with food, I remain to be convinced that they really do much that is positive for each other.

So, what of the future? The boom that was evident at the end of last century, when every aspect of Madeira life appeared to be prospering and the outlook for the trade was fairly rosy, was shattered in 2008 and the effects of the crash run on. Mercifully for madeira, although trade faltered it has turned out to be more of a stumble than a headlong fall. Ingenious solutions to cope with new difficulties—like the unprecedented growth in the sale of miniature bottles of madeira, which can be carried in suitcases with relative safety, after the air travel ban on liquids in cabin baggage—have helped to keep things steady. More important has been the underlying subsidy provided by POSEIMA. Of particular interest is a scheme to assist in the improvement of the quality of madeira whereby, if a shipper agrees to age his wine for at least five years, he is paid a minimum of €0.05 per hectolitre per day for the period of participation in the scheme. According to one shipper, without it all shippers' finances would be in the red. However, relatively encouraging figures for tourism and wine sales over the last few years should not be allowed to disguise the fact that thirteen years into the new century, the economy of Madeira, like that of Portugal as a whole, is in pretty poor shape. Money for further development has run out, so the construction cranes which for the last twenty years towered above parts of Funchal have all but disappeared. Apartment blocks stand uncompleted or empty—some estimates put the number of unsold apartments as high as 20,000. No new hotels seem to be under construction and, both in Madeira and on Porto Santo, several have closed. While work on the new harbour continues, work on completing the *via rapida* appears to have stalled, and there are indications everywhere, in the form of empty shops and closed or three-quarters empty supermarkets, of an economy in distress. There are at least a dozen new shops in Funchal offering to buy gold, and unemployment is in excess of twenty per cent. A small gathering of people in the street may not seem significant to the passing tourist, but they are waiting for a distribution of free food. The wine trade, like tourism, has been lucky to have been relatively unscathed amid the surrounding economic gloom. If the market remains somewhat flat in the immediate future, having weathered the storm the madeira trade should be poised, and I believe is poised, to prosper once the economic clouds have cleared. It will not be the first time it has made a come-back after a dip in its fortunes. I think it is fair to say that IVBAM and the shippers recognize that madeira will remain something of a niche market: the glory days of the eighteenth century are never going to be recaptured. But I believe there will always be a core of discriminating wine enthusiasts able to recognize and celebrate madeira's unique place in the fine wine spectrum.

APPENDICES

APPENDIX I

MADEIRA

SOME BASIC INFORMATION

Geological origins and formation

Of long-extinct volcanic origin, Madeira is the tip of a vast plateau more than three-fifths submerged in the sea. Its terrain is rugged and mountainous, the highest point being 1,862 m above sea level. Of the total land area, 47 per cent is above 700 m; 66 per cent has gradients of more than 2.5 per cent; and barely 11.5 per cent has gradients of less than 16 per cent. By far the greater part (about 80 per cent) of the coastline consists of cliffs, and nearly one third of these are considerably over 100 m in height. The highest cliff is Cabo Girão, just west of Câmara de Lobos: at 589 m, it is often claimed to be the second highest in the world (but at least six other higher sea cliffs are listed on Wikipedia).

A central, east-west spinal ridge has a shallow convex orientation towards the south-west, its extremities curving slightly in opposite directions. The central region, the principal area of volcanic activity, consists of spectacular rocky peaks with a conical formation reminiscent of Java. The summits here (Pico Ruivo, Pico do Arieiro, Pico da Torre) are over 1,800 m in height.

To the west of this central region, the island is divided from north (São Vicente) to south (Ribeira Brava) by extended re-entrants which are connected at the pass of Encumeada (1,004 m), over which what used to be the main road connecting the north and south of the island passes. The main highway now passes through a tunnel under the col. Further to the west again there is an extensive plateau, only a little lower than the peaks (Paúl da Serra, 1,400 m), while to the east the mountains gradually give way to less accentuated slopes.

On both the north and south sides of the island, the central mountain ridge is marked in places by considerable erosion, giving indentations or basins separated from each other by vast shoulders of land. Where there are small rivers, their rate of descent can be as steep as 10 per cent.[1] In consequence, the rapidity of their torrential winter flow precludes any alluvial deposit and their paths are marked by deep valleys or ravines with steep, wall-like sides.

Three other features of the landscape are worthy of special note. Where beds of lava in the uplands have been exposed by erosion, they often form mini-plateaux, known as *achadas*, on the slopes of mountains and the sides of valleys. Occasionally—and especially between Paul da Serra and the south coast—rivers with almost parallel courses have between them level or slightly convex areas that slope gently towards the sea; these are called *lombos* or *lombadas*. Finally, both along the coast and inland, erosion has caused landslips at the foot of cliffs, and the resulting tongues of land, known as *fajãs*, are noted for their fertility. All these terms are frequently used in place names.

On account of this geomorphic formation, populated areas are mainly confined to the coastline—especially where there are basins (generally the sites of towns and villages)—to those valleys and re-entrants which have hospitable contours, and inland to *achadas, lombos* and *fajãs*. The island has a total area of 768 sq km (296.5 sq mi).

Climate

The island's climate is largely determined by the north-westerly winds, which prevail for almost the entire year, and the central mountain ridge, which shelters the south coast from the winds to which the north coast is directly exposed.

During the summer these winds carry anticyclonic air masses from the Azores, thereby ensuring a long dry season. This nevertheless remains temperate owing to the cooling effect of the surrounding ocean—except when occasional east winds from Africa produce suffocating conditions by suddenly increasing the temperature and reducing humidity to dramatically low levels (13 per cent). At other seasons, Madeira can be subject to westerly winds, sometimes violent, whose cyclonic character produces abundant rain. The passage of the seasons is less evident at coastal level than at higher altitudes, where seasonal differences become more marked the higher one gets.

Typically, the centre of the island is covered with cloud for much of the year. Temperatures are generally relative to altitude, and as the land temperature along the south coast increases each day, so masses of air rise from the valleys, provoking condensation and cloud formation at about 500 m in winter and slightly higher in summer. In the middle of the day this cloud barrier reduces the heating effect of the sun and helps to maintain, even in summer, a moderate temperature. In the evening the air cools and the process is reversed, as winds push the humid masses into warmer zones where the clouds rapidly dissipate.

On the north coast, by contrast, the dominant wind pushes the humid masses of air against the mountain barrier and they are obliged to rise rapidly. The resultant cloud forms at about 400 m or even lower. This affects both the local temperature and humidity—the former being on average 1.5°C lower than on the south of the island and the latter as much as 10 per cent higher. The clouds also ascend to 1,200–1,400 m and give rise to precipitation, which approaches 3,000 mm each year. The central peaks and Paul da Serra often remain above cloud level, surrounded by a white tablecloth of cloud, and for that reason are much drier than the areas only slightly below them.

Nevertheless, the irregularity of the island's relief gives rise to many microclimates. The hottest areas are the *fajãs* of the south coast. Snow on the peaks is not uncommon in winter. Temperature varies with altitude and exposure, ranging from an average of 16°C in February to 22.3°C in August, giving an annual average of around 19°C on the south coast and 17.5°C on the north. Precipitation also varies with altitude, and normally ranges from 500 mm on the south coast, through 1,200 mm on the north coast, to 3,000 mm in the central part of the island. In Funchal, for example, 63 days of rain would be a typical annual figure. However, the number of rainy days varies widely from year to year. Thus, in Funchal over a thirty-year period the total ranged from 26 to 111 days, while during the same period the total precipitation ranged from 200 mm to 1,138 mm—a clear reminder that we are dealing with a climate that in some respects verges on the tropical, and which has since the eighteenth century subjected the island to fourteen catastrophic floods, the latest of which occurred in 2010.[2] Relative humidity varies from an average 65 per cent in March to 72 per cent in July, with an all-year average of 69 per cent.

Population

The population of Madeira shows fluctuations in size as measured in the ten-yearly census. According to the 2011 census, the total number of inhabitants was 267,302, compared with 245,011 in 2001 and 248,720 in 1990.[3] However, in 1960 the figure was 265,432 (similar to that for 2011), while in 1940 it was 247,000 (comparable to the figures for 1991 and 2001). Although the birth rate is declining, emigration plays a part in swelling the population. In 2009 there were over 7,000 legal immigrants on the island (mainly from South America and the Ukraine). It must also be remembered that emigrants frequently come back to the island in retirement, and even second generation emigrants often return home from Brazil and Portuguese ex-colonies.

The *concelho* of Funchal, the capital, is the largest nucleus of population: 111,892 (41.86 per cent). This is followed by other *concelhos* along the south coast: 43,005 (16.09 per cent) live in Santa Cruz; 35,666 (13.34 per cent) in Câmara de Lobos; and 21,828 (8.17 per cent) in Machico. Only 16,153 (6.04 per cent) live in the north of the island (Santana, São Vicente and Porto Moniz). 5,483 (2.05 per cent) live in Porto Santo.

Political organization

The RAM (Região Autónoma da Madeira)—which includes the whole of the archipelago—was established under the 1976 Constitution as an autonomous region within the Republic of Portugal. It is divided into eleven *concelhos* (councils): Funchal, Câmara de Lobos, Ribeira Brava, Ponta do Sol, Calheta, Porto Moniz, São Vicente, Santana, Machico, Porto da Cruz and Porto Santo. Councils are further subdivided into *freguesias* (parishes).

The autonomous region is governed by a Regional Legislative Assembly, elected for a four-year term by direct universal suffrage on the basis of proportional representation. Each of the eleven councils elects a deputy to the Legislative Assembly for each 3,500 electors (or fraction over 1,750). The Regional Government is formed by a president, nominated in the light of the electoral results, and by the regional secretaries of each government department. It is competent to legislate on a wide range of regional concerns, but in national matters the Lisbon central government prevails. The island is a net recipient of finance from Portugal.

APPENDIX 2

CONTROL OF THE WINE INDUSTRY

Instituto do Vinho, do Bordado e do Artesanato da Madeira

In June, 2006, the Instituto do Vinho da Madeira (IVM) and the Instituto do Bordado, Tapeçarias e Artesanato da Madeira (IBTAM) were merged to form the Instituto do Vinho, do Bordado e do Artesanato da Madeira (IVBAM). IVBAM has, therefore, taken over all the responsibilities regarding the island's wine that were formerly exercised by the IVM. It is integrated with the regional government of the island.

IVBAM is a hierarchical organization consisting of four Directorates and a number of Divisions governed by a Management Council (*Conselho Directivo*) consisting of a President and two other voting members. In this account emphasis is naturally placed on the aspects of the organization that deal with the wine sector, so the parts of IVBAM that are relevant to handicraft (embroidery and wickerwork) are not considered in detail. It should be noted, however, that several of the Divisions that are mentioned have responsibilities for handicrafts as well as the wine sector.

The structure of IVBAM consists fundamentally of two arms. The first provides administrative support to the Management Council, and the second consists of four Directorates (*Direções*) answerable to the Management Council, and a number of units called Divisions (*Divisões*), which are controlled by the Director of which they are a part. The structure of the first arm is as follows. There are four departments that service the Management Council by providing administrative, legal, planning, and computer and communications support. Together these form the Assessory and Support Services (*Serviços de Assessoria e Apoio*). There are additionally three other Divisions which are directly controlled by the Management Council. These are the Division for the Management of Finance, Budgeting and Human Resources (*Divisão de Gestão Financeira, Orçamental e de Recursos Humanos*)—GFORH; the Promotional Division (*Divisão de Promoção*)—Div. Prom—which includes public relations; and the Division of Artistic Creation (*Divisão de Criação Artística*)—Div. CA—which designs exhibitions, makes videos of events, maintains a library of images, and so on.

The second arm, called the Executive and Operative Services (*Serviços Executivos e Operativos*), consists of four Directorates (*Direções*), each with a number of Divisions (*Divisões*). One of the Directorates, the Directorate of Handicraft (*Direção de Artesanato*), the DSART, deals with the island's embroidery and wickerwork industries, and will not be discussed further here. The other three have a responsibility for different aspects of the control and administration of grape and wine production, other alcoholic products, and their commercialisation. Here they are, with their constituent parts. (1) The Directorate of Control and Certification (*Direção de Serviços de Controlo e Certificação*)—the DSCC—comprising the Department of Control (*Departamento de Fiscalização*)—DF, and the Division of Technical Verification (*Divisão de Verificação Técnica*)—Div.VT. (2) The Directorate of Vitivinicultural Services (*Direção de Serviços de Vitivinicultura*)—the DSVV—comprising the Viticultural Division (*Divisão de Viticultura*)—Div.VITI, and the Department of Wine-Production (*Departamento Vinícola*)—DV. (3) The Directorate of Support for Quality Services (*Direção de Serviços de Apoio á Qualidade*)—the DSAQ—which has, under its umbrella, IVBAM's laboratories in Funchal and at the Adega de São Vicente, and the Tasting Panel (*Câmara de Provadores*).

The titles of the Directorates and Divisions and their component parts are more or less self-explanatory. They work in conjunction with each other in discharging their day to day tasks in a rather more complex, interactive way than in the days of the IVM, which had a simpler structure. The scope of each Directorate's responsibilities and how they are discharged is briefly summarized below.

The Directorates

(1) **The Directorate of Control and Certification (DSCC)** exercises operative control through its Divisions over the following aspects of all DOP fortified wine, DOP and IGP table wine, rum and other alcoholic drinks produced in the archipelago—hereafter referred to collectively as 'alcoholic products'.

Its wide-ranging responsibilities encompass the following: the administration of the vintage and all paperwork associated with it; accounting for the existence and movement of all alcoholic products, including their bottling; the control of spirit and rectified concentrated must used in wine production; the maintenance of current accounts for all registered alcoholic products; the collection of samples for analysis and coordination of controls relating to their quality, including organoleptical and laboratory analysis of samples (in conjunction with DSAQ) and the issue of certificates of analysis; the validation and issue of guarantee seals; the issue of certificates of origin, and other documentation relating to the movement and sale of alcoholic products; the control of brands, labelling and packaging; the registration of producers of and dealers in alcoholic products; the authorization of the retail sale of imported alcoholic products; the control of the activities of all wine trade sectors and the circulation of all alcoholic products made in the archipelago; the control of taxation relating to alcoholic products and the pursuit of infringements thereof; collaboration with other operative services of IVBAM in the development and revision of the technical regulation of alcoholic products; the making of proposals regarding the norms, procedures and administrative arrangements regarding all of the preceding matters; the application and enforcement of all the rules applicable to the sector and the supply of appropriate technical advice when necessary; the administration of EU aid available to grape growers and wine producers; the collection of economic information and preparation of forecasts for planning purposes; the preparation of technical and statistical reports for purposes of administrative control. The Director is a graduate in chemical engineering and has one technical assistant.

The Department of Control (DF), as its name suggests, enforces all legal norms and standards relating to alcoholic products, including their production, storage, movement, marketing and taxation. This is done through the implementation of an Annual Control Plan (*Plano de Controlo Annual*) which comprehensively encompasses the entire process of wine production, including installations, from the reception of grapes until wine is certificated and commercialized.

The Division of Technical Verification (Div.VT) verifies the quality of all alcoholic products and validates it by issuing certificates of origin, guarantee seals, and supporting documentation.

(2) **The Directorate of Vitivinicultural Services (DSVV)** has responsibility for controlling the culture of the vine so as to ensure the production of quality wines. Its mandate is to manage the island's viticultural heritage, administer the current programme of restructuring, and to carry out research on the results of which future policy can be based. Specifically, it promotes what it considers to be best viticultural practice and gives technical advice to growers; it maintains experimental stations (used for demonstration purposes) at which a wide variety of matters such as, for example, clonal selection, vine training systems, pruning methods, etc., are investigated; and it plants and maintains vineyards to preserve the genetic heritage of the varieties planted in them. The Director is a graduate in agricultural engineering, and there is one technical assistant, one co-ordinator, one technical coordinator, and six operational assistants.

The Viticultural Division (Div.VITI) administers the Grower's Card; it controls the granting of planting and replanting licenses; it gives technical assistance to growers; coordinates regional planning to implement national and EU viticultural improvement programmes; it collaborates with other operative services of IVBAM in the technical regulation of the sector; it promotes and regulates the gradual phasing out of direct producers; it administers and maintains the vineyards of the experimental and demonstration research stations; and it maintains the stations from which IVBAM is licensed to provide vegetative viticultural material.

The Department of Wine-Production (DV) maintains and manages the wine-production units belonging to IVBAM—specifically the Adega de São Vicente and the winery in Funchal, where it vinifies a small amount of wine for promotional purposes. Its mandate is to raise the quality of the wines made in these units; to advise on the technical requirements of equipment in these units; to maintain a register of users of these units and to regulate the hiring of their facilities.

(3) **The Directorate of Support for Quality Services (DSAQ)**. This Directorate is responsible for running IVBAM's laboratories—the Nucleus of Laboratories (*Núcleo de Laboratórios*)—NLs. There is one in Funchal, and one in the Adega de São Vicente. It is also responsible for the IVBAM Tasting Panel (*Câmara de Provadores*). DSAQ's role is mainly a supporting one, insofar as it carries out the physico-chemical and organoleptical tests which are an essential element of establishing the quality of an alcoholic product seeking certification. However, it is empowered to support any research, studies or experiments undertaken by any component of IVBAM, or by IVBAM in collaboration with other entities, and it may make proposals regarding its internal functioning, such as proposing new methods of analysis, or regarding the functioning of the Tasting Panel. The operation of the Tasting Panel is explained elsewhere.[1]

Although IVBAM now has its headquarters in the Rua Visconde do Anadia, the rather exotic building which formerly housed the IVM in the Rua 5 de Outubro still belongs to IVBAM. This was originally one of the houses of Henry Veitch, the British consul at the turn of the eighteenth and nineteenth centuries. Veitch carried out his wine trade here, and since then the building has from time to time housed other shippers—including Isidro Gonçalves, Cossart Gordon and the Companhia Vinícola da Madeira. It was the headquarters of the Delegation of the Junta Nacional do Vinho between 1940 and 1979. When it was in IVM hands it housed a small but interesting museum of madeira wine, now alas gone. It was severely damaged in the floods of 2010 and is now empty and somewhat forlorn looking. It is to be hoped that it will not be left to go to rack and ruin. Space in three surviving warehouses can, nevertheless, be rented by shippers for storage of over-spill stocks, and IVBAM continues to use it to store the wine it itself makes.

APPENDIX 3

EXPORTS DURING THE NINETEENTH
AND TWENTIETH CENTURIES

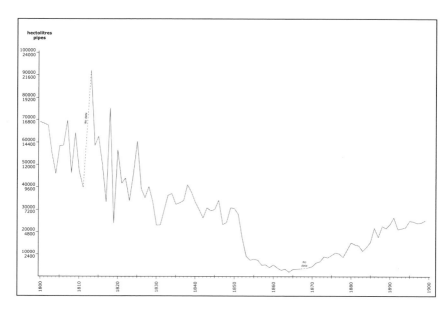

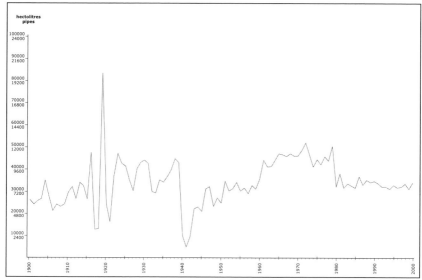

Source: Based on Vieira (4), pp. 470–2.

APPENDIX 4

PRODUCTION AND MARKETS

1995–2010

Table 1: Production of must from 1995–2010.

Year	1995	2000	2005	2010
Number of growers	2,284	2,257	1,650	1,504
Sercial	627.52 (1.03%)	855.04 (1.37%)	950.77 (2.36%)	417.35 (1.22%)
Verdelho	520.29 (0.86%)	936.84 (1.50%)	476.16 (1.18%)	657.60 (1.92%)
Boal	583.50 (0.96%)	1,940.69 (3.11%)	1,945.74 (4.82%)	1,099.69 (3.20%)
Malvazia	1,085.83 (1.79%)	2,231.91 (3.58%)	1,859.38 (4.61%)	1,016.68 (2.96%)
Other European varieties	29,863.81 (49.36%)	50,551.00 (80.97%)	33,220.91 (82.32%)	28,512.74 (83.08%)
European varieties sub-total	32,680.95 (54.02%)	56,515.48 (90.53%)	38,452.96 (95.28%)	31,704.06 (92.38%)
Direct producers	27,812.77 (45.98%)	5,913.51 (9.47%)	1,903.28 (4.72%)	2,613.88 (7.62%)
Total	60,493.72	62,428.99	40,356.24	34,317.94

Quantities are given in hectolitres.
Percentages indicate the proportion of the total production.
Figures supplied by the IVBAM, IP-RAM.

285

Table 2: Summary of markets from 1995–2010. The trend is indicated by a breakdown of figures at five yearly intervals.

Country	Total amount imported (A)	% of total (A)	Total amount in bottles (B)	% of (A)	% of (B)	Total amount modified and disqualified wine (C)	% of (A)	% of (C)
1995	37,528.75	100.00	15,609.93	41.59	100.00	21,918.82	58.41	100.00
France	12,530.61	33.39	857.59	6.84	5.49	11,673.02	93.16	53.26
Portugal[1]	5,459.08	14.55	5,459.08	100.00	34.97	0.00	0.00	0.00
Germany	4,803.22	12.80	494.37	10.29	3.17	4,308.85	89.71	19.66
Britain	3,485.19	9.29	3,118.64	89.48	19.98	366.55	10.52	1.67
Belg./Lux.	2,220.02	5.92	222.67	10.03	1.43	1,997.35	89.97	9.11
Japan	2,044.19	5.45	2,044.19	100.00	13.10	0.00	0.00	0.00
Sweden	1,599.28	4.26	323.22	20.21	2.07	1,276.06	79.79	5.82
USA	1,193.04	3.18	1,169.12	98.00	7.49	23.92	2.00	0.11
Holland	1,158.40	3.09	357.14	30.83	2.29	801.26	69.17	3.66
Denmark	1,003.94	2.68	457.96	45.62	2.93	545.98	54.38	2.49
Switzerland	727.32	1.94	7.38	1.01	0.05	719.94	98.99	3.28
Others	1,304.46	3.48	1,098.57	84.22	7.04	205.89	15.78	0.94
2000	40,176.46	100.00	15,976.18	39.77	100.00	24,200.28	60.23	100.00
France	14,510.02	36.12	565.14	3.89	3.54	13,944.88	96.11	57.62
Portugal[1]	6,325.19	15.74	6,325.19	100.00	39.59	0.00	0.00	0.00
Germany	5,438.18	13.54	398.11	7.32	2.49	5,040.07	92.68	20.83
Belg./Lux.	3,191.58	7.94	111.23	3.49	0.70	3,080.35	96.51	12.73
Britain	2,853.44	7.10	2,496.24	87.48	15.62	357.20	12.52	1.48
Japan	2,084.07	5.19	2,084.07	100.00	13.04	0.00	0.00	0.00
Sweden	1,623.51	4.04	516.13	31.79	3.23	1,107.38	68.21	4.58
USA	1,361.09	3.39	1,328.59	97.61	8.32	32.50	2.39	0.13
Holland	722.04	1.80	297.04	41.14	1.86	425.00	58.86	1.76
Denmark	697.44	1.74	497.44	71.32	3.11	200.00	28.68	0.83
Finland	297.51	0.74	297.51	100.00	1.86	0.00	0.00	0.00
Others	1,072.39	2.67	1,059.49	98.80	6.63	12.90	1.20	0.05

2005	33,983.64	100.00	26,309.63	77.42	100.00	7,674.01	22.58	100.00
France	9,561.04	28.13	5,350.30	55.96	20.34	4,210.74	44.04	54.87
Portugal[1]	6,224.96	18.32	6,224.96	100.00	23.66	0.00	0.00	0.00
Germany	4,013.84	11.81	2,177.38	54.25	8.28	1,836.46	45.75	23.93
Britain	3,247.00	9.55	2,455.00	75.61	9.33	792.00	24.39	10.32
Japan	2,252.51	6.63	2,190.16	97.23	8.32	62.35	2.77	0.81
USA	1,727.15	5.08	1,677.15	97.11	6.37	50.00	2.89	0.65
Belgium	1,716.75	5.05	1,466.79	85.44	5.58	249.96	14.56	3.26
Sweden	1,280.21	3.77	1,280.21	100.00	4.87	0.00	0.00	0.00
Holland	852.65	2.51	567.15	66.52	2.16	285.50	33.48	3.72
Denmark	557.52	1.64	372.72	66.85	1.42	184.80	33.15	2.41
Canada	411.04	1.21	411.04	100.00	1.56	0.00	0.00	0.00
Others	2,138.98	6.29	2,136.78	99.90	8.12	2.20	0.10	0.03

2010	32,776.15	100.00	23,678.15	72.24	100.00	9,098.00	27.76	100.00
France	11,213.97	34.21	4,463.97	39.81	18.85	6,750.00	60.19	74.19
Portugal[1]	4,570.81	13.95	4,560.81	99.78	19.26	10.00	0.22	0.11
Germany	3,406.71	10.39	2,588.31	75.98	10.93	818.40	24.02	9.00
Britain	2,704.73	8.25	2,123.93	78.53	8.97	580.80	21.47	6.38
Japan	2,177.79	6.64	2,070.29	95.06	8.74	107.50	4.94	1.18
Belgium	1,715.50	5.23	1,465.50	85.43	6.19	250.00	14.57	2.75
USA	1,458.23	4.45	1,413.23	96.91	5.97	45.00	3.09	0.49
Sweden	1,177.22	3.59	1,177.22	100.00	4.97	0.00	0.00	0.00
Switzerland	1,142.74	3.49	1,086.84	95.11	4.59	55.90	4.89	0.61
Holland	844.58	2.58	654.58	77.50	2.76	190.00	22.50	2.09
Denmark	610.73	1.86	320.33	52.45	1.35	290.40	47.55	3.19
Others	1,753.15	5.35	1,753.15	100.00	7.40	0.00	0.00	0.00

Quantities are given in hectolitres. Figures supplied by IVBAM. IP-RAM.
[1] Includes all national markets (Continental Portugal, Madeira and Azores).

APPENDIX 5

REGIONAL TABLE WINE

Although this is a book about traditional fortified madeira, it would not be adequate to make no more than a passing reference to table wine production. Apart from *vinho seco*, about which a passing reference is more than enough, this is a relatively new phenomenon, and the ideas driving the project forward are clear. Does the island not welcome tens of thousands of largely wine-drinking tourists every year? Large amounts of table wine consequently have to be imported (mainly from mainland Portugal) to cater for their require-ments. Would it not, therefore, make sense to make this table wine locally, turn restructured vineyards of direct producers to profitable use, improve the economy of the island, and complement the tour-ist's image of Madeira with an attractive local product?

As far back as the 1970s studies were begun to try to determine which grape varieties from France, Italy, Germany and mainland Portugal might prove suitable for making table wine on the island. Three experimental stations at Calheta, Preces and Arco de São Jorge run by the Divisão de Viticultura (DV), part of the Dirreção Regional da Agricultura, were planted in 1984 with what were thought to be the most suitable candidates, and a clonal selection programme was started. In 1994, the experimental stations replanted vines of the varieties which had shown most potential in the first phase of the studies, and further investigations (lasting until 2003) were begun. At the same time, at its winery at Bom Sucesso

Grape Varieties for the Production of Madeira Table Wine

Authorized varieties for DOP Madeirense

Red and Rosé

Bastardo, Cabernet Sauvignon, Complexa, Deliciosa, Malvasia Cândida Roxa (*Malvasia Roxa*), Maria Feld, Merlot, Tinta Barroca, Tinta Negra, Touriga Franca (*Touriga Francesa*), Syrah, and Touriga Nacional.

White

Arnsburger, Carão de Moça, Chardonnay, Chenin Blanc, Terrantez (*Folgasão*), Lilás (*Alvarinho Lilás*), Malvasia Bianca, Malvasia Branca de São Jorge, Malvasia Cândida, Boal (*Malvasia Fina*), Rio Grande, Sauvignon, Sercial, Tália (*Ugni Blanc*) and Verdelho.

Authorized varieties for IGP Terras Madeirenses

Red and Rosé

Bastardo, Cabernet Sauvignon, Complexa, Deliciosa, Malvasia Cândida Roxa (*Malvasia Roxa*), Maria Feld, Merlot, Tinta Barroca, Tinta Negra, Touriga Franca (*Touriga Francesa*) and Touriga Nacional.

White

Arinto, Arnsburger, Chardonnay, Chenin Blanc, Terrantez (*Folgasão*), Malvasia Branca de São Jorge, Malvasia Cândida, Boal (*Malvasia Fina*), Sauvignon Blanc, Sercial, Tália (*Ugni Blanc*) and Verdelho.

(near the Botanical Garden in Funchal) the DV began making micro-vinifications from about a score of candidates. In the meantime, the MWC had introduced Madeira's first commercial *Vitis vinifera* table wine—'Atlantis'—at first, in 1992, as a rosé made from Tinta Negra, then in 1994, as a white wine made from Verdelho. Both are still in production and pleasant, if undistinguished. They provided the models which the IVM hoped would lead the way.

As the results of the experiments began to be disseminated, in 1993 a few adventurous growers began to plant table wine varieties. However, the investigations of the DV did not produce particularly promising results. Verdelho was the only white madeira grape that produced a reasonable table wine; Sercial certainly did not. Tinta Negra was disappointing and suitable, it was judged, only to be part of a blend.

In 1999, the first regulations governing the production of table wines in the archipelago were published.[1] These authorized a Madeiran VQPRD table wine (Quality Wine from a Determinate Region): DOP 'Madeirense' (Protected Denomination of Origin 'Madeirense'). To qualify for this classification, white and rosé wines have to have a minimum of 10.5 per cent alcohol, and red wine has to have a minimum of 11 per cent alcohol. These regulations were supplemented in 2004, when another VQPRD wine was introduced.[2] This class, IGP 'Terras Madeirenses' (Protected Geographic Indication 'Terras Madeirenses') has the lower requirement of a minimum of only 10 per cent alcohol for all wines. The grapes for both DOP and IGP wines have to be grown on Madeira or on Porto Santo, and must be on the authorized list of varieties recognized for its class. These can be seen on the table opposite.

At the same time that it became possible to produce DOP 'Madeirense' wine (1999), as an incentive to small producers lacking the facilities to make their own wine, the (purpose-built) Adega de São Vicente (ASV) opened its doors in time for the vintage, but was not officially inaugurated until 2000. The ASV was built by, owned by, and operated by the staff of the IVM and later taken over by IVBAM. Starting with 100,000 litres, its fermentation capacity has now grown to 300,000 litres. The equipment is up-to-date and has digital temperature control, there are two pneumatic presses, chilling equipment (used, for example, to give Verdelho low temperature skin maceration for from twelve to twenty-four hours), stainless steel storage, and a bottling line. There are also a small laboratory and a tasting room.

There is a resident winemaker, who normally supervises between seven and eight workers, although this goes up to ten or eleven for the harvest. During the harvest the ASV handles around forty fermentations. The minimum amount accepted for vinification is 2 tonnes for white and rosé, and 3.5 tonnes for red. The largest single amount ever handled was 60 tonnes, and 15 tonnes a day is not uncommon.

The ASV offers a complete service. Producers have the choice of making the wine with their own wine-maker, or having it done for them by, and in consultation with, the resident ASV winemaker. In addition, bottles, labels, corks and pallets can be supplied. Some storage is also available. The customer has to supply his own casks if the wine is to be cask aged. Because of cost this is not the usual option, and wood treatment of red wines is normally by using oak chips or staves.

The total area producing grapes for table wines is currently estimated to be 44 hectares. In 2011, 1,285 hL of wine were produced, of which 1.108 hL were DOP 'Madeirense', and 177 hL were IGP 'Terras Madeirenses'. It cannot be said that the production of table wine has taken off in a very big way. The madeira shippers, apart from the MWC and Justino's, have turned their backs on it, and at the time of writing only twelve producers are registered with IVBAM—a figure that has been static for three years. The volume of wine produced at the ASV tells its own tale. From 1999 there was a steady build up until 2005, when production peaked. In 2008 it dropped back again, and remains fairly constant.

As far as the potential for good quality wines is concerned the jury is still out. The general impression I have formed of the wines currently on offer is, to put it as politely as possible, disappointing. Francisco Albuquerque's Primeira Paixão, a wine first made in 2008 in conjunction with Rui Reguinga, an Alentejo wine-maker who, since 2010, has been a consultant to the ASV, is the exception. It shines out like a beacon and shows what can be done with Verdelho. A biological wine, the grapes are sourced from Estreito de Câmara de Lobos. In my opinion none of the other white varieties, particularly Arnsburger, has so far made anything to write home about. I have also found the reds mostly very disappointing, with one modest exception, Terras do Avo Grande Escolha, made from Tinta Roriz, Syrah and Touriga Nacional. A recurrent problem with other reds is the wood treatment. The handling of oak chips or staves is not very subtle, resulting in non-integrated raw, woody flavours. At least one producer invests in French barriques but, frankly, I cannot see Madeira producing musts of sufficient quality to justify this considerable expense. The sad fact is that, because costs of production are already relatively high, local wines do not really compete on price with imports from mainland Portugal. When I asked the ASV wine-maker his opinion, he replied that he believes there is a future for Syrah (if well grown) and Touriga Nacional (again depending on where it is grown). Francisco Albuquerque is excited by the quality of the grapes grown at Caniçal, where he has Merlot and Touriga Nacional. IVBAM, on its website, concedes that, despite the long lists of recommended varieties, 'the varieties suitable for this type of wine are very much restricted.' This truthful admission continues: 'In reality the varieties suitable for white wine are in practical terms limited to Verdelho and Arnsburger, and similarly for red wines, to Touriga Nacional, Merlot, Cabernet Sauvignon, Aragonez and Tinta Negra'. There is a long road ahead if Madeira is to produce table wines of average interest or above, but a start has been made. We shall see—but I'm not putting any bets on it.

APPENDIX 6

THE 1792 VINTAGE AND THE NAPOLEON MADEIRA

Undoubtedly the most celebrated of all madeiras is the so-called 1792 'Napoleon' vintage. Several mid-nineteenth-century moulded bottles have survived into this century. They bear a small cream label, generally scuffed and often no longer legible, measuring about 8.6 cm across and 4.8 cm deep; it reads 'BLANDY/ *Madeira*/1792–1840'. The first date is that of the vintage and the second is the date of bottling. The bottles have undoubtedly been recorked from time to time and have wax seals.

The connection with Napoleon was first mentioned in print by André Simon in *Madeira, Wine, Cakes and Sauce*, published in 1933. It was also touched on by Rupert Croft-Cooke and Noël Cossart in their books on madeira, and has been recounted, more or less inaccurately, many times since. According to Simon, he was told by Michael Grabham on his ninety-third birthday in January 1933, when the 1792–1840 madeira was drunk, that 1792 was the year his father had been born. The story continued: 'When, in 1815, Napoleon I called at Madeira, on his way farther south to St Helena, this 1792 wine was picked out as likely to become very fine with age,[1] and it was bought for the fallen Emperor, to help him forget the duress of exile. But, as you know, they found out that he suffered from some gastric trouble—some said that it was cancer of the stomach—and they would not let him drink this wine. As a

295

matter of fact, the Emperor died in 1820, and this 1792 was hardly ready by then. The curious thing about it was that nobody had paid for the wine. That is to say, the English Consul at Funchal, a Mr Veitch, had paid the merchant who had put the wine on board His Britannic Majesty's ship, in 1815, but he, Veitch, had never been able to get the money refunded. So he did the next best thing. He claimed the pipe of 1792 as his own, and he got it back in Madeira, in 1822, when he sold it to Charles Blandy. His son, John Blandy, bottled the wine in 1840, and that happens to be the year when I was born. I married his daughter; that is how the wine came to me, and why I can give it to you today.'[2]

The story, even if true in essentials, is certainly wrong in detail. Charles Blandy was only ten years old in 1822—when, according to Grabham, Veitch sold him the pipe of madeira. John Blandy, who is said to have bottled the wine in 1840, only joined the firm in 1841. It may have been a fabrication. Croft-Cooke, basing his opinion on a letter written by Grabham's son Walter, thought it was; Cossart, on the other hand, did not. The fairest thing to do, therefore, is to let Walter Grabham and Noël Cossart speak for themselves.

In a letter to Graham Blandy dated 13 November 1941, Walter Grabham wrote: 'I am afraid that during his last years, my father embroidered some of his statements ... This Blandy, 1792–1840 Madeira wine of which my father in 1930 still possessed about 15 dozen bottles, never had any association with Napoleon. In a letter dated 30 Aug. 1930, to Col. Arthur Cossart about some wines he was selling, my father referred to this wine: "1792–1840: a grand old wine; our family wine, the dates strangely coinciding with the birth year of my father and myself." There is no taint of Napoleon about that, and he would hardly have omitted it if it had been a fact. I never heard my father associate Napoleon with this wine but about the same time there was a younger wine, either 1902 or 1923 or both, which he referred to as "Faraday wine". When I taxed him with this perversion, he just replied that it pleased him.'

In a letter to Richard Blandy dated 26 July 1982, Noël Cossart put his point of view: 'In my book I am telling the story as I heard it from Uncle Michael, Uncle Arthur, and confirmed by André himself. When André left Pommery & Greno in 1933 he was P.R. to the M.W.A for a short time, and that is when he got the story. I remember having a long discussion about the Blandy 1792–1840 with him at the Academy of Ancient Madeira Wines at Water Lane in 1959. Walter had a peculiar quirk of discrediting his father whenever possible, I presume because he had always been suppressed by him. He was a wicked old man, but I am convinced his story is true. The fact that in his letter to Uncle Arthur he did not mention the Napoleon connection was because Uncle Arthur knew it.'[3]

My own view inclines sharply towards scepticism. All the evidence points to Michael Grabham having been the sole source of the story. In another letter to Richard Blandy, dated 12 July 1982, Cossart says: 'In their notes both uncle Michael Grabham and my grandfather say that it was John who bottled the famous Blandy "Napoleon Madeira" in 1840. In the absence of these 'notes' there is no independent confirmation of the story, so when Cossart writes, 'I can guarantee the story he told about his 1792 madeira was no leg pull and is fact',[4] he appears to overstate his case. The truth, I believe, is that Cossart was a good raconteur who enjoyed a good story, and he was convinced by this story because he wanted to be.

Other discussions about the Blandy 1792–1840 have left considerable confusion in their wake. The first thing to be clear about is that, in addition to the vintage wine, there is also a Blandy 'Extra Reserve—Solera 1792'. The first mention of the solera is by Vizetelly (1877): 'A powerful choice old reserve from the same district [Cama de Lobos], the solera of which was founded as far back as 1792.'[5] It seems probable that this solera was created from the same 1792 vintage, part of which was bottled in 1840, though the only evidence to support this is negative: Blandy's have no records of a second wine. It seems a little unlikely, however, that there would have been two different 1792 vintages, one of which was bottled in 1840, the other being used for the solera. The final bottling, which finished off the solera, was in 1957. The bottles have embossed lead capsules, body labels and neck labels, and typed or printed back labels which state: 'This famous old Solera was laid down in the year 1792 and matured in its original casks. In 1957, the year of the State visit of Her Majesty Queen Elizabeth II and the

Duke of Edinburgh to Portugal, the remainder of this wine was drawn from the casks and bottled.' There was a total yield of 1,228 bottles, each individually numbered.

The labelling of neither the straight vintage nor the solera indicates from which grape variety the wine was made, suggesting that it was (like most eighteenth-century madeira) generic. Vizetelly's mention of Cama de Lobos might suggest a fairly rich, Boal type of wine. Cossart, possibly following Vizetelly, also refers to both wines as from Câmara de Lobos,[6] but the labelling does not support this. Nor does it support the not infrequent description in auction catalogues (since 1977) of both the vintage and solera wines as Boal.[7] Nor is there any evidence that Blandy's ever marketed a 1792 Boal in addition to the 1792–1840 madeira.

Despite the fact that Christie's, in a sale on 25 September 1980, listed as Lot 383 'Sercial—1792. Blandy. Bottled 1840', I am disinclined to think either that the 1792–1840 madeira was a Sercial or that there was a separate 1792 Sercial (coincidentally bottled in 1840). This mention is unique, apart from Croft-Cooke's assertion that the wine drunk by Churchill at Reid's in 1950 was a Sercial,[8] which is clearly just a mistake. On the other hand, there is more convincing evidence of the existence of a 1792 Solera Malvazia. Cossart refers to one having been 'bottled [in] 1957 on the occasion of HM the Queen's state visit'. Not only is this at odds with his assertion that the solera bottled for the Queen's visit was from Câmara de Lobos[9]—there has never been any suggestion that two different soleras, one from Câmara de Lobos and the other Malvazia, were bottled for the Queen—but, like the Câmara de Lobos assertion, it is unsupported by the labelling of the solera bottled in 1957. I would dismiss this as a confusion similar to Croft-Cooke's over Sercial, were it not that a Malvazia Solera 1792 was sold at Sotheby's in 1972[10] and Michael Broadbent reports drinking one— the same bottle?—in his *Great Vintage Wine Book*.[11] These are, however, the only references I have been able to find to this wine, and there have never been any other suggestions, so far as I know, that the 1792–1840 vintage might have been made from Malvasia.

All things considered therefore, I am inclined to the view that Blandy's 1792–1840 vintage and Extra Reserve Solera 1792 came from the same source, and that (on the authority of Vizetelly) this was a wine which may well have originated in Câmara de Lobos, although we cannot now say whether it was made from a single grape variety, or if it was, what that might have been.

APPENDIX 7

VIDONHO AND VIDONIA

AN UNSOLVED MYSTERY

We first met with Vidonho in Chapter One. It has cognate terms in other languages: Vidueño and Viduño (Spanish); Vidogne (French); Vidonia (English) and Vidogna (possibly an alternative spelling of Vidonia). In the following discussion I shall use these terms interchangeably, matching the term to the original language of any texts quoted.

Vidonia was a wine produced in the Canary Islands from the early Middle Ages until the end of the nineteenth century, when it seems to have disappeared. This was caused not by phylloxera, which never reached the islands, but by *Oïdium tuckeri*, which wiped out about 90 per cent of the Canary Islands' wine production during the second half of the century.[1] In Chapter One, following Galindo's discussion of the meaning of Vidueño in his book *La Vid y el Vino en Tenerife en la Primera Mitad del Siglo XVI*, I contended that in the sixteenth century, as in Tenerife, the term Vidonho was used in Madeira to indicate a type of wine made from a blend of white varieties other than Malvasia. Galindo discusses in considerable detail the possibility that Vidueño was a specific grape variety and not just a blend, and he decisively rules it out. 'We can affirm that during the period under examination there is no documentary evidence of any grape variety called *vidueño* and, consequently, of any wine made from it.'[2]

I have suggested that, at least in the seventeenth and eighteenth centuries, references to Vidonia were an extension of this usage. In references to Vidueños in writings about the wine of Tenerife the contrast is almost entirely with Malvazias. According to Juan Henríquez, in the mid-seventeenth century there were three classes of wine: Malvazias, a medium quality, and Vidueños, the last being the cheapest.[3] Amongst references to Vidonho in Madeira, the following references are typical. In the Funchal Câmara registers for June 1641 we find that it was proposed that Vidonho should be valued at 4,000 réis per bica.[4] And whereas in 1620 only 287 pipes of Vidonho were exported, in 1650 we find that the export figure for Vidonho had grown to an amazing 2,381 pipes.[5] Bolton, writing at the beginning of the eighteenth century, makes three references to the shipping of Vidonia;[6] and in 1723 the *London Gazette* refers to '31 Pipes…of…White Vidonia Madera Wine'.[7] Bell's Weekly Messenger advertised Vidonia at £3 per pipe on 29 December 1799.[8] There is one reference in the Condell Innes Notebook, in the entry for 5 April 1809: 'At foot we note the Shipping prices as/agreed upon at the Meeting of Factory on 31 Xbr last/Vidoho. 65/-'.[9]

It is possible that by 1809—the date of the last quotation—what was being referred to was not always a blend of white varieties, although this established usage continued. The term Vidonho was frequently and clearly used in this generic sense in many nineteenth-century writings about wine, as in this example from 1865: 'The varieties (vidonhos) which are cultivated on trees are, for the most part, Verdelho, Sercial and Tinta.'[10] Although the most recent use of the word in this sense that I have come across was in 1956, it still appears in many standard Portuguese dictionaries as the second of three meanings:[11] (1) 'a new vine shoot which is cut together with a piece of the wood of the mother vine'; (2) 'grape variety'; (3) 'a certain variety of grape'. The first definition (known only to one Portuguese wine-maker I have spoken to) may be discarded for the purpose of our discussion. It was a method of propagation which became redundant after phylloxera, when root-grafting became general. The second sense is obsolete or at best obsolescent, having been replaced by *videira* and *cepa*. This is the generic meaning of *vidonho*, indicating a grape variety in general. It is worth mentioning that a wine is currently marketed in Tenerife as Vidueño Seco, and it is indeed a table wine made from a blend of various white varieties.[12] The third meaning of *vidonho* refers to a specific grape variety and, as Vidogna and Vidogne, we start to find it not only appearing in nineteenth-century lists of Madeira grape varieties but also, as Vidueño, regularly stated to be the grape variety used in Tenerife to make Vidonia.

In 1824 Cyrus Redding wrote: 'What is called Vidonia is properly the dry Canary wine, best known as Teneriffe. Perhaps it was so called because it was derived from the *vidogna* grape.'[13] In 1864 we find Thomas Shaw writing 'It is within the recollection of many that there was a large trade in Tenerife, more usually called Vidonia, owing to the principal grape being the Vidogne'.[14] Vizetelly, visiting the Canaries in 1877, indicated that it was still much in vogue: 'To-day the favourite vine in Tenerife is the vidueño, or vidonia, as it is sometimes called, the fruit of which is a juicy round white grape, the bunches seldom exceeding a pound and a half in weight. There is also a black variety of the vidueño, but this is very rare, and is mainly grown in the valley of Orotava.'[15] He goes on: 'We tasted a variety of growths shipped under the name of Vidonia (the grape from which they are produced being so called), commencing with the vintages of 1876 and 1875, which, however, had not yet developed any especial characteristics.'

References to the specific grape variety start at about the same time. Thus Jullien, whose *Topographie de Tous les Vignobles Connus* was published in 1816 and translated into English in 1824, includes Vidogne in his list of grape varieties to be found on Madeira and says (rather obscurely) that it makes 'a wine drier than the white *Burgundy*, but not so sharp as the *Rhenish*'.[16] Redding, in his *A History and Description of Modern Wines* published in 1824, also includes Vidogna in his list of Madeira grape varieties,[17] and finally Thudichum and Dupré include it in the list of Madeira varieties given in their *Treatise on the Origin, Nature and Varieties of Wine* published in 1872. 'In [Madeira] lives the genius of the Malvasia and Vidogna grapes', they say, remarking of the Vidogna that it is similar to Chasselas.[18]

From these references it is clear that Madeira Vidonia was a type of wine like the Canaries Vidonia—a dry wine usually contrasted with Malvazia—and that in the nineteenth century it was apparently made from a specific grape variety called Vidonho or Vidogna. The question therefore arises: was the grape variety used to make Madeira Vidonia the same as was used for the Canaries Vidonia—that is, Vidueño—and, if so, what was it?

We may take as our starting point Viala and Vermorel's *Ampélographie* published in Paris at the beginning of the twentieth century, where we find the following confirmation of the third dictionary definition of the word: '*Vidonho. Cépage portugais de la Beira Baixa, très répandu à l'île de Madère, d'après certains auteurs identiques à Vidogne ou Chasselas, différent d'après d'autres et bien spécial.*'[19] A further entry under 'Vidogne' confirms its identity with Chasselas, and the entry for 'Chasselas Doré' indicates that this variety was grown in Tenerife.[20] More recently, Pierre Galet in his *Dictionnaire Encyclopédique des Cépages* confirms the identification with Chasselas[21]—but he may just be following Viala and Vermorel. Unfortunately, Wikipedia does not include any variant of Vidonia amongst more than two hundred listed synonyms for Chasselas.

I know of only one reference which records the presence of Chasselas on Madeira, and this expressly states that 'it is a recently (1921) introduced variety cultivated only in the surroundings of Funchal'.[22] When Thudichum and Dupré mention the Vidogna in Madeira, they compare it, but do not identify it, with Chasselas. The absence of any other evidence to suggest that Madeira Vidonia was originally made from Chasselas appears to rule out this possibility entirely, and we must conclude that, even if Canaries Vidonia was made from Chasselas, what was called Vidonia in Madeira was not.

Noël Cossart states that Verdelho 'was also once known as Vidonia'[23] and, presumably following him, so do Lemps[24] and Robinson.[25] It is interesting, therefore, that Cossart himself tells us that the wine made from Verdelho in the mid-eighteenth century was called 'Verdia', not Vidonia.[26] However, the only evidence I have discovered for identifying Verdelho with Vidonia is purely circumstantial. In two cases, writers who mention Vidogne/Vidogna in their surveys of the grape varieties in Madeira, perhaps significantly, fail to mention Verdelho. These are Jullien and Thudichum and Dupré. Both of them list Malvasia, Boal, Sercial and Vidogne/Vidogna. To what then, if not Verdelho, could they possibly be referring? Moreover, Viala and Vermorel say that the Vidonho is '*très répandu à l'île de Madère*'. Again, what could they possibly mean if not Verdelho, the preponderant variety on the island at the time of phylloxera? Nevertheless, even if Vidonia or Vidogna possibly came to be used as alternative names for Verdelho, it does not follow that we can be certain that references to Vidonia in the eighteenth century and to Vidonhos in the sixteenth and seventeenth centuries were to wine made from Verdelho. Indeed, convenient though it might be to accept the simple identification of Vidonho with Verdelho in the context of Madeira, there are at least three reasons for caution. Firstly, in listing the grapes grown in Madeira, Redding[27] mentions both Verdelho and Vidogna, making it difficult to see how they could be one and the same. Richard Burton, writing in 1883, also mentions both: 'The favourite of the Canaries is, or was, the *vidonia*, a juicy berry, mostly white, seldom black: the same is the case with the muscadels …The valuable *Verdelho*, preferred at Madeira, is, or was, a favourite; and there are, or were, half a dozen others'.[28] Vizetelly when speaking of the Canaries[29] likewise mentions both Verdelho and Vidogna. However, as they are both referring to the Canaries, this is of course consistent with the Vidogna in the Canaries being the same as the Chasselas Doré). Secondly, Viala and Vermorel indicate, without further explanation, that the Madeira Vidonho is thought by some to be *bien spécial*— that is, not to be identified with any other variety, and certainly not with Verdelho, about which they have a lot to say without a hint of identifying it with Vidonho. And thirdly, André Simon, who was an extremely knowledgeable wine historian of this period, clearly distinguishes Verdelho from Vidonia when listing the types of wine made in Madeira when Bolton was writing his letters. Compare 'A smaller quantity of ordinary beverage White Wine was made, from the Verdelho grape' and 'In certain specially favoured vineyards … richer species of grapes, chiefly the Malvazia and Vidonia, were grown and gathered later than the common beverage grapes'.[30] It is not clear upon what basis Simon asserts that there was Verdelho in

Madeira at this time (though there probably was); and he may have made the distinction between Verdelho and Vidonia only because he appears to have considered Vidonia as predominantly a sweet wine—wrongly, in my view—which he would therefore have to distinguish from a dry beverage wine.[31]

To make the puzzle even more confusing, in their recent *Wine Grapes*, Robinson, Harding and Vouillamoz give Vidueño as a synonym for the Perruno grape.[32] This Spanish variety, which two centuries ago apparently comprised half the vineyards in Jerez, is now much less common but is still encountered in the making of sherry. According to José Vouillamoz, to whom I am indebted for much of the following information, this identification was made on the basis of an entry in the Vitis International Variety Catalogue (*www.vivc.de*). The VIVC is an inventory, originally sponsored by the OIV, which was started in 1983 by the Institute for Grapevine Breeding Geilweilerhof and has been available online since 1996. It is a continuously updated catalogue of the genetic resources of *Vitis vinifera* species, varieties and genotypes, and grape varieties are allocated identifying numbers.

The VIVC distinguishes between the following: Vidueño—a synonym for Perruno (9185); Vidueño Blanco—a synonym for Beba (22710); and Vidueño Negro—a synonym for Garnacha Tinta (4461). All three are registered European varieties, the first Spanish, the second Portuguese, and the third is registered in Spain, but also in Italy as Alicante/Cannonau/Tocai Rosso, and in Austria as Grenache. José Vouillamoz, in view of this confusing multiplicity, now thinks that Vidueño should be discarded as a synonym for Perruno.

More surprising, however, is the fact that VIVC lists Vidonho as a Portuguese variety (13065). It has not yet been studied and there is no ampelographical information available about it. It has not been registered as a European variety. It turns out on investigation that the appearance of Vidonho in VIVC is based on nothing more substantial than its appearance in Viala and Vermorel's *Ampélographie* and in Pierre Galet's *Dictionnaire Encyclopédique des Cépages*, which follows Viala and Vermorel in identifying Vidonho with Chasselas. Although I invited the OIV to comment on Vidonho, and more particularly on Viala and Vermorel's assertions, it apparently did not feel confident enough to venture any opinion.

It is difficult to know how best to sum up this discussion, let alone devise a theory that will square with all the facts. I am inclined to take as my starting point the clear parallels between Madeira and the Canaries as wine-producing areas. They both produced Malvazia and dry wines, and were in competition with each other. They had cognate terms (Vidonho and Vidueño) to describe their dry wines, and for many years these terms indicated a type of wine. It does not take too much imagination to think of the British merchants in Funchal, as it became more general to make dry wines from Verdelho, making a transfer of the name for the wine to the Verdelho grape. It would, in these circumstances, be a natural extension of this generalized use of 'Vidonia' to employ the same word as a synonym for Verdelho. A similar thing might well have happened in the Canaries, accounting for the Vidueño there becoming synonymous with Chasselas and explaining why, by the nineteenth century at any rate, the grape varieties referred to as Vidogna in the Canaries and in Madeira were not one and the same. It appears to be merely an accident that in the Canaries the word Vidonia, signifying a type of wine, appears to have lasted much later into the nineteenth century.

Unfortunately, this theory does not easily explain away Redding's mention of both Vidogna and Verdelho in Madeira, unless he was confused or misinformed. But given that many grape varieties do have synonyms, confusion is by no means an impossible explanation. If some islanders referred to the grape by the one name and some by the other—which is consistent with my theory—it is possible that they could mistakenly have been thought to be two separate varieties, especially if they were in fact two separate varieties in the Canaries. It would be like someone hearing about Sercial in one context and Esgano Cão in another, and not realizing that they are the same variety.

What my theory does not explain, however, is the fate of the grape variety mentioned by Viala and Vermorel, let alone what it was. It may simply have disappeared, perhaps since the publication of their *Ampélographie*, which lists at least eight Madeira grape varieties apparently no longer to be found on the island.[33] It is only by chance, after all, that Terrantez and Bastardo survived into the twentieth century. What I am most convinced of, however, is that this is not the last word on Vidonia and Vidonho.

Postscript

We know that Vidueños (and Malvazias) were produced in Tenerife right up until the latter part of the nineteenth century, and that they died out between then and World War I. The Casa del Vino Wine Museum (La Baranda) at El Sauzal displays some old labelled bottles, but none with a vintage date later than 1915. Production of traditional Malvazia has only quite recently re-started. By contrast with Madeira, therefore, there are no long-established firms with old vintage reserves, and it seems that few of the families who originally owned the estates with the vineyards from which these wines were made have retained bottles from the century before last in their cellars.

Imagine my excitement when I was in Tenerife in 2004 and I learned of the recent discovery of a cache of bottles of late nineteenth century wine belonging to the Benitez de Lugo family on their estate in the northwest of the island. The wine had apparently been found bricked up in a farm building which they were renovating. At the time of my visit the local government was considering the purchase of the bulk of the 136 remaining bottles as part of the island's patrimony. Very fortunately, I persuaded the family to part with a bottle of Vidueño Seco 1882 and a bottle of Malvasia del Rincon (Orotava) 1894.

I opened these bottles at a lunch for wine friends in March, 2005. I knew that the bottle of Vidueño would certainly prove to be interesting, and I had a vague hope that it might shed a little light on the mysteries I had grappled with when originally writing this book. Alas, the hope was vain.

The Vidueño Seco 1882 was in a late nineteenth century heavy, green glass, slightly tapered bottle. The neck and shoulder had a covering of very thin hard grime, suggesting that it had been stored standing up, and this was confirmed by the remains of crusting within the bottle which extended into the neck without reaching the level of the bottom of the cork. The top of the bottle had been recently recoated with a bright crimson wax over the remains of the original darker red wax seal. The exposed top of the presumably original cork showed no signs of ullage, but the cork disintegrated while being extracted. Patches of translucent crusting adhered to the sides of the bottle, but the crust was heaviest at the base of the punt, which again confirmed that the bottle had been stored vertically. The small, discoloured rectangular paper label (5.3 x 4.3 cm) had had its corners trimmed at 45°. On it in faded black ink was written 'Vidueño seco/1882'. The wine fill was just into the neck.

The wine was decanted and came out of the bottle entirely cleanly. There appeared to be no loose sediment, the crust in the punt being totally consolidated. It was tasted an hour or so later. My tasting note is as follows:

Pale medium amber; bright, clear and colourless on the rim. Slightly muted and faded on the nose, but nevertheless a gentle, harmonious and agreeable bouquet, though without any defined or recognizable varietal character. Very up-front entry; minimal fruit, rather watery, and lacking in any body or weight. Quite dry. Persistent, generalized fortified wine rancio residue in the mouth, but with a very short finish. Sound, not at all unpleasant to drink, but nondescript and quite unremarkable. No real clues as to variety.

I have never tasted an old madeira quite so pallid as this wine. One guest was reminded of old sherry—but that, I thought, was an insult to sherry. So, the wine was disappointing, to say the least. Clearly my expectations had been too high. Even in the second half of the eighteenth century Vidonia from the Canary Islands was considered second rate. The East India Company, finding that the supply of genuine madeira was insufficient to meet demand from the East Indies, tried to make up the shortfall with Canaries Vidonia (without, however, trying to pass it off as genuine madeira). It met with strong customer resistance–a 'general dislike' because it was much inferior to the Madeira which had 'more body'.[34] Nineteenth-century commentators were of the same opinion. Thomas Shaw, points out that it resembled madeira, but is quick to add 'though far from possessing its flavour or body'.[35] Burton remarks that the 'white wines are rather grape-ciders than real wines'.[36] He goes on to say: 'If [Tenerife wine] developed none of the highest qualities of its successful rivals, it became, after eight to twelve years' keeping, a tolerable wine, which many in England have drunk, paying for good madeira. The shorter period sufficed to mature it, and it was usually shipped when three to four years old. It kept to advantage in wood for a quarter of a century, and in bottle it improved faster … I found Canary bearing the same relation to madeira as marsala bears to sherry: the best specimens almost equalled the second or third-rate madeiras'.[37] This was published in 1883, the year after the vintage of Vidueño I was fortunate enough to taste. By then the consequences of *oïdium* were at their worst, musts were weaker than ever, and exports had collapsed to the extent that Burton was even able to speak of Canary wine as 'unknown to the English market'.[38] In other words, containing a wine that was only rated as comparable to second or third-rate madeira, and made from must of a considerably inferior and lighter quality than in the best days of Tenerife wine, the contents of my bottle of Vidueño Seco were probably not at all impressive to start with and never had the potential to survive for over a hundred years. The same was sadly true of the Malvasia del Rincon 1894.[39] The wines proved similar insofar as they had both lost whatever fruit they had ever had, leaving the packaging of a fortified wine without the content.

APPENDIX 8

THE CONDELL INNES NOTEBOOK

The Condell Innes manuscript is bound into a copy of *Account of the Island of Madeira* by N. C. Pitta, published in 1812. There is no apparent connection between the book and the manuscript, which consists of 254 pages numbered 9–83, 83 (repeated), 85–177 and 179–263. Several of the pages are blank apart from the page number and a date. The information contained in the notebook relates to a shipping company in Funchal called Condell, Innes & Co. (later, from 1809, Duncan, Innes, Lewis & Co.) and appears to consist of statistical information copied from other sources, including parts of letters to the firm's correspondent in London. The paper on which the manuscript is written bears an 1810 watermark. One may surmise therefore that the notebook was written by a partner of Duncan, Innes, Lewis & Co. some time after 1810 and was used to record interesting information concerning the firm, which dealt in corn, cereal and flax imports from the United States and India, imports of foodstuffs from England, and in wine exports mainly to these three countries.

The major part of the text, which starts on page 27, is headed 'Extracts from Madeira' and, apart from fifteen pages concerning trade with the East India Company between 1808 and 1812, comprises a chronologically arranged notebook covering the period from 30 September 1789 to 13 January 1821. There are no entries for 1790. The contents are miscellaneous but maintain a more or

311

less regular pattern, at least for some years at a time. The entries until 1803 are very brief (one or two pages a year), but thereafter they become increasingly longer and more detailed. Apart from the earlier years, the information generally provided includes: (1) a list of exports to the East India Company, which appears to have been the firm's best customer; (2) a list of the prices of the various qualities of wine as decided by the British Factory; (3) the company's stock position (until 1807); (4) extracts from letters covering the prospects for each year's vintage and how it turned out, indications of the state of the cereals market in Funchal, the difficulties and costs of letters of credit drawn on London, and complaints—all occasionally interspersed with pieces of unrelated information, such as the total exports for the year, imports of corn and cereals, lists of merchandise, analyses of the profit structure of the company, comments on noteworthy events on the island (notably the great flood of 1803 and the visit of Napoleon), etc.

The Condell Innes Notebook reminds one irresistibly of the Bolton Letters in its scope, and is full of interest to economic historians of the period. It deserves to be published, but as its contents would be of more interest to the specialist than the general reader, this may not happen soon. The Notebook belongs to Blandy's Madeiras, Lda, and I am most indebted originally to Mr James Symington and now to Mr Christopher Blandy for generously permitting me to quote from it.

APPENDIX 9

SUPPLIERS

All madeiras (including vintage wines) which are currently being shipped may be located by contacting the shipper concerned, who will direct you to his importing agent for your area, who in turn can give you a list of retail suppliers. Artur de Barros e Sousa, Lda, have no overseas agents but will send wine by post. All telephone and fax numbers have the following country prefix: 351–291.

Artur de Barros e Sousa, Lda, Rua dos Ferreiros 109–111, 9000–082 Funchal, Madeira. (Tel: 220622) *www.vinosmadeira.com*; email: *absl@netmadeira.com*.

Cooperativa Agrícola do Funchal (CAF), Caminho de São Martinho 56, São Martinho, 9000–273 Funchal, Madeira. (Tel: 702457/700900) *www.cafmadeira.com*.

H. M. Borges, Sucrs., Lda, Rua 31 de Janeiro 83, PO Box 92, 9050–011 Funchal, Madeira. (Tel: 223247; Fax: 222281) *www.hmborges.com*; email: *info@hmborges.com*.

J. Faria & Filhos, Lda, Travessa do Tanque, 85/87, 9020–258 Funchal, Madeira. (Tel: 742935) *www.jfariaefilhos.pt*; email: *jfariaefilhos@sapos.pt*

Henriques & Henriques, Vinhos, SA, Sítio de Bélem, 9300–138 Câmara de Lobos, Madeira. (Tel: 941551; Fax: 941590) *www.henriquesehenriques.pt*; email: *henriquesehenriques@net madeira.com*.

Justino's, Madeira Wines, SA, Parque Industrial de Cancela, 9125–042 Caniço, Santa Cruz, Madeira. (Tel: 934257; Fax: 934049) *www.justinosmadeira.com*; email: *justinos@justinosmadeira.com.*

Madeira Wine Company, SA, Rua dos Ferreiros 191, PO Box 295, 9000–082 Funchal, Madeira. (Tel: 740100; Fax: 740101) *www.madeirawinecompany.com*; email: *semerces@madeirawine company.com.*

P. E. Gonçalves, Lda, Caminho Bela Vista 36, 9300–027 Câmara de Lobos, Madeira. (Tel: 942813; Fax: 941510).

Pereira D'Oliveira (Vinhos) Lda, Rua dos Ferreiros 107, 9000–082 Funchal, Madeira. (Tel: 220784; Fax: 229081) email: *perolivinhos@ hotmail.com.*

Vinhos Barbeito (Madeira) Lda, Estrada da Ribeira Garcia, Parque Empresarial de Câmara de Lobos—Lote 8, PO Box 264, 9300–324 Câmara de Lobos, Madeira. (Tel: 761829; Fax: 765832) *www.vinhosbarbeito.com*; email: *info@barbeito.com.pt.*

Information about UK importers of madeira can be found at: *www.thebft.co.uk/index.php/business-directory/category/ distributors.*

Apart from buying directly from someone with a private cellar of madeiras there are, in general terms, three other possible sources of older wines.

Commercial wine auctions are regularly held in Britain, USA, Holland, Switzerland, Hong Kong, Japan and some other countries, and old madeiras turn up from time to time. In Britain the principal wine auctioneers are Christie's (*www.christies.com*) (UK Tel: 44–(0)20 7839 9060; Fax: 44–(0)20 7839 1611. USA Tel: 1–212.636.2000; Fax: 1–212.894.1990), and Sotheby's (*www. sothebys.com*) (UK Tel: 44–(0)20 7293 5000; Fax: 44–(0)20 7293 5989. USA Tel: 1–212.894.1990; Fax: 1–212.606.7880). In the United States the principal auctioneers are Zachys in New York (*www.zachys.com*) (Tel: 1–914.448.3026; Fax: 1–914.206.4544) and Hong Kong (*asia@zachys.com*) (Tel: 852–2810.9906; Fax: 852–3014.3838); Hart Davis Hart Wine Company in Chicago (*www.hdhwine.com*) (Tel: 1–312.482.9996; Fax: 1–312.335.9096); Acker Merral and Condit of New York (*www.ackerwines.com*)

(Tel: 1–877–225.3747; Fax: 1–877.225.3724) and Hong Kong; Spectrum Wine Auctions (online) (*www.spectrumwine.com*): USA (Tel: 1–949.748.4845; Fax: 1–949.567.1360) and Hong Kong (Tel: 852–2116.1103); The Chicago Wine Company (*www.tcwc.com*) (Tel: 1–630.594.2972; Fax: 1–630.594.2978); Morrell and Co., in New York (*www.morrellwineauctions.net*)(Tel: 1–212.307.4200; Fax: 1–212.247.5242); and Heritage Auctions (*www.wine.ha.com*) in New York (Tel: 1—212–486–3500; Fax: 1–212–486–3527) and in San Francisco, Beverley Hills and Dallas (Tel: 1—800.872.6467).

Here are three specialist madeira wine merchants who will mail madeira worldwide. Apart from stocking vintages still for sale in Madeira, they also sell vintages and old soleras (often sourced from private cellars) which are otherwise unobtainable.

In Britain: *Patrick Grubb Selections*, Orchard Lea House, Steeple Aston, Bicester, 0X6 4RT. (Tel: 44–1869 340229; Fax: 44–1869 340867). On average, there are over 200 vintage wines in stock.

In USA: *The Rare Wine Company*, 21468 Eighth Street East, Sonoma, California 95475. (*www.rarewineco.com*) (Tel: 1–707 996 4484 or 1–800 999 4342.; Fax: 1–707 996 4491). On average, there are over 100 vintage wines in stock.

In Belgium: *The Madeira Collection*, Bert Jeuris, Kaaistraat 62a, 8800 Roeselare, Belgium. (*www.themadeiracollection.be*) (Tel: 32–477.52.79.46).

In Britain there are a few wine brokers who, while not in any way madeira specialists, often have old vintage and solera madeiras on their lists. Stocks at any one time can vary greatly. Orders can be sent abroad. Of these, the following are worth trying:

Bowes Wine Ltd, P.O. Box 2272, Melksham, Wiltshire, SN12 6ZG. (*www.boweswine.co.uk*) (Tel: 44–1380 827291)

Corney and Barrow (Broker Services) Ltd, 12 Helmet Row, London, EC1V 3QJ. (*www.corneyandbarrow.com*) (Tel: 44–171 5122; Fax: 44–171 9371).

Finest and Rarest, P.O.Box 340, Burgess Hill, West Sussex, RH15 5AP, UK. (*www.finestand rarest.com*) (Tel: 44–845 299 7991; Fax: 44–207 681 2740). Top bottles, but at top prices.

Hedonism Wines, 3–7 Davies Street, London, W1K 3LD. (*www.hedonism.co.uk*) (Tel: 44–207 290 7870).

Reid Wines, The Mill, Marsh Lane, Hallatrow, Bristol, BS18 5EB. (Tel: 44–1761 452645; Fax: 44–1761 453642).

Turville Valley Wines, The Firs, Potter Row, Great Missenden, Bucks, HP16 9LT. (*www.turville-valley-wines.com*) (Tel: 44–1494 868818; Fax: 44–1494 866680).

NOTES

PREFACE TO THE FIRST EDITION

1. Saintsbury, pp. 18–19. Saintsbury rated madeira higher than either port or sherry: 'The very finest Sherries of the luscious kind … cannot touch it' (p. 18); '[Red port] has not the … transcendental qualities of Burgundy and Madeira' (p, 32).
2. See also p. 205.
3. In 1986 the island provided 10,996 beds and recorded 319,419 visitors. In 1995 there were 17,492 beds and 649,132 visitors. See Anon. (6), p. 125.
4. Mayson (1), p. 222.

1. EARLY HISTORY

1. Albuquerque and Vieira, p. 1.
2. Silva and Meneses, II, p. 171a.
3. Ibid., II, p. 172b.
4. See, for a case in point, the Torre Bella family, pp. 124–6.
5. Albuquerque and Vieira, p. 56.
6. Silva and Meneses, II, p. 241b.
7. Albuquerque and Vieira, p. 38.
8. The Italian original is quoted in Henderson, footnote to pp. 248–9. Alvise da Mosto is known in Portugal as Cadamosto.
9. Silva and Meneses, III, p. 406a.
10. Tavares, p. 7.
11. Silva and Meneses, I, p. 37a.
12. Ibid., I, p. 14b.
13. Ibid., II, p. 281a.

14. Ribeiro, p. 49.
15. Ibid., p. 48.
16. Vieira (5): Vieira, A. 'A Vinha e o Vinho na Madeira nos Séculos XVII-XVIII', p. 105.
17. Simon, II, p. 217.
18. An Italian wine made from a noble grape variety of Greek origin.
19. Quoted in Italian in Aragão, pp. 63–4.
20. Ibid., p. 126.
21. *Voyage of Lopes*, 1588, in *Purchas' Pilgrimages*, quoted in Johnson, p. 81.
22. Galindo, pp. 168–9. All these varieties are still to be found on the island.
23. Ibid., p. 172.
24. Ibid., pp. 168–71.
25. Ibid., p. 171.
26. Ribeiro, p. 51.
27. Ibid., p. 52.
28. See Map No. 2 on p. 14.
29. This river runs between the Rua 5 de Outubro and the Rua 31 de Janeiro.
30. It seems likely, for geographical reasons, that this is the *fajã* that later became famous as the Fajã dos Padres. See also Silva and Meneses, II, p. 446a, where Manuel de Noronha is mentioned as owning *in sesmaria* the land which later became the Quinta of the Fathers of the Society [of Jesus]—i.e. Quinta Grande.
31. Canhas.
32. Extracted from Fructuoso, pp. 58–134. Given the close parallels between the wine cultures of Madeira and the Canaries, it is curious that Fructuoso, who also visited the Canaries, uses the term Vidonhos extensively in his description of Madeira but fails to use it when describing the latter. He mainly mentions Malvasias and *vinhos* ('vines' in mediaeval Portuguese), though he also tells us that at the parochial church of São João, near Terras de Santa Luzia and Ponta Chã, 'there are good vines which are there called Granel and Sabinal'—two varieties not mentioned by Galindo.
33. Duncan, p. 48, though note the reservations about his methods expressed in the next chapter.
34. Cossart, p. 32.
35. See Bolton (1), p. 17; Croft, p. 23.
36. Croft, p. 24.
37. Jeffs, p. 23.

318

38. Simon, III, p. 322.
39. Henderson, p. 301.
40. Ibid., p. 303.
41. Ibid., p. 194.
42. Quoted in Lemps, p. 37.
43. See Croft, p. 23; Henderson, p. 250; Redding, p. 230; and Driver, Appendix, p. xiii.
44. See p. 155.
45. Galindo, pp. 161–66.
46. Ibid., p. 161.

2. MADEIRA COMES OF AGE

1. Vieira (5), p. 105.
2. Ibid., p. 107.
3. See glossary under Pipa for the volume of a pipe, and also remarks in the preface to the second edition.
4. Duncan, pp. 46–7.
5. Ibid., pp. 46–8.
6. Mauro gives different figures for this year, derived from different sources, which illustrates clearly the risks incurred by relying on any one set of figures. See p. 18.
7. Jeaffreson, pp. 171–2.
8. Ovington, pp. 9–10.
9. Aragão, pp. 66–7.
10. Ovington, p, 14.
11. Duncan, pp. 54 and 58.
12. See Simon and Craig, pp. 9–18.
13. Ovington, pp. 12–13.
14. Bolton (1), pp. 15–16, and Duncan, p. 71.
15. See Bolton (2), p. 32.
16. Ibid., p. 23.
17. Duncan, pp. 40–1.
18. See under *milreí* in the glossary for an explanation of Portuguese currency.
19. Duncan, p. 39.
20. Ibid., p. 45. Note, however, that Mauro, using different sources, asserts that out of a total of 2,619 pipes exported, 238 were Malvazia (p. 356, quoted in Lemps, p. 32). According to Mauro, therefore, Malvazia amounted to 9 per cent of the wine exported, which is two

and a half times the amount suggested by Duncan. Clearly, more research is needed.

21. Bolton (1), p. 78.
22. Bolton (2), p. 75.
23. Ibid., pp. 23–4. André Simon in his transcript of the letters also suggests that 'the richest Old wine', offered by Bolton as a substitute for Malvazia, is in fact Vidonia. See ibid. p. 74. He may have suggested this, however, because he regarded Vidonia—I think erroneously—as a sweet wine. Whereas Bolton always refers to Malvazia as 'rich' (and never as 'sweet'), Redding describes Vidonia (quoted in Appendix 6 on p. 250) as 'of good body'.
24. Ibid., p. 78. Cf. pp. 47, 60 and 72.
25. Sloane, I, p. 10.
26. Ovington, pp. 8–9. This passage is perhaps better known from the quotation André Simon gives of it in his introduction to his edition of the Bolton Letters (see (1), pp. 19–20) from the English edition of Savary's *Universal Dictionary of Trade and Commerce* published in 1755. Simon does not indicate that he knew Savary had virtually transcribed this passage word for word from Ovington, and that it had been published more than sixty years earlier.
27. Bolton (1), p. 160.
28. Ibid., p. 17.
29. Yeasts can remain active in environments of less than 17° alcohol. As completely fermented out madeira would not reach this concentration of alcohol on its own, a certain instability would always be present. Anticipating a little, it is because fortification with brandy brought the alcohol level over this critical figure that the problem of instability was subsequently cured.
30. Bolton (2), p. 45. He also reports (Bolton (1), p. 87) that, of a consignment sent to America, 'an abundance of wines have turned vinegar'.
31. Croft-Cooke, p. 66.
32. Duncan, p. 38.
33. Bolton (1), pp. 91, 144 and 151.
34. Bolton (2), p. 50.
35. See pp. 126–9.

3. THE EIGHTEENTH CENTURY

1. Lemps, pp. 34–5.
2. Vieira (4) lists both production figures (pp. 290–2) and export figures (pp. 470–2), without indicating his sources for the former. Although

export figures based on customs house totals may be assumed to have some claims to accuracy, production figures at this time are not generally based on systematically maintained records and must, therefore, be approached with considerable caution. The note in the first edition read as follows: 'Biddle, II, p. 194, lists total annual shipments from 1774–1896 with some gaps. These figures appear to be based on customs house totals, but the already mentioned unreliability of the figures as a basis for calculation remains.'

3. Atkins, p. 24.
4. Lemps, p. 52.
5. Cossart, p. 43.
6. See de Sousa, p. 65. Lemps quotes (p. 45) from Castro e Almeida: *Arquivo da Marinha e Ultramar: Inventario: Madeira e Porto Santo* [2 vol., Coimbra, 1907–9] an annual average of 13,523 pipes for the period 1790–99.
7. Ibid.
8. Silva and Meneses, II, p. 36b.
9. The information in this paragraph is from the de Freitas MS.
10. Anon. (1), p. 9.
11. Anon. (2), II, p. 392.
12. Forster, p. 24.
13. Barrow, p. 20.
14. Staunton, p. 69.
15. Detailed figures for each parish are given in E. de Castro e Almeida, op. cit., 1, p. 93, and quoted in Lemps, p. 44.
16. Ibid., p. 56.
17. Silva and Meneses, III, p. 414a.
18. The de Freitas MS. I am indebted to Dr Ricardo de Freitas for drawing it to my attention.
19. Vieira (2), p. 91.
20. See ibid., pp. 34–5.
21. Ibid., pp. 39–44. See especially sections 13–18.
22. Silva and Meneses, III, p. 414b.
23. Vieira (2), pp. 86–7.
24. The de Freitas MS.
25. Lemps, p. 46.
26. Silva and Meneses, III, p. 414b.
27. Barrow, p. 21.
28. Ibid., pp. 38–9.
29. Croft, pp. 24–5.
30. Vieira (2), p. 59.

31. Anon. (1), pp. 5–6.
32. Apart from 1771, these figures are taken from Cossart, p. 247–8.
33. Other firms which do not now exist, even in name, but which survived into the twentieth century were: Shortridge, Lawton & Co., founded in 1757; and Welsh and Cunha (latterly Welsh Brothers), founded in 1794.
34. Vieira (2), p. 19.
35. Staunton, p. 70.
36. See Robertson, p. 28.
37. Cossart, p. 139.
38. Ibid.
39. Anon. (1), p. 8.
40. Croft, p. 23.
41. Cossart, p. 138.
42. Croft, p. 23.
43. Croft-Cooke, p. 66.
44. Jullien, pp. 232–3.
45. Vieira (2), p. 32.1: cf. Vieira (1), pp. 49–51 and Silva and Meneses, I, p. 425b.
46. Leacock's way of writing 5 milréis, I presume.
47. Originally quoted by kind permission of William Leacock.
48. Ibid. Particular was one of the qualities of wine shipped to England. See p. 47.
49. Penning-Rowsell (1), pp. 12–13. See also Penning-Rowsell (2,), p. 819. Further fascinating information about sales of madeira at Christie's from 1777–81 can be found in *Christie's Wine Review* for 1977–80 and in *Christie's Wine Companion* for 1981.
50. Anon. (3), p. 14.
51. Hawkesworth, II, p. 133.
52. Vieira (2), p. 25.
53. Ibid., p. 26.
54. Anon. (1), p. 8.
55. Anon. (3), p. 15.
56. Forster, p. 23.
57. Anon. (3), pp. 15–17.
58. Vieira (2), p. 31.
59. See ibid., pp. 40–42.
60. Lemps, p. 53.
61. Ibid.
62. Bolton (2), pp. 42 and 43.

63. Croft-Cooke, p. 136.
64. Staunton, p. 69.
65. See Cossart, pp. 146–7.
66. Croft-Cooke, p. 60.
67. Cossart, p. 145.
68. MWC MSS.
69. Croft-Cooke, p. 59.
70. Cossart, pp. 36–7.
71. Lemps, pp. 38–9.
73. Hawkesworth, II, p. 11.
74. Dunmore and Brossard, I, p. 244a; compare II, p. 17.

4. THE NINETEENTH CENTURY I

1. Driver, p. 37.
2. Hodgson, p. 14.
3. Nash, p. 131.
4. See Silva and Meneses, III, pp. 40–1, and Gregory, pp. 103–4.
5. Binney, p. 15 and p. 19.
6. Condell Innes Notebook, p. 220.
7. Gregory, pp. 30–1.
8. See Appendix 8, pp. 313–4.
9. Biddle, p. 194.
10. According to Alvaro de Azevedo, exports rose to an *average* of 20,000 pipes a year between 1810 and 1815 (Silva and Meneses, II, p. 156b.), but this is a huge over-estimate.
11. Condell Innes Notebook, p. 147. Most of this appears to have gone to India.
12. Ibid., p. 176.
13. Ibid., pp. 174–5.
14. Alternative round figures are provided by Taylor, but as they cannot in general be reconciled to what the Condell Innes Notebook tells us, they are probably inaccurate. See Taylor, p. 74.
15. Condell Innes Notebook, entry dated 31 December 1820, p. 261.
16. Vieira (2), p. 90.
17. Ibid., p. 53.
18. Condell Innes Notebook, pp. 51–2.
19. Vieira (2), p. 219.
20. Ibid., pp. 95 and 116.
21. See ibid., pp. 49–51.

22. Ibid., p. 120.
23. Ibid., p. 59.
24. Ibid., p. 98.
25. Holman, p. 23.
26. Vieira (2), p. 73.
27. Ibid.
28. Ibid., p. 61.
29. Ibid., p. 73.
30. Ibid., p. 74.
31. Condell Innes Notebook, p. 220.
32. Anon. (4), pp. 53–4.
33. Vieira (2), pp. 137 and 141.
34. Ibid., p. 278.
35. Ibid., p. 138.
36. Ibid., p. 91.
37. See Vieira (4), p. 19.
38. Vieira (2), p. 107.
39. Ibid., p. 89.
40. Ibid., p. 97.
41. Ibid., p. 87.
42. See Biddle, p. 194.
43. Hodgson, p. 3.
44. Cossart MS.
45. See Silva and Meneses, I, pp. 95–6. It is now known as ACIF, being a commercial and industrial association.
46. See Silva and Meneses, I, pp. 391–2.
47. Silva and Meneses, I, p. 392a.
48. The potato had first been planted in Madeira in 1760. See Silva and Meneses, III, p. 306b.
49. Quoted in Gregory, p. 106. Coincidentally, 1846 was also the year of the Irish potato famine.
50. Ibid., p. 176.
51. Silva and Meneses, II, pp. 329–30.
52. Alternative figures abound. According to Eduardo Dias Grande, the production between 1847 and 1852 was as follows. 1847:19,572 pipes. 1848: 13,795 pipes. 1849: 14,508 pipes. 1850: 13,020 pipes. 1851: 9,217 pipes. 1852: 2,124 pipes. This gives an average production in the four years to 1851 of 12,635 pipes. (See Vieira, p. 304.) According to João Andrade de Côrvo, on the other hand, Madeira and Porto Santo had a combined production of 19,487 pipes in 1847

and 14,445 pipes in 1849. (See ibid., p. 289.) Again, according to statistics published in the Semanario Oficial for 24 June 1854, the annual average of production for the years 1847 to 1852 was 13,690 pipes, contrasting with an average, according to Grande, of 12,039 pipes. In 1852 this number dropped to 2,110 pipes, and in 1853 to 690 pipes. These figures make for an even more sensational proportional drop in production. (See ibid., p. 181.)

53. That is, 151 hL, again according to Grande. (See ibid., p. 303, from which the production figures up to 1859, which are given below, are also derived.)

54. Thudichum and Dupré, p. 694.

55. Burton, p. 71.

56. João de Andrade Côrvo, the investigator mentioned below. Vieira, p. 288.

57. Cossart asserts that the reduction was from seventy to fifteen British merchants (p. 116), stating in his Appendix IV (p. 251) that the number of British shippers had increased to seventy-one by December 1828. He lists only seventeen British firms as active in the year leading up to December 1828—apparently implying that fifty-four new traders set up shop within a year. This is just incredible. Given the economic situation by 1828, there were no incentives for new merchants to come to the island, and the trade (reduced to average exports of 7,649 pipes a year) simply could not have supported such a number. Cossart previously claims that 'the wine-growing industry of the islands flourished until 1851'. Flourish it certainly did not.

58. Gregory, p. 104.

59. Printed in Vieira (2), pp. 280–302.

60. Ibid., p. 302.

61. Ibid.

62. See Vieira (2), p. 187, and Anon. (5), pp. 11–13 and 72–3.

63. See Biddle, p. 147.

64. See Vieira (2), pp. 182–190.

65. Vizetelly, p. 201.

66. See Vieira (4), pp. 31–2 and 97.

67. Gregory, p. 108.

68. See p. 6.

69. Silva and Meneses, II, p. 33b.

70. Vieira (1), p. 61.

5. THE NINETEENTH CENTURY II

1. For a detailed account of phylloxera, see Ordish. For a brief account, see the article on Phylloxera in Robinson (2), pp. 725–8.
2. Vizetelly, p. 202.
3. Some extracts from the minutes of the Commission's meeting are reprinted in Vieira (2), pp. 127–31. See also Silva and Meneses, II, pp. 32–3.
4. See Biddle, p. 147.
5. Vieira (2), p. 321.
6. Silva and Meneses, II, p. 159a.
7. See Biddle, p. 147.
8. For the Blandy's case see Croft-Cooke, pp. 12–13. For the Anglo-Portuguese treaty see Gregory, pp. 27–8. 'Madeiras' were, however, manufactured at Massandra in the Crimea during the period of the USSR, and in Australia until quite recently. Several are still produced in U.S.A., such as *King's Cross*, American Madeira, Château St. Cyr Cellars, Batavia, NY 14020. On this see 'Defesa da denominação de origem' by Palma, C. in Vieira (5), pp. 179–184.
9. See Vizetelly, p. 158.
10. See Vieira (2), pp. 281–3.
11. See p. 43.
12. Ibid.
13. Bowdich, pp. 110–11.
14. See Vieira (2.), pp. 285–7.
15. White, p. 55.
16. Harcourt, p. 99.
17. See pp. 115–16.
18. Vizetelly, p. 173.
19. Taylor, p. 75.
20. See Vizetelly, p. 75.
21. See Vieira (2), p. 281.
22. White (1851), p. 56.
23. Vizetelly, p. 159.
24. See Anon. (3), pp. 18–19, and Harcourt, p. 99. A consequence of this use of gypsum would also have been to make the wine more acid. On this see p. 155, and Jeffs, pp. 270–1.
25. Thudichum and Dupré, pp. 692–3.
26. Johnson, p. 87.
27. Cossart (p. 134) says that Cossart Gordon was doing so in 1907.
28. See Cossart, p. 83.

29. See Simon and Craig, pp. 22–3.
30. Vizetelly, p. 96.
31. See Vieira (2), p. 326.
32. See ibid., p. 172. However, cf. Vieira (4), p. 240, where the total in 1848, presumably for the island, is stated to be 27.
33. Vizetelly, p. 183.
34. For extracts of Portuguese texts of *A Brief Notice on the Treatment of Wine by Heat* (1882) and *The Three Systems of Treatment for Madeira Wine* (1900), see Vieira (2), pp. 313–27.
35. White (1851), p. 57.
36. Johnson, p. 90.
37. See p. 153.
38. Driver, Appendix, p. xii.
39. Holman, p. 18.
40. Bowdich, p. 109. Compare Driver, *loc. cit.*
41. Lyall, p. 363, and Redding, pp. 2301.
42. Vizetelly, p. 174.
43. See Harcourt, p. 98.
44. See for example Driver, Appendix, p. xiii.
45. White (1851), p. 61. It is also known as *vinho pálido* and *palhetinho*. Vizetelly, however, distinguishes rainwater from *palhetinho*.
46. Driver, p. 75, and Wortley, p. 309.
47. See White (1851), p. 61. This may have been the liqueur mentioned by Bowdich (p. 111), made from the first pressing of the grapes after treading with the addition of an equal quantity of brandy.
48. Vizetelly, p. 190.
49. See Cossart, pp. 77–8.
50. See Harcourt, p. 98.
51. Vieira (2), p. 316.

6. THE TWENTIETH CENTURY AND BEYOND

1. See Tavares, p. 34.
2. Pestana, IX, p. 233.
3. For this account I am indebted to Chapter 9 of Gregory's book, in which a more detailed account of the matter may be found.
4. See Gregory, pp. 127–8.
5. Quoted ibid., p. 12.5.
6. See Silva and Meneses, II, pp. 405–6.
7. See ibid., I, p. 292a. The provisions of the law of 18 September 1908

are printed in Monarchia, No. 226 (7 October) for 1908, and the regulations for Madeira in No. 59 (16 March) for 1909.

8. Ibid., II, p. 160b.
9. See Pereira, I, p. 565.
10. Cossart, p. 111.
11. See Silva and Meneses, I, p. 99b.
12. See Tavares, pp. 34–5.
13. See ibid., p. 35.
14. Here is a complete list of members of the 1934 Association, with dates of joining: Vinhos Viúva Abudarham & Filhos, Lda (1934); Aguiar Freitas & Cª Sucrs Lda (1936); A. Nobrega (Vinhos da Madeira), Lda (1953); A. Pries Scholtz & Co (not known); Barros, Almeida & Cª (Madeira), Lda (1936; this company had been set up in 1935 by the Madeira Wine Association and Barros, Almeida & Cª the port firm in Vila Nova de Gaia, the latter transferring its shares to Sr José T. de Freitas a week later); Bianchi's Madeira, Lda (1953); Blandy's Madeiras, Lda (1934); Cossart Gordon & Co Lda (1953); Casa dos Vinhos Vasconcelos, Lda (1951); E. A. Cunha (not known); F. F. Ferraz & Cª Lda (1937; having been founded in 1915 and dissolved in 1931, it was reconstituted in 1937 by the Madeira Wine Association and Turquands, Barton, Mayhew & Co); Funchal Wine Company, Lda (1934; the date on which it was constituted by the Madeira Wine Association and Turquands, Barton, Mayhew & Co); Freitas Martins, Caldeira & Cª Lda (1960; Martins, Caldeira & Cª Lda being dissolved and reconstituted under the new name); Gibbs & Co (not known); J. B. Spinola, Lda (1936); Krohn Bros. & Cª Lda (1951); Leacock & Co. (Wine), Lda (1934); Luiz Gomes (Vinhos), Lda (1953); Madeira Victoria & Co Lda (1936; having been constituted in 1934 by the Madeira Wine Association and Sr José T. de Freitas); Miles Madeiras, Lda (1969; although the right to use its trademarks was ceded to the Association in 1951); Power Drury (Wine), Lda (1934); Royal Madeira Company, Lda (1936; the company having been constituted in 1934 by The Madeira Wine Association and Sr José T. de Freitas); Rutherford & Miles, Lda (1951); Sociedade dos Vinhos Madeira Menéres, Lda (1936); Sociedade Agrícola da Madeira, Lda (1937; this company, founded in 1928 by Salomão da Veiga França and Maurílio Ferraz e Silva, should not be confused with the Sociedade Agrícola Madeirense of the previous century, long since defunct); Tarquinio T. da Camara Lomelino, Lda (1936; the company joined the Association in two stages, when separate shareholders ceded their shares to it in 1934

and 1936 respectively, although the second Association had been given the right to develop the name and trade of the company in 1933); Vinhos Donaldson & Co Lda (1934); Vinhos Shortridge Lawton & Co Lda (1934); Welsh Bros (Vinhos), Lda (1934). Turquands, Barton, Mayhew & Co was the firm of accountants which audited the Association's accounts. It had a token shareholding in each of the companies to make up the minimum of two shareholders required by Portuguese law, and these were ceded to the Royal Madeira Company in 1982.

15. See Tavares, p. 35.
16. Ibid.
17. The other Dukes used for brands, all extinct dukedoms—Sussex, Cambridge and Cumberland—made their appearance on the market in the 1950s. The brand still exists.
18. Writing in 1933, even André Simon had to report that Boal 'is not, as a matter of general practice, made from one kind of grape alone, and that grape the Boal'. See Simon and Craig, p. 40.
19. Cossart, pp. 148–9.
20. See Lemps, p. 119.
21. See p. 178.
22. Pereira, I, p. 588.
23. See Lemps, p. 119.
24. From 15,000 hL in 1973 to 37,000 hL in 1980. See Cossart, p. 112.
25. The JNV itself continued in being until 1986, when it was renamed the Instituto da Vinha e do Vinho (IVV). Because Madeira is an autonomous province, however, the IVV has no jurisdiction over the IVM's successor organization, IVBAM, although IVBAM deals with the EU through the IVV.
26. The Direcção de Serviços de Produção Agrícola no longer has this responsibility.
27. At the time this norm properly applied only to quality table wines; it has now been incorporated into the legislation covering madeira production.
28. See Mayson (2), p. 210.

7. THE SOIL AND THE GRAPES

1. See p. 70.
2. See p. 116.
3. See Cossart, p. 99.

4. Silva and Meneses, III, p. 412a.
5. Cossart, p. 73.
6. Terrantez madeira allegedly from the eighteenth century survives to the present day.
7. Viala and Vermorel, VII, p. 316.
8. Silva and Meneses, III, p. 412a.
9. Microsatellite analysis is a way of determining whether grape varieties have the same genetic character by extracting and comparing their DNAs.
10. Cossart, pp. 99–100; Robinson (1), p. 218.
11. Anon. (3), p. 15.
12. Cossart, p. 99.
13. It is described in detail in Silva and Meneses, III, p. 410b.
14. See http://fringewine.blogspot.co.uk/2013/03/know-your-malvasia-malmsey-malvasia.html.
15. See http://madaboutmadeira.org/2013/01/complexa-authorized-but-any-good.
16. Brazão, p. 7.
17. See also p. 132.
18. Silva and Meneses, III, p. 410a.
19. See under 'Vinhas' in Silva and Meneses, III, pp. 406–12.
20. Viala and Vermorel, VI, p. 376.
21. Cossart, p. 104.
22. See p. 279.
23. Cossart p. 104.

8. THE VINEYARDS

1. Various (2), Vol. 1, pp. 34, 37 and 45.
2. Redding, p. 234.
3. See p. 38. Gordon apparently kept meticulous records of the results of the vintage of all his vineyards, but sadly these appear to have disappeared.
4. See p. 6.
5. See p. 92.
6. See p. 272 for an explanation of the term *Fajã*.
7. See p. 318, note 30.
8. Bowdich, p. 59.
9. Driver, p. xii. *Fazenda* is another word for 'farm' (note that *Fajã* is not an abbreviation of *fazenda*). 'Giram' is an anglicized version of Girão.

10. See p. 31.
11. Ibid.
12. Vizetelly, p. 174.
13. Silva and Meneses, II, pp. 6b–7a.
14. Cossart, p. 194.
15. Pereira, p. 563. On Dermot Bolger, see above.
16. The other, at Ponta Delgada, belongs to Ricardo França, and was constructed at the same time. See pp. 136–7.

9. VITICULTURE AND THE VINTAGE

1. See pp. 44–5.
2. See p. 73.
3. 1 tonne=1,000 kg (1 ton=1,016 kg). The amount of must obtainable from 1 tonne depends on many variables: type of grape, amount of juice, degree of pressure in pressing, etc. In general, 130 kg of red grapes and 150–160 kg of white grapes are needed to produce one hectolitre of must (see Robinson (2), pp. 1080–2.) This means, for example, that one hectare of Sercial produces around 65 hL of must.
4. Cossart, p. 107.
5. For further information about IVBAM and its component parts see Appendix 2 (pp. 277–82).
6. In 2012, the regional government bought from around seventy farmers whose grapes failed to reach the minimum degree. It paid €0.60 per kg for 69,000 kg in total, all of which were used in alternative ways—for example, distillation.
7. *Contas correntes* came into being under the legislation of 11 March 1901 (Art. 13). Shippers had to inform first the Customs, then the Delegation of the JNV, of their purchases during the vintage and of their sales. Only the total amount of wine in stock was monitored. In 1973 the Delegation introduced *contas correntes* for bulk wines by variety but without date of making, and for vintage (*garrafeira*) wines. The present detailed system was introduced by the IVM in 1980.

10. MAKING AND MATURING THE WINE

1. As late as 1985 the MWC was purchasing *mosto* from the north of the island.
2. Caramel is still, though decreasingly, used to colour wines.
3. Cossart, p. 133.

4. Mayson (2).

5. The use of concentrated must has been regulated since 1991.

6. Since 1989 vinification sufficient to produce 4° of alcohol must take place before fortifying alcohol is added. See pp. 169 and 176 for the official sweetness tolerances for each type.

7. The lowest legal limit is 15.5°.

8. These are destined to become *colheitas*, as is explained in Chapter 11.

9. See Cossart, p. 140.

10. Cossart, however, indicates (p. 133 and pp. 150–1) that vintage madeiras used to be given *estufagem*.

11. For technical explanations of maderization, oxidation, rancio, aceto-bacter and the effect of oxygen on wine, see under these headings in Robinson (2).

12. Cossart, p. 142.

13. If this were not done the wine would become a kind of *solera*.

14. Cossart, p. 192.

15. Total acidity in wine refers to the test that yields the total of all acids present. (Strength of acidity is measured according to pH, and the lower the pH, the higher the acidity in the wine.)

11. FROM CASK TO CUSTOMER

1. Portaria No. 40/82 of 15 April.

2. Article 6 of Portaria 40/82, quoted in *Jornal Oficial* for 18 March 1994.

3. Portaria No 125/98 of 29 July.

4. A *garrafeira* is a wine cellar, and a *frasqueira* is a cellaret or domestic receptacle for holding wine bottles.

5. Portaria No. 39/2001 of 8 May.

6. Despacho Normativo No. 3/2001 of 5 June.

7. A meq is a milliequivalent, or a one thousandth (10^{-3}) of a gram equivalent of a chemical element, an ion, a radical, or a compound.

12. THE MADEIRAS OF TODAY AND YESTERDAY

1. Most of the wines shown to Vizetelly in 1877 were less than ten years old.

2. Portaria No. 125/98 dated 29 July.

3. Portaria No. 40/82 of 15 April.

4. Article 6 of Portaria No. 40/82 of 15 April.

5. Bottles of madeira sold at auction over four decades, together with the prices they have fetched, have been usefully recorded by Emanuel Berk in Appendix III of his edition of Cossart's *Madeira The Island Vineyard*. See Cossart, pp. 219–36.
6. See Cossart, pp. 83.
7. The reader will notice that one of the wines awarded a rosette for quality in the next chapter is, although very old, not a vintage wine.
8. See p. 132.
9. Simon and Craig, p. 29.
10. Nevertheless, there are examples of so-called 'bottle-aged madeiras'. These are bottles of ordinary madeiras originally intended for fairly immediate consumption (generally in the United States) which happen not to have been consumed and have survived down the ages. They are of variable interest. The better ones, in my experience, have a sort of lean elegance, but many are pallid and rather feeble.
11. Cossart, p. 199.

13. NOTES ON SOME VINTAGE MADEIRAS

1. See p. 193.
2. This information, confirmed by Avery's, is taken from the catalogue of Christie's wine sale on 29 September 1977, Lot No 364.
3. Cossart, p. 189.
4. See pp. 191 and 203.
5. See Cossart, pp. 187–9.
6. See ibid., p. 161.
7. Ibid., pp. 168 and 170.

14. THE PRODUCERS

1. The name Barros e Sousa does not indicate the combination of two family names for business purposes (like, for example, Marks & Spencer), but is a single surname—rather like a double-barrelled family name such as Abel Smith.
2. See Silva and Meneses, II, p. 281b.
3. The family still maintains a remarkable private cellar. See p. 216.
4. Cossart Gordon acquired a Terrantez 1846 from him in 1900. See p. 211.
5. See pp. 85–6. It would be impossible to do justice to all the firms that have been part of the MWC without turning this profile into a complete

history of the company and thereby unbalancing the book. The history of Cossart Gordon—though not the rather sad way its London branch was absorbed into the MWC—is adequately dealt with in Noël Cossart's book, and that of Leacock in Croft-Cooke's book. Henry Price Miles, aged one and a half, arrived in Madeira with his mother in 1852. At twelve he was apprenticed to a firm called Rutherford and Brown. Shortly thereafter the Browns went to South Africa and the Rutherfords decided to return to England. They sold the business to Henry Miles, then nineteen, on condition that exports to London would be exclusively to them. Thus in Madeira, Rutherford and Brown became H. R. Miles, later (in 1935) H. R. Miles & Co, while in London the name of Rutherford & Miles was registered. H. R. Miles & Co joined the MWA in 1969. Rutherford and Miles's most famous brand, Trinity House Bual, is now owned by the MWC but is no longer in production. The Miles family's activities are now centred on brewing, being part owners of the Empresa de Cervejas da Madeira, which produces the excellent Coral beer.

6. For more detail about the history of the family, see Marcus Binney's book *The Blandys of Madeira*.
7. Already in existence in Fructuoso's time.
8. Binney, pp. 167–8.
9. See pp. 293–4.
10. See Vieira (3), pp. 105 and 172.

15. TODAY AND TOMORROW

1. See p. 122.
2. First edition, p. 153.
3. Lewis, p. 30.

APPENDIX 1: MADEIRA: SOME BASIC INFORMATION

1. Ribeiro, p. 22.
2. Ibid., p. 36. Much of this account is directly derived from Ribeiro, but with more up-to-date values derived from Anon (6)—see Bibliography.
3. Ibid., p. 111.

APPENDIX 2: CONTROL OF THE WINE INDUSTRY

1. See p. 177.

APPENDIX 5: REGIONAL TABLE WINE

1. Portaria No. 68/99 of 12 May.
2. Portaria No. 86/2006 of 2 April.

APPENDIX 6: THE 1792 VINTAGE AND THE NAPOLEON MADEIRA

1. This point is elaborated by Cossart: 'The wine was considered hardly ready for drinking ... so it was only bottled ... in 1840' (Cossart, p. 155). Apart from the unlikelihood of Napoleon being offered a wine that would only reach maturity at best in his extreme old age, the wine would have been 33 years old when it returned to Madeira (if the story is true)—which by the standards of the time, when madeira was still sold the year after the vintage, would have been a very old wine indeed.
2. Simon and Craig, pp. 35–6.
3. This and Walter Grabham's letter are quoted, originally by kind permission of Richard Blandy and now by kind permission of Andrew Blandy, from the originals in his possession.
4. Cossart, p. 322, footnote 55.
5. Vizetelly, p. 191.
6. See Cossart, pp. 169 and 197.
7. Cf. these entries from Christie's catalogues. 1 December 1977: Lot 411, 'Bual—Believed Vintage 1792. Blandy'. 25 September 1980: Lot 385,'Believed Bual—Vintage 1792'. 18 June 1992: Lots 469–73,'Bual Vintage 1792', with a note referring back to Lot 433, which is Blandy's Vintage 1792, itself with a note about the Napoleonic association.
8. Croft-Cooke, p. 126.
9. Cossart: cf. p. 91 with p. 169.
10. Cossart (1984 edn), p. 162.
11. Broadbent, I, p. 397.

APPENDIX 7: VIDONHO AND VIDONIA: AN UNSOLVED MYSTERY

1. Meyers, Vol 9, p. 142; Shaw, p. 450; Burton (2), Vol. 1, p. 257.
2. Galindo, p. 178.
3. Henríquez, p. 96.
4. Mauro, p. 443.
5. *Ibid.*, p. 415.

6. Bolton (2), pp. 23, 24 and 64.

7. *London Gazette*, No 6173/3: quoted in the OED entry for Vidonia.

8. Simon and Craig, p. 31.

9. Condell Innes Notebook, p. 69.

10. Vieira (2), p. 305.

11. See for example, Costa and Meio's *Dicionário da Lingua Portuguesa*.

12. Vidueño Seco (63% Marmajuelo, 12% Malvasía, 20% Moscatel, 5% Verdello y Gual) produced by Bodega Contiempo.

13. Redding, p. 194.

14. Shaw, p. 449.

15. Vizetelly, pp. 206–7.

16. Jullien, p. 231. Of the Canaries Vidonia he says, on page 229, that it 'is made with raisins before they are ripe, whence their harshness and dryness' and adds that 'they improve much by age, and become similar to *Madeira* wine, particularly when imported into warm climates'.

17. Redding, p. 229

18. Thudichum and Dupré, pp. 692 and 693.

19. Viala and Vermorel, VII, p. 341b. 'Vidonho. Portuguese grape variety from Beira Baixa, very extensive on the island of Madeira, according to certain authors identical to Vidogne or Chasselas, according to others different and very special.'

20. Ibid., II, p. 7.

21. Galet, p. 833.

22. Silva and Meneses, III, p. 411a.

23. Cossart, p. 100.

24. Lemps, p. 96.

25. Robinson (1), p. 248.

26. Cossart, p. 322, fn 45.

27. Redding, p. 229.

28. Burton, pp. 254–5.

29. Vizetelly, p. 207.

30. Bolton, p. 17.

31. André Simon appears to suggest that Vidonia was sweet when he writes (Simon and Craig, p. 19): 'Madeira produced mostly red wines and some white wines ... as well as a very limited quantity of Malvasia or Malmsey, and even less Vidonia or Vidogna, sweet dessert wines'. I know, however, of no other evidence to support this view. In any case, the export figure of 2,381 pipes for 1650 quoted above

hardly accords with 'even less' Vidonia than the 'very limited quantity' of Malvazia, given that in 1650 only 238 pipes of Malvazia were exported; see Mauro, p. 415.

32. Robinson (3), p. 782–3.
33. See pp. 114–5.
34. Hancock (2), p. 156.
35. Shaw, p. 450.
36. Burton, p. 254.
37. Ibid., p. 256.
38. Ibid., p. 252
39. Deep amber gold; true Malvasia nose, reasonably full and positive, typical caramel and vanilla; concentrated rancio flavours on the palate, but hollow and lacking fruit; austere and uncompromisingly dry with a very short finish. The attractive bouquet indicated something interesting and enjoyable, but the wine was totally dried out and failed to deliver.

GLOSSARY

ACIF	Associação Comercial e Industrial do Funchal. Local trade association which has a *Mesa dos Vinhos*, a sub-section to which shippers who export wines generally belong.
Adega	Winery.
Agua pé	Light refreshing drink made by mixing water with *bagaço* (q.v.).
Aguardente	Strictly speaking a word for spirits, but universally used in Madeira to indicate the type of rum made from sugar cane. Wine spirits are *aguardente do vinho*.
Americanos	American vines, or more specifically the variety called *Isabela* (*Vitis labrusca*).
Armazem	Store or lodge.
Armazem de calor	A form of *estufa*, being an artificially heated store.
Arrobo	Boiled-down must used for sweetening.
Bagaço	Grape skins, pips and stalks after fermentation and/or pressing.
Balseira	Method of growing vines up trees common in the north of Madeira until the twentieth century.
Bardos	Fences made from the branches of shrubs—normally *urze*, a giant heather—to protect the vines from wind damage and sea spray.

Baumé	The name for the most generally used scale of measurement of the sugar content of a solution whose values are determined by using a hydrometer at a temperature of 15°C.
Bentonite	An absorbent clay compound used for fining (i.e. clarifying and stabilizing) wine.
Bica aberta	Method of fermenting wine in open-topped wooden casks.
Borracheiro	Man who carries a *borracho*.
Borracho	Sack made from a goatskin and retaining the shape of the animal, used for transporting must and wine.
Cadastro	Register. In a wine context, a census of vineyards recording, *inter alia*, area and grape varieties.
Calda	Syrup made from boiled-down sugar.
Canteiro	Trestle upon which a cask rests. See *Vinho de canteiro*.
Carvão	Charcoal.
Castas boas	Former name for recommended varieties of grape.
Castas nobres	Former name for classical varieties of grape.
Cepa	Grape variety.
Concelho	Local council.
Contrato de colonia	Type of land leasehold whereby the lessor pays a proportion of the land produce in rental.
Cuba de calor	Tank, often of concrete lined with epoxy resin, used for heating wine during *estufagem*.
Cuba de fermentação	Tank, often of concrete lined with epoxy resin, used for fermenting wine.
Direct producers	Ungrafted vines of American origin, not authorized for use in making madeira but used to make *vinho seco* (q.v.).

Escudo	Portuguese national monetary unit (PTE) prior to the introduction of the euro on 1 January, 1999. At the point of transition 1 euro was equivalent to 200.482 PTE.
Espaldeira	System of training vines on wires between posts.
Estágio	Period of time during which wine is stored and rested.
Estufa	Room or building in which *estufagem* takes place.
Estufagem	Process of heating wine to simulate ageing.
Frasqueira	Private store or cellar for wine. Alternative name for *garrafeira* in both the senses given (q.v.).
Freguesia	Parish.
Garrafão	Glass demijohn, generally covered with wicker, used for storing wine; of varying capacities up to 15 litres.
Garrafeira	Private store or cellar for wine. The name by which madeira which has been cask aged for at least twenty years is known. See *Frasqueira*.
Granel	Youngest and cheapest type of madeira which was exported in bulk until 2002.
IVBAM	Instituto do Vinho, do Bordado e do Arte-sanato da Madeira, IP (The Wine, Embroidery and Handicraft Institute of Madeira), government body which presently controls the wine trade in Madeira.
IVM	Instituto do Vinho da Madeira (Madeira Wine Institute), government body which controlled the wine trade in Madeira prior to IVBAM.
Inox	Stainless steel.
JNV	Junta Nacional do Vinho. The controlling body which preceded the IVM.

Lagar	Tank or trough, in Madeira often made from wood, in which the grapes are trodden at the vintage.
Latada	Trellis, generally low-lying, which supports vines.
Levada	A channel with a gentle gradient cut into hillsides in Madeira to collect water for irrigation. Small levadas feed larger levadas at lower altitudes, and combine to form an extensive water-supply network.
Lodge cask	Cask or pipe holding around 600 litres used for storing madeira.
Lote	Specific parcel of wine; in English, a 'lot'.
Maderization	Oxidation of wine through exposure to air, more generally applied to table wines which have oxidized than to those aged in cask.
Malvina	Malvidina. A substance thought to be injurious to health found in American hybrid vines.
Mangra	Madeiran word for *oïdium* or powdery mildew.
Mercaptan	Evil-smelling substance produced by bacteria after fermentation.
Milréi	Basic unit of Portuguese currency until the twentieth century. The relevant money table is as follows: 1 conto = 1,000 escudos; 100 centavos = 1 escudo; 10 réis = 1 centavo; 400 réis = 1 cruzado; 1,000 réis = 1 milréi (now 1 escudo). See also under *Escudo*.
Morgado	Estate which is entailed and descends as a unit to whoever inherits it.
Mosto	Must, or grape juice before fermentation.
MWA	Madeira Wine Association, former name of the Madeira Wine Company.
MWC	Madeira Wine Company.
OIV	Office International de la Vigne et du Vin.

Organoleptic	An adjective applied to tests on wine carried out by means of the senses (smell, taste, etc.), as opposed to chemical analysis.
Partidista	Trader who buys or makes wine in order to mature it and sell it on to a shipper or other trader.
Patamars	Vineyard terraces without retaining walls that have been constructed by bulldozing the soil.
Pipa	Wooden cask or pipe. A madeira pipe differs in volume from a port pipe and contains 110 'old' gallons, 92 imperial gallons, or 418 litres. Previously there were shipping pipes (*pipas de embarque*), also of 418 litres; handling pipes (*pipas de carreteira*) of 500 litres (used for moving madeira around the island); and some shippers still use lodge pipes, which are half as big again as shipping pipes, for storing and maturing wine.
Poio	Terrace with retaining stone wall. See also *Socalco*.
POSEIMA	Programme of Options for the Remoteness and Insularity of Madeira and the Azores. An EU scheme of economic support for projects within the programme (*Programa de Opções Específicas para fazer face ao Afastamento e á Insularidade da Madeira e dos Açores*).
PRODERAM	Programme of Rural Development within the Madeira Region (*Programa de Desenvolvimento Rural da Região Autónoma da Madeira—2007-2013*).
Produtores direitos	'Direct producers': American and hybrid vines not authorized for madeira production.
Quinta	Farm: often used in Madeira to signify an estate with a large house.

Socalco	Terrace with a retaining stone wall. See also *Poio*.
Solera	A system of fractional blending whereby a small amount is drawn from a reserve and replaced with younger but similar wine, which is then allowed to blend and mature with the remainder of the reserve before subsequent repetitions of the sequence.
Tetrahybrid	A hybrid generated from three varieties.
Tonel	(plural *tonéis*) Large vat.
Tornaviagem	'Round trip'. See *Vinho da roda*.
Vinha da pé	Vineyard in which the vines are grown on the ground with minimal or no support.
Vinho abafado	Literally 'smothered wine': wine to which alcohol has been added before fermentation has stopped.
Vinho claro	Madeira after fermentation but before fortification.
Vinho da roda	From the seventeenth to the twentieth centuries, wine that had been shipped on a round sea voyage. Much esteemed because of the improvement this treatment made to the wine.
Vinho de canteiro	Wine matured in cask without *estufagem* (q.v.).
Vinho seco	Table wine made for local consumption from direct producers (hybrid vines), so called because it has been fermented dry.
Vinho surdo	Grape must to which alcohol has been added before the start of fermentation. Formerly a sweetening agent.
VIVC	Vitis International Variety Catalogue, administered by the Geilweilerhof Institute for Grape Breeding (Institut für Rebenzüchtung Geilweilerhof) in Siebeldingen, Germany.

BIBLIOGRAPHY

This bibliography is very selective, for the most part containing only books that are referred to in the text or which may be useful to the reader.

Albuquerque, L. de, and Vieira, A. *The Archipelago of Madeira in the XV Century*. Funchal, 1988.

Anon, (1) *A Journal of a Voyage Round the World in His Majesty's Ship Endeavour in the Years 1768, 1769, 1770, and 1771*. London, 1771.

———— (2) *A Collection of Voyages round the World performed by Royal Authority, Containing a Complete Historical Account of Captain Cook's First, Second, Third and Last Voyages*. 6 vols. London, 1790.

———— (3) *A Guide to Madeira, containing a short account of Funchall*. London, 1801.

———— (4) *An Historical Sketch of the Island of Madeira*. London, 1819.

———— (5) *125 Anos de Cerveja na Madeira* [by José Adriano Ribeiro]. Funchal, 1996.

———— (6) *20 Anos de Autonomia e Desenvolvimento*. Funchal, 1996.

Aragão, A. *A Madeira Vista por Estrangeiros*. Funchal, 1981.

Asher, G. *Vineyard Tales*. ('Malmsey: A Revival'). San Francisco, 1996.

Atkins, J. *A Voyage to Guinea, Brasil and the West-Indies*. 2nd. ed., London, 1737.

Barrow, J. *A Voyage to Conchinchina in the Years 1792 and 1793*. London, 1806.

Biddle, A. J. *The Land of the Wine, being an account of the Madeira Islands*. 2 vols. Philadelphia, San Francisco and London, 1901.

Binney, M. *The Blandys of Madeira 1811–2011*. London, 2011.

Bolton, W. (1) *The Bolton Letters. Letters of an English Merchant in Madeira 1695–1714*. Edited by A. L. Simon. London, 1928.

———— (2) *The Bolton Letters. The Letters of an English Merchant in Madeira. Vol. II, 1701–1714*. Produced by G. Blandy, Funchal, 1960. Reprinted in 1976 and 1980.

Bowdich, T. E. *Excursions in Madeira and Porto Santo*. London, 1825.

BIBLIOGRAPHY

Brazão, João do S. *Análise ao Sector Vitivinícola da Região Autonoma da Madeira*. Madeira, 1994.

Burton, R. F. *To the Gold Coast for Gold*. 2 vols, London, 1883.

Cossart, N. *Madeira the island vineyard*. London, 1984. 2nd ed. with new material by Emanuel Berk, Sonoma, 2011.

Croft, J. A. *Treatise on the Wines of Portugal*. York, 1787.

Croft-Cooke, R. *Madeira*. London, 1961.

Dillon, F. *Sketches in the Island of Madeira*, London, 1850.

Driver, J. *Letters from Madeira in 1834*, London and Liverpool, 1838.

Duncan, T. B. *Atlantic Islands. Madeira ... in Seventeenth-Century Commerce and Navigation*. Chicago and London, 1972.

Elliott, T. *The Wines of Madeira*. Gosport, 2010.

França, I. de, *Journal of a Visit to Madeira and Portugal (1853–1854)*. Funchal, [1970].

Forster, G. *A Voyage Round the World in His Britannic Majesty's Sloop RESOLUTION, commanded by Capt. James Cook, during the Years 1771 ... 2 vols.*, London, 1777.

Fructuoso [Frutuoso], G. (1) *Livro Segundo das Saudades da Terra*. Ponta Delgada, 1968.

—— (2) *Las Islas Canarias (de 'Saudades da Terra')*. La Laguna de Tenerife, 1964.

Galindo, P-M. M. *La Vid y el Vino en Tenerife en la Primera Mitad del Siglo XVI*. La Laguna (Tenerife), 1998.

Galet, P. *Dictionnaire Encyclopédique des Cépages*. Paris, 2000

Gonsalves, A. B., and Nunes, R. S. *Ilhas de Zargo. Adenda*. Parte I. Funchal 1990.

Gregory, D. *The Beneficent Usurpers*. London and Toronto, 1988.

Hancock, D. (1) *Oceans of Wine*. New Haven and London, 2009.

—— (2) "An Undiscovered Ocean of Commerce Laid Open": India, Wine and the Emerging Atlantic Economy, 1703–1813' in Bowen, H. V., Lincoln, M. and Rigby, N. *The Worlds of The East India Company*, Woodbridge (UK) and Rochester, NY (USA), 2002.

Harcourt, E. V. A *Sketch of Madeira*. London, 1851.

Hawkesworth, J. *An Account of the Voyages undertaken by the order of his Present Majesty for making Discoveries in the Southern Hemisphere*. 2 vols, the second vol. being *An Account of a Voyage Round the World in the Years 1768, 1769, 1770 and 1771 by Lieutenant James Cook, Commander of his Majesty's Bark the Endeavour*. 4th ed., Perth, 1787.

Henderson, A. *The History of Ancient and Modern Wines*. London, 1824.

Henríquez, J. *Vinos de Tenerife*. Santa Cruz de Tenerife—Las Palmas de Gran Canaria, 2002.

Hoare, M. *The Quintas of Madeira*. Funchal, 2004.

Hodgson, S. *Truths from the West Indies*. London, 1838.

Holman, J. (1) *Travels in Madeira*. 2nd ed., London, 1840.

——— (2) *A Voyage Round the World, Vol. 1, 1827–1832*. Reprinted, Teddington, 2007.

Jeaffreson, J. C. *A Young Squire of the Seventeenth Century*. 2 vols. London, 1878.

Jeffs, J. *Sherry*. 4th ed., London, 1992.

Johnson, J. Y. *Madeira, Its Climate and Scenery*. 3rd ed., London, 1885.

Jullien, A. *The Topography of all the known Vineyards*. London, 1824.

Lemps, A. H. de, *Le Vin de Madère*. Grenoble, 1989.

Lewis, R. A. *The Wines of Madeira*. Tring (UK), [1968].

Lyall, A. *Rambles in Madeira and in Portugal in the early part of M.DCCC. XXVI*. London, 1827.

Mauro, F. *Le Portugal, Le Bresil, et l'Atlantique au XVII Siecle (1570–1670)*. Paris, 1983.

Mayson, R. (1) *Portugal's Wines and Wine Makers*. Chapter 17. London, 1992.

——— (2) 'Does anyone know how to make madeira?' Article in *Decanter*, May 1991.

Meyers, R.J., ed. *Meyers Konversations-Lexikon*. 4th ed., 9 vols., Leipzig and Vienna, 1885–92.

Nash, R. *Scandal in Madeira*. Lewes, 1990.

Ordish, G. *The Great Wine Blight*. London, 1972. New ed., London, 1987.

Ovington, J. *A Voyage to Suratt In the Year*, 1689. London, 1696.

Pamment, D. 'An Intricate Art.' Article in *Decanter Magazine's Guide to Madeira*. 2nd ed., 1987.

Penning-Rowsell, E. (1) 'Christie's wine auctions in the 18th century.' Article in *Christie's Wine Review 1972*. London, 1972.

——— (2) 'Auctioning Wine in the 18th Century.' Article in *Country Life*, 6 October 1966.

Pereira, E. C. N. *Ilhas do Zargo*. Vol. I, 4th ed., Funchal, 1989.

Pestana, E. A. *Ilha da Madeira*. 2 vols. Funchal, 1965, 1970.

Redding, C. *History and Description of Modern Wines*. London, 1833

Ribeiro, O. *A Ilha da Madeira ate Meados do Seculo XX*. (This is a geographical study.) Lisbon, 1985.

Robertson, G. *Port*. London, 1978.

Robinson, J. (1) *Vines, Grapes and Wines*. London, 1986.

——— (2) ed. *The Oxford Companion to Wine*. Oxford and New York, 1994.

——— (3) with, Harding, J. and Vouillamoz, J. *Wine Grapes*. London, New York, Toronto, etc., 2012.

Saintsbury, G. *Notes on a Cellar-Book*. London and Basingstoke, 1978.

Shaw, T. G. *Wine, the Vine and the Cellar*. 2nd ed., London, 1864.

Silva, F. A. da, and Meneses, C. A. de, *Elucidário Madeirense*. 3 vols. Funchal, 1922. Reprinted 1940 and also in facsimile, Funchal, 1984.

Simon, A. L. (1) *The History of the Wine Trade in England*. 3 vols. London, 1964.

——— (2) and Craig, E. *Madeira—Wine Cakes & Sauce*. London, 1933.

BIBLIOGRAPHY

Sloane, H. *A Voyage to the Islands Madera ... and Jamaica.* 2 vols. London, 1707.

Sousa, J. J. A. de, 'O Porto do Funchal e a Economia da Madeira no Seculo XVIII.' Article in *Das Artes e da História da Madeira.* Vol. VII, No. 37, 1967.

Staunton, G. *An Authentic Account of An Embassy from the King of Great Britain to the Emperor of China.* London, 1797.

Tavares, J. *Subsídios para o Estudo da Vinha e do Vinho na Região da Madeira.* Funchal, 1952.

Taylor, E. M. *Madeira: Its scenery and how to see it.* London, 1882.

Thudichum, J. L. W., and Dupré, *A Treatise on the Origin, Nature and Varieties of Wine.* London, 1872.

Various. (1) *Decanter Magazine's Guide to Madeira.* 2nd ed., 1987.

———— (2) *Recenseamento Agrícola—Análise dos principias resultados.* Lisbon, 2011.

Viala, P., and Vermorel, V. *Ampélographie.* 7 vols. Paris, 1901–10.

Vieira, A. (1) *Breviário da Vinha e do Vinho na Madeira.* Ponta Delgada (Azores), 1990.

———— (2) *Historia do Vinho da Madeira.* Funchal, 1993.

———— (3) *A Rota do Açúcar na Madeira / The Sugar Route in Madeira.* Funchal, 1996.

———— (4) *A Vinha e o Vinho na História da Madeira Séculos XV a XX.* Funchal, 2003.

———— (5) ed. *Os Vinhos Lícorosos e a História.* Funchal, 1998.

———— (6) with Palma, C. and Homen-Cardoso, A. *Madeira Wine (Encyclopedia of the Wines of Portugal, Vol. V).* Lisbon, n.d. [1998]. Also published as *O Vinho da Madeira (Enciclopédia dos Vinhos de Portugal, Vol. V).* Lisbon, n.d. [1998].

Vizetelly, H. *Facts about Port and Madeira.* London and New York, 1880. Reprinted in facsimile, Baltimore, n.d.

White, R. *Madeira Its Climate and Scenery.* London and Madeira, 1851. 2nd ed., rewritten with the addition of much new matter by J. Y. Johnson. Edinburgh, 1857.

Wortley, E. S. *A Visit to Portugal and Madeira.* London, 1854.

Manuscript sources

References to these unpublished sources are indicated in the text by means of the abbreviations shown here in square brackets.

Cossart, P. *Journal. From leaving Madeira 14 July 1833 to my return to it 15 May 1835.* Formerly in the possession of John Cossart, Esq. [Cossart MS]

Freitas, R. D. V. de. *Madeira no Século XVIII (1759–1779) Economia e Sociedade.* Dissertation, University of Lisbon, preserved in the Arquivo da Marinha e Ultramar, Funchal, Caixa II, Documento No. 311. [de Freitas MS]

BIBLIOGRAPHY

Newton, Gordon & Murdoch account books, ledgers, etc. in the archives of the Madeira Wine Company. [MWC MSS]

Anon. Manuscript account of the trading of Condell, Innes & Co (later Innes, Duncan, Lewis & Co), a firm of madeira wine-shippers, 1789–1821. 235 pp. In the possession of Blandy's Madeiras, Lda. [Condell Innes MS]

Internet sources

The following selected sites provide information about many aspects of the history and production of madeira.

www.ivbam.gov-madeira.pt A range of information, including the organization of IVBAM, how it functions, the legal framework of, and up-to-date statistics about, grape and wine production, exports, etc.

www.madeirawineguide.com A very comprehensive, unofficial site, containing information about wine production, shippers, history, the island, blogs and a selection of miscellaneous writings about madeira.

http://portuguesefeast.com/page/madeira-wine-history A short history of madeira wine.

www.vinhomadeira.pt This site contains information about the history and production of madeira as well as an on-line shop for wine, books and other merchandise associated with the island.

Sadly, websites are seldom kept up to date, and the reader is cautioned that a great deal of misinformation appears on all of these sites.

The URLs of individual wine producers are shown in Appendix 6.

INDEX